Psychology, Religion,
and Human Need

Psychology, Religion, and Human Need

*A Guide for Ministers, Doctors, Teachers,
and Social Workers*

by

W. L. CARRINGTON, M.D.

LONDON : THE EPWORTH PRESS

THE EPWORTH PRESS
(FRANK H. CUMBERS)

25–35 City Road, London, E.C.1

MELBOURNE   CAPE TOWN
NEW YORK   TORONTO

SET IN MONOTYPE IMPRINT AND PRINTED IN
GREAT BRITAIN BY BUTLER AND TANNER LTD
FROME AND LONDON

To

MY WIFE

Contents

SECTION THREE

The Healing Ministry

SECTION FOUR

The Evangelistic Ministry

Introduction

THE SECOND World War provided, among other things, a unique opportunity for the study of the general and religious attitudes of a true cross-section of an important age-group of the male (and to a smaller extent the female) populations of many countries. It seems to have been the general experience of military and other chaplains that about one in every ten service men had any close connexion with the regular worship and other activities of the Christian Church. And yet it would be generally agreed that almost ten out of ten would have been willing to risk their lives, if the occasion arose, for their fellow men. They were at least capable of the 'greater love' which is at the centre of the Christian Faith. Here surely is the great hidden spiritual wealth of our time.

The general worship, the preaching, the sacraments, and the various social and cultural activities of the Christian Church seem to have lost much of their appeal to millions of people, however valuable they may still be to the faithful. Because of this the leadership of the Church in many social, national, and international affairs has greatly declined, even allowing for the unassessable influence of the Church through broadcasting and the public Press.

But more and more people everywhere are feeling the need for personal encouragement, help, and guidance in the complex problems and difficult dilemmas of modern life, in the everyday problems of personal relationships (especially in the intimate relationships of marriage and parenthood), and in the various problems of mental and physical illness and abnormal behaviour. They are also feeling the need for help in their inner emotional tensions and conflicts, their intellectual bewilderment and confusion, and their volitional frustration and indecisiveness.

Can the Christian Church regain its rightful leadership in the community, and if so, how? In the view of the author of this book the key to the situation is in the fullest possible development of the pastoral work of the whole Church: ministers and laymen. If the Church is to be 'the Body of Christ', it must surely live and work among people as One who serves. To carry out this great calling it cannot afford to be insensitive to the deepest needs of people, or

ix

to offer any but the very best kind of understanding and help to them.

There are many indications that we are at the beginning of a very great period of expansion of Christian Pastoral work, in which the educated and trained Christian layman will find more and more opportunities for valuable service. It may well be that this will bring the revival for which the Church is constantly praying, to the greater glory of God and the increasing welfare of all mankind.

This book is an attempt to give an account of the kind of pastoral ministry to which it is believed the Christian Church is being called in these days, for which 'the fields are white already unto harvest'. Some already overworked ministers may feel that the book covers a field which is too wide for them to cover, even with some rearrangement of priorities. The author would suggest two considerations in answer to any such objections. The first is that we must ask ourselves whether in the face of the urgent and increasing burden of human need, the Church can remain deaf to the call and continue to exert any adequate leadership in the community. The second is the practical consideration that the author himself is actively carrying out all the different aspects of pastoral work described in his book in the midst of a busy medical practice. Every practical activity discussed in the book is the product of his own practical experience, very greatly inspired, enlightened, and assisted by many people, personally and in their writings.

The material of the book has gradually taken shape over the last sixteen years in regular courses of lectures to the Theological Students of Ridley College, the Anglican Theological College of Melbourne, to which theological students of many other denominations have accepted the invitation to come. Some of the material has also been given in 'post-graduate conferences' to groups of ministers of most of the Christian denominations. The giving of these lectures, and the full and free discussions which have followed them, have helped the author to mould the material into its present shape.

It may have some symbolic significance that a 'layman' should make bold to write a book on Pastoral Ministry. If this work is to be done in such a way as to cope with even a fraction of the need, the Christian layman must have a vital part in it. The author has no desire to tell the members of a 'sister profession' what they should be doing, but rather to use his own experience and opportunities to the fullest extent in the service of God.

To acknowledge all the many sources of help in this project would be beyond the author's power, and beyond the available space. Many of them are acknowledged in the actual text, but there are some who must receive special mention. Bishop Donald Baker, Principal of Ridley College until 1953, first invited the author to lecture to his students, taking the risk of inflicting a very immature and uncertain lecturer upon them. He has given unstinted and most generous encouragement and support throughout the whole period, which has been carried on by his successor the Very Reverend S. Barton Babbage, Dean of Melbourne.

The Very Reverend Kenneth Jones, Dean of Armidale, New South Wales, has given far more help than he can possibly realize in the portion of the book which deals with pastoral visiting, and in the ideas which are offered on the subject of worship.

The Reverend Dr Kenneth T. Henderson, Director of Religious Broadcasts for the Australian Broadcasting Commission, has also been of great help and encouragement, particularly in his genius for conjuring up subjects and titles which have called forth the most vigorous and heart-searching thought from the author.

The publishers, The Epworth Press, and their London Editor, Dr J. Alan Kay, have given most generous encouragement and help. Mr E. E. Bartholomew, of the Epworth Press Melbourne Staff, has also been most gracious in his co-operation and encouragement.

Lastly the author would pay a special tribute to his wife for her most valuable part in the project: for putting up with long periods during which her husband was glued to his typewriter. The book is appropriately dedicated to her.

SECTION ONE

*The Modern Psychological and Religious Approach to
Human Need*

CHAPTER ONE

The General Nature and Scope of Personal Help

I. THE MODERN CHRISTIAN MINISTRY

WHAT, AFTER all, *is* Christian ministry, male or female, lay or ecclesiastical? It is, or should be, just the attempt of someone who cares supremely about God to cherish and help in one way or another the souls that are loved by God, to be as one that serveth. And moreover it is an attempt that is made, not because we feel like it or choose it, but because we are decisively pressed, called, put to it. 'You have not chosen me, but I have chosen you.' The word 'vocation' does not mean that we do the calling. It is true, alas, that we often seem to see this principle ignored; but is it worth while to consider the sort and degree of pastoral work which we *might* do, unless we are prepared to do everything which comes our way from that centre?

These words of Evelyn Underhill [1] provide a fitting introduction to any consideration of the nature and scope of pastoral work and its relationship to the total vocation of Christian ministry. They emphasize the important, and often forgotten fact, that all Christian people, male and female, laymen and ministers, are called to some kind of Christian ministry, inspired and directed by Jesus Christ whose words to Peter, 'Lovest thou me? Feed my sheep', have been at the centre of all Christian ministry to this day.

This wide calling divides itself naturally into two different, but closely related parts: the public ministry to people assembled in groups, or linked together indirectly by the written or broadcast word, and the private ministry to individuals.

The public ministry, which reaches out to the hearts, minds, and wills of people in groups, may be thought of from four different aspects. There is a priestly ministry which leads people in worship and in the sacraments of the Church; a preaching and teaching ministry which sets out to educate, inspire, and develop them in their faith, and in its application to their daily living; a prophetic ministry which extends their range of vision and stirs them to creative action;

[1] *Mixed Pasture* (Methuen, 1933).

and finally an organizing ministry through which the ecclesiastical and social services of the Church are planned and carried out.

The private ministry to individuals may be thought of as three different activities, which correspond with the three parts of the work of the Eastern Shepherd, from which the whole conception of pastoral ministry has been derived. In the shepherd's daily work there is the general care and supervision of the sheep, and especially the lambs, the special care of the sick, injured, and worn-out sheep and lambs, and the seeking, finding, and bringing back the lost and strayed. All this work is directed to the goal of keeping each individual sheep an effective member of the flock, or bringing it back into the flock.

In the same way the pastor is called first of all to the general care and supervision of the people committed to his charge. He is to be their 'guide, philosopher, and friend', to know and understand them, to share their joys and sorrows, to stand by them in important events, such as marriage, parenthood, tragedy, separation, and bereavement. On these occasions, and in the many every-day meetings with people, he has the privilege and the unique opportunity for much quiet educational work as well as that of personal comfort and encouragement. The right word spoken in love at the right time will often have far-reaching influence for good. In this, and all his work, he will give special help to the children.

The second part of the pastor's work is the special care of the sick, injured, and worn-out people in his charge. He will offer personal help and comfort to the physically and mentally ill in their homes, or in hospitals or institutions, not forgetting other people with whom he may thus be brought into contact. He will also offer help to people in their sorrows, anxieties, and dilemmas, and their frustrations and failures.

The third part of the work is the seeking and finding of the 'lost or strayed'; offering to them in attitude and word the redeeming love of Jesus Christ, the Great Saviour and Healer, and attracting them into the Christian 'flock'.

These three aspects of Pastoral work—the personal and educational, the therapeutic or healing, and the evangelistic—are all completely inter-related. The shepherd of souls is at the same time a physician of souls, and always a seeker of souls. They are also completely inter-related with the whole of the public ministry, and Jesus used both public and private ministry as the occasion demanded. Each aspect of the work will open the door in some way to the other, and make it more effective.

In that general setting we are to consider the private pastoral ministry of both ministers and laymen. To an unfortunate extent it has been left to the ordained minister to do, and for him it has become rather crowded out by the claims of the public ministry. If the Church is to meet even a part of the need of people there must be a real awakening, and a great expansion of this private pastoral ministry. It may well be that when this happens the Church will experience a great and thrilling revival, and human society will advance to the highest level of order and freedom in all history.

Every minister and layman is not gifted for pastoral work to the same extent, but Jesus called all His followers to be the light of the world and the salt of the earth. It seems therefore to be an essential part of the Christian vocation, and opportunities for helping other people in this way cannot be evaded by any Christian. It ought therefore to be cultivated and developed to the fullest possible extent in every person who accepts the Christian Gospel and way of life, in the spirit and power of the Great Shepherd.

Some of the more gifted people will undertake special training, and give up the greater part of their time and devotion to the more complex pastoral work, and to the training of others in the pastoral part of their vocation. We need the specialist here, as in many other vocations. But the specialist is unable to be fully effective unless he is in constant close fellowship with other ministers and laymen who are doing the work.

There are operations in surgery for which the fully trained specialist is needed, and at the other end of the scale simple 'cut fingers' well within the competence of the relatively untrained parent or friend. In the care of the human soul there are also activities within the competence of all Christian people as well as the deeper and more complex work for those with special gifts, training, and experience. Pastoral work is wide enough in range to provide a part for every Christian in response to the bidding of Jesus: 'Lovest thou me? Feed my sheep' (John 21¹⁷).

All helping work is most effective when there is co-operation and fellowship between those who do it. Ideally, pastoral work is carried out by the whole congregation under the leadership of the trained minister, and this would facilitate better co-operation between it and the more 'secular' helping activities of medicine and the social services.

B

Jesus came that men and women 'might have life, and that they might have it more abundantly' (John 10^{10}). The goal of all pastoral work in His name is therefore the Christian ideal of abundant personal life, which overflows into continually expanding fellowship. The Word was uniquely made flesh in Jesus but is continually to be 'made flesh' in His followers. When we pronounce or listen to the Benediction, the 'good saying', do we remember that it is for us to convey to people as well as wish them 'the Grace of our Lord Jesus Christ, the Love of God, and the Fellowship of the Holy Spirit', that these great gifts are to be 'made flesh' in all of us?

The pastor, minister, or layman is intended to be the apostle of Christian Fellowship, and our failures in this great calling are probably at the root of many of the difficulties in modern Church organization, and much of the decay in church-going in these days. People assemble in and around our church buildings, but all too often their real needs are not touched. Many of them need healing as well as education and religion.

Education, psychotherapy, and religion have been described by David E. Roberts [1] as the only resources which can transform man's internal character-structure, and thus 'assist him to bring forth from within himself the resources for changing the patterns of contemporary civilization'. They have already been described as the three inter-related parts of the Christian Pastoral Ministry, corresponding with the three great parts of the work of Jesus as Teacher, Healer, and Saviour.

Until people are freed from the domination of emotional tensions and conflicts they are generally unable to experience abundant life or to take part in real fellowship. This needs more than the most eloquent and sincere words. The most potent of all forces for the overcoming of emotional tensions and the reconciling of emotional conflicts is Christian Love, made flesh and expressed in expert Christian Counselling, and multiplied in spontaneous Christian fellowship. Our rooted individualism has made it difficult to understand the infinite creative and healing power of a Religion which is social to its very core.

The general standard of pastoral work today in most countries falls far short of these ideals and goals. We find ministers insufficiently trained in the theory and practice of their pastoral ministry, lacking

---

[1] *Psychotherapy and a Christian View of Man* (Charles Scribner's Sons, 1950), p. 7.

also in time and money and help, compelled to be 'jack of all trades' in the ecclesiastical field, and trying faithfully with sacrificial devotion to minister to those who need them. Their influence is hindered to some extent by the fact that they have not sufficient contact with people outside their congregations.

Christian laymen, on the other hand, have good contact with people outside the congregation, in their daily work, and in their various social activities. But they are generally unable or unwilling to make any real use of it, and feel no responsibility or calling for pastoral work. Their 'religion' is mostly of a 'private' or 'individual' nature, and often a little vague and formal.

And yet, though they may not often realize it, people are hungry for what Christianity offers, and what the whole Church, ministers and laymen, should be offering in more obvious and tangible form. Their hunger takes them to many different possible sources of help. We find them in doctors' surgeries and hospital out-patient departments, looking not only for 'medical' help, but even more for 'peace of mind', often expecting to find it in a bottle of medicine.

We find them also buying and reading books and articles on psychology, and going to lectures, plays, and moving pictures about psychological themes. We also find them in increasing numbers buying religious books and going to plays on religious themes. Handel's *Messiah* is still the most popular and the most frequently performed major musical work, and the Bible is still the world's 'best seller', even in many unexpected places.

Add to this the number of people whose hunger drives them, often despairingly, to all kinds of 'escape mechanisms', particularly to alcohol, drugs, and gambling, and we can begin to grasp the magnitude of the hunger. As Jesus observed in His own day: 'The fields are white already unto harvest' (John 4³⁵).

How is the situation to be tackled?

To give the necessary leadership the Christian minister will need a first-class pastoral training for the personal and educational, the healing, and the evangelistic parts of his pastoral work. It should be possible to select enough men of special gifts and the right temperament for this work, and to train them through lectures and clinical work to become specialists in the work and teachers of future pastors.

If we put the specialists into the best places for their work, such as hospitals and universities and theological colleges, their influence will develop and spread widely. The hospital work will enable them to add further to their knowledge and experience, and the academic opportunities will lead to better training of students, to first class post-graduate courses for ministers, and to further dissemination of their knowledge through lectures, books, preaching, and broadcasting.

The art of being a physician of souls does not necessarily come with 'Holy Orders'. It has to be well learnt, and, as with education in general, the learning is never complete. Careless or slipshod work is no more excusable in the physician of souls than it is in the medical physician. 'General practitioners' and specialists are needed in the pastoral field as well as in the medical, and each has a special and valuable work to do.

The Christian layman appears to be the key to the whole problem of contact with the non-churchgoer, and laymen will of necessity provide the required manpower for any worth-while extension of pastoral work. It is well to remind ourselves that the Communist 'layman' knows, lives, and gives out the Marxian answer to the human situation, and he is a red-hot propagandist for his faith. The Christian layman is relatively inarticulate and inactive, partly perhaps because he does not receive enough strong and inspiring leadership. As Archbishop Temple once remarked: 'We must move nearer to a state of affairs where the minister stands for the things of God before the congregation, while the congregation stands for the things of God before the outside world.' [1]

Can enough competent laymen be found and trained to make an effective contribution to the pastoral needs of their community? The National Marriage Guidance Council of Great Britain, and similar bodies in other parts of the world, have provided an unmistakable answer to that very practical question. Large numbers of laymen (and this term always includes lay-women) are doing excellent work in this important part of the pastoral field, and their numbers are increasing year by year.

It may well be that the familiar phrase, 'The priesthood of all believers', will soon be joined by another one: 'The pastorhood of all believers'.

II. THE INNER RESOURCES NEEDED

In any Christian pastoral work the pastor, minister, or layman may be regarded as a kind of channel between God and man, through

[1] *The Hope of a New World* (SCM Press, 1941), p. 106.

which God may find His way into men and women, the doors of whose hearts may have been closed to Him for one reason or another. If he thinks of himself always in this way he will be saved from the awful strain of 'trying to play God'. He will avoid any undue sense of frustration when things do not go as he would have expected or liked, and he may be less prone to undue pride when things go well. Above all, this concept of the pastoral function clarifies the necessary inner qualities to be cultivated in the pastor.

There are three essential parts of the channel from God through the pastor to man, each of which needs to be kept open if the Spirit of God is to flow freely. The first is that between God and the pastor, which can only be kept open by a regular and constant devotional life. Then there is the channel through the pastor himself, which is kept open by disciplined humility and self-understanding. And finally there is the channel between the pastor and the person he is helping, which is kept open by virtue of the pastor's understanding outgoing Christian Love.

With this in mind the necessary inner resources may be summarized under the three general headings of ability, faith, and love, recognizing that they are needed on an ascending scale as we go from the 'rank-and-file' Christian layman to the highly trained specialist.

The pastor's ability will include a reasonable and growing knowledge of Jesus Christ, the Christian Gospel, and the Christian Faith, as well as the power to express and communicate these great insights and inspirations in terms which have meaning for ordinary people. It will also include a reasonable understanding of people, some knowledge of the main principles of psychology, and of the modern ideas and methods of interviewing and counselling, backed up by a reasonable and growing understanding of himself, his own emotional needs and prejudices.

The pastor also needs a firmly based faith in God and in people to vitalize and sustain all his work. This is helped by a personal experience of the Gospel and a deep conviction of the relevance and power of the Christian way of life. Every modern pastor who sets out to 'overcome evil with good' will soon find with St Paul that 'our wrestling is not against flesh and blood, but against the principalities, against the powers, against the world-rulers of this darkness, against the spiritual hosts of wickedness in the heavenly places' (Ephesians 6[12]). Like St Paul, too, he will feel the need of 'the shield of faith', and indeed 'the whole armour of God', God's own power, patience, and persistence.

The third and greatest inner quality needed by the pastor is the love of God, of an intensity which cannot help overflowing into the love of all God's other children. Without this, as St Paul observed, all kinds of other excellent qualities are of no value. This kind of love can only be awakened in and remain with any human being when he experiences in some way or another the love of God for him as shown supremely in Jesus Christ. At the end of a long life, and from a unique experience of the loving companionship of Jesus, St John summed up his deepest insights into the nature and power of love in seven simple words: 'We love, because He first loved us' (1 John 4[19]).

This love, of 'the Two Great Commandments' kind, will be felt, and will show itself, as an unquenchable passion for the highest welfare of all other people, even the ungrateful and unattractive. It will inspire the pastor to a wide interest in people for their own sakes, which will never give the impression that he is wanting to 'save' them or get something from them. It will enable him to 'feel into' other people, and to accept their feelings, and to become aware of their hidden good qualities, as Jesus did with Zacchæus. It will also generate a healthy objective Christian humility, which will prevent the pastor from the real danger of taking himself and his work too seriously, and save him from over-dogmatism, pride, or over-shyness.

It is clear then that all these inner resources of the good pastor are those of Jesus Christ, 'the pastor pastorum', the great Shepherd, Physician and Seeker of Souls. In a very real sense He is allowed to live in and to shine out through the pastor, whose radiance and power are generated and sustained by his full response to the Christian vocation. 'The hireling fleeth because he is an hireling; and careth not for the sheep' (John 10[13]).

It is difficult to find a more appropriate word picture of this indwelling Christ than the prayer of St Paul on behalf of his friends at Ephesus:

'That he [God] would grant you, according to the riches of his glory, to be strengthened with might by his spirit in the inner man; that Christ may dwell in your hearts by faith; that ye, being rooted and grounded in love, may be able to comprehend with all saints what is the breadth, and length, and depth, and height; and to know the love of Christ, which passeth knowledge, that ye might be filled with all the fulness of God' (Ephesians 3^{16-19}).

III. MAKING CONTACT AND WINNING CONFIDENCE

The possession of these inner qualities will of itself establish contact with many people, but there are many ways in which this can be greatly extended and deepened for the better fulfilment of the pastoral function. We may think first of the use of existing facilities associated with the work of the minister, and to a smaller extent open to the layman, as opportunities for pastoral work. We shall then consider the opportunities for pastoral work provided by the attitudes, actions, or experiences of other people, and lastly some opportunities we can make for ourselves.

Of existing facilities one of the best and most frequent is to be found in the regular worship of the Church. Every Church service is worth all the detailed and devoted care that can be given to make it mean something real to people, to make Jesus Christ more real through it. This is greatly helped by simple natural speech, and by constant care with phrasing and emphasis. It would help many ministers and laymen to hear tape-recordings of their conduct of services, and to have them assessed and criticized by experts. Members of congregations might also be encouraged to offer ideas and suggestions about the general conduct of services.

A very great opportunity, not generally used well enough, is to be found in the special services which make contact with non-church-goers, such as those in connexion with baptism, marriage, funerals, and services of public commemoration or dedication. It is difficult, but most important, for the minister to think supremely of the attitudes and needs of the many people in the congregation who may be quite untrained in the art of public worship, who may have little or no real understanding of the conventions and symbols, and many of the words associated with the particular service. If he is to make the best use of this opportunity, which in many cases 'knocks but once', he will need wherever possible to make his words and actions clear enough and natural enough to have meaning and relevance to the visitor, who may have come for reasons unconnected with Christian worship. Is the Church always awake to this kind of opportunity? The vivid portrayal of the feelings of a cynical but pathetically groping university professor at the funeral service for his wife in

Lloyd Douglas's book *Disputed Passage* will provide much to think about.

Broadcast services offer a particularly important opportunity of this kind, the possibilities of which are being slowly realized. In these, and all other 'religious' broadcasts, the needs and attitudes of the 'untrained' listener cannot rightly be ignored. Jesus Himself gave His message in such terms that 'the common people heard Him gladly'.

The conduct and 'atmosphere' of the whole service provides a great pastoral opportunity, but even more direct contact with people can be made through preaching and teaching, especially when the 'atmosphere' of the whole service provides a real sense of worship. Preaching and teaching should demonstrate the pastor's sympathetic understanding of men and women—and children—and inspire in them the feeling that here is someone they could easily confide in. The pastor's message should meet them where they are. As someone has pointed out, the pastor should tell people on Sunday what they have been telling him during the week.

This personal contact with people can be further helped by the use of suitable pamphlets, booklets, articles in Church and 'secular' papers, and many other similar devices.

The visiting of people in their homes affords perhaps the most intimate and personal of all the existing opportunities for making contact with people and winning their confidence. The minister has always had the privilege of entry into people's homes as a welcome visitor, without necessarily waiting for a special invitation. In routine visits, and in special visits to the sick, dying, and bereaved there are pastoral opportunities far beyond the people actually visited. The same applies to visits to schools, universities, factories, jails, and many other institutions, and particularly to hospitals.

Another existing pastoral opportunity is provided through the many church organizations and societies, and through various community projects in which there may be co-operation with other denominations and organizations. The use of related community services in appropriate situations—medical and psychiatric, legal, political, educational, and social—will also bring many more opportunities of this kind.

Lastly, among the existing facilities are those linked up with the various kinds of counselling when people come to interview the pastor for any reason. Counselling may be mainly educative, for example, to those about to be married, to parents, and in any kind of vocational guidance. Or it may be mainly therapeutic, such as in personal trouble, inter-personal difficulties in marriage or in industry or other social activity, and in certain 'institutional' problems, such as are met with in reformatories.

The attitudes, actions, and experiences of other people provide many golden opportunities for making pastoral contact and winning their confidence.

When they abuse, criticize, or even injure us, can we see in these things a positive opportunity for Christian witness? If we can accept the other person's right to his own opinions and attitudes, and tell him that we are sorry he should have reason to think that about us, and we hope that some day he will have reason to think differently, it will generally bring a more 'healing' spirit into the situation, and may well help to change an enemy into a friend. This acceptance will also make it easier for us to look again at our own attitudes and actions in the light of his opinion, to see if there may have been any good reason for the enmity. To love one's enemies is a difficult but essential part of the Christian attitude. There are dangers in limiting our associations to friendly people or to those with whom we have much in common, and we miss many opportunities of urgently needed pastoral work by doing so.

When we meet other people who are in trouble, or have committed some wrong, we can make good use of the opportunity if we think of the attitude of Jesus to the woman in adultery, or to Zacchæus, and follow His teaching: 'Judge not.' It is worth while at this point to remind ourselves that all His attitudes and all His teaching were based on the solid and enduring foundation of the way life works. They were never merely arbitrary or expedient attitudes. He still speaks with authority, 'and not as the Scribes'.

When people make requests of us, perhaps at very inconvenient times, they provide good opportunities for pastoral contact by what Jesus described as 'going the second mile'. This is a genuine expression of the Christian spirit, which may have far-reaching consequences.

When people grumble it is tempting to try to 'cheer them up' or to argue them out of their self-pity. But much better pastoral contact will be made by the acceptance of their feelings and the willingness to allow them to 'let off steam' without being criticized or given 'advice'.

Many good pastoral opportunities are provided by other people as a result of previous help given to someone they know, or have heard about. As Jesus maintained, we are known by our fruits, not so much by our methods or our words.

Finally, there are many pastoral opportunities that we can make for ourselves, through our own creative initiative.

Spontaneous acts of friendship and service will always achieve far more than their intrinsic value. Giving 'a cup of cold water' in the name of Christ will bring some of His spirit into the personal contact, and may lead to all kinds of opportunities for later pastoral work.

If we have misunderstood someone, or wronged him in any way, an honest admission of the wrong and a suitable apology and restitution will often open the door to later pastoral work. 'First be reconciled to thy brother' (Matthew 5²⁴).

Another pastoral opportunity we can sometimes make for ourselves is in the handling of ordinary conversation. This is an art which demands a delicacy of touch and a sensitivity to other people's reactions if we are to be good 'fishers of men'. Any idea that religion is being dragged into the conversation will generally generate resistance or even opposition in the mind of the listener.

Lastly, we can make many pastoral opportunities through the various kinds of public witness, from platform, pulpit, and through writing and broadcasting.

Anyone who attempts pastoral work must be prepared for many apparent frustrations. There will be many times when he will become overwhelmed with the sense of the vastness of the problem, and of his own inadequacy and unfitness, especially when the results seem pitifully small compared with the time and effort expended on it. But if our pastoral work is well conceived and faithfully carried out there will be good enough fruit to provide the necessary inspiration to keep on in faith.

CHAPTER TWO

The General Psychological Background

I. THE SPRINGS OF HUMAN ATTITUDE AND CONDUCT

WE HAVE seen that one of the essential conditions for pastoral work is that the pastor should have a reasonable and growing understanding of people, and of himself. This involves an awareness of the complicated pattern of inner motives and external goals from which the various kinds of human attitude and conduct are built up.

Human attitude and conduct may be regarded as resulting from the progressive dynamic interaction of two powerful and complex sets of influences: natural instinctive urges, which are the 'raw material' of attitude and conduct, and an enormous range of controlling influences, external and internal, by which they are 'harnessed' and directed to fit in with the many and varied goals and purposes of human endeavour.

The natural instinctive urges are closely associated with bodily constitution, physical and chemical. They belong to biology rather than to psychology. Some of them we have in common with most animals, for example, the urge to suck, without which our babyhood would be fraught with the danger of starvation, and the sexual urge, without which the propagation of the species would be impossible. Others are of a more individual character, and seem to be part of our racial or personal inheritance. Men and women are as different in their 'psychic constitution' as they are in their physical appearance and structure.

Whether we call these urges instincts, propensities, or anything else, they can be divided into three convenient groups from the point of view of their apparent function or purpose. In the first group are those which seem to be directed toward self-preservation, in the second group are those which seem to govern the preservation of the species, and in the third, somewhat related to the other two, are the urges to associate with others in groups, often called 'the herd instinct'.

It seems that the instinctual endowment of any animal, including man, is accurately fitted to the natural needs of early life. Ian D. Suttie begins a profound study of the child mind with the reasonable assumption that 'the child is born with a mind and instincts adapted to infancy, or in other words so disposed as to profit by parental nurture'.[1] Instead of the bundle of co-operating and competing instincts characteristic of primitive animals who soon have to fend for themselves, the child mind appears to him to be dominated from the beginning by the need to retain the mother, and a sense of acute but probably indiscriminate discomfort in isolation.

Suttie also believes that the instinct of self-preservation, though directed first to the mother, is socialized, and with play, co-operation, and shared interests, it is diverted to the need for others (the herd instinct) in an expanding social environment.

Sigmund Freud regarded these instinctive urges as purely sexual. He used the term sex in a wider sense than most authorities, which included practically all desire ('*libido*' or lust). He described infantile sexuality as an unfolding desire, centred in succession about the mouth, anus, and genitals, and mainly concerned with pleasure and gratification.

C. C. Jung saw '*libido*' as instinctive energy, will-power as well as desire, capable of being directed into various channels, religion, art, and social feeling, as well as sex. His psychology has been described as the nearest approach to religion, in that it introduces the recognition of man's religious need into psychology.[2]

Alfred Adler thought of this instinctive energy in more superficial terms as a kind of 'will to power', or desire for significance, a reaction to the human infant's realization of its helplessness.

The particular pattern of an individual's inborn dispositions is called his 'temperament', and the various kinds of temperament have been classified in different ways. The ancient 'philosophers' described four temperaments: sanguine, choleric, phlegmatic, and melancholic. They attempted to link them up with the four 'humours', and thought of them as brought about by an excess of blood, bile, phlegm, and spleen respectively. Plato described three types, the sensual, active, and thoughtful.

In more recent times Jung [3] has divided people into extraverts and

---

[1] *The Origins of Love and Hate* (Kegan Paul).
[2] J. Gebser, quoted by Hans Schaer in 'Introduction' of *Religion and the Cure of Souls in Jung's Psychology* (Routledge & Kegan Paul, 1951).
[3] *Psychological Types*.

introverts. Attempts have also been made to correlate the different 'temperaments' with the physical build and chemical structure of the body. Kretschmer [1] classified them as cycloid and schizoid, and tried to link these temperaments with bodily shape and structure. The cycloid or 'mercurial' personality often occurs in people of 'pyknic' bodily type, of medium height, with fat rotund body and face, short fat neck, and prominent abdomen. The schizoid, introvert personality often occurs in people of 'asthenic' type, with long thin body and face, a long, narrow, protruding nose, and a small chin. He described two other bodily types, the 'athletic', with strong well-proportioned frame covered by big muscles, and the 'mixed' or 'dysplastic' type, in which he placed all that would not fit into his other groups.

More recently W. H. Sheldon and S. S. Stevens of Harvard University have produced a three-fold classification of temperaments, [2] the 'viscero-tonic', the 'somato-tonic' and the 'cerebro-tonic', reminiscent of Plato's sensual, active, and thoughtful types. They are linked with bodily characteristics in that the viscero-tonic have large body cavities, the somato-tonic are of athletic build, and the cerebrotonic are generally thin and 'asthenic'. The viscero-tonic personality is supposed to be centred round the viscera, and to be dominated by love of food, comfort, affection, and company. The somato-tonic personality is dominated by muscular and bony development, and by vigorous bodily assertiveness, and the cerebro-tonic personality is dominated by the thoughtful, attentional, and inhibitory functions of the brain.

There is a general similarity between all these classifications, and it is generally agreed that they have much evidence to support them. It is recognized, however, that most people are mixtures of types, and that human personality is too complex to be pigeon-holed completely in any such rigid fashion.

It is also very difficult to separate any inborn tendencies of body or mind from the many and varied effects of the early environment of a person and from the complex chemical stimuli of ductless gland hormones.

From this consideration of the natural instinctive urges and the different kinds of temperament we must therefore pass on to look at some of the external and internal controlling influences that help to mould human attitude and conduct.

[1] *Physique and Character*.
[2] W. H. Sheldon, *The Varieties of Temperament*

The external controlling influences come from the total environment, physical, biological, personal, cultural, and spiritual, and are admitted into the personality partly through the alimentary and respiratory systems (food and air), and mostly through the five senses. They continually interact with the natural instinctive endowment, and become experienced as perceptions, emotions, ideas, and memories. In this way they become organized into acquired dispositions, of great number and variety: internal controlling influences which dispose us to act in certain ways in a wide range of situations.

These acquired dispositions tend to undergo progressive organization in the personality as the child grows and develops in awareness and in the power of relating events and experiences to one another and to the unfolding pattern of his life experience. As they do so the individual becomes less and less dominated by his environment. As J. A. Hadfield has pointed out, 'he himself affects and changes his environment'.[1]

The first level of organization is into sentiments, which are acceptable to the self, and complexes, which are unacceptable, or which, as Hadfield suggests, 'compel the individual to behave in an abnormal manner'. Sentiments and complexes are arranged around some kind of symbol, an object such as a flag, a person, something associated with a person or an experience, or an idea or mental image. They are held together and endowed with energy by emotion, and may be evoked by all kinds of external and internal stimuli. In some cases the response is so uniform that it may be looked on as a conditioned reflex, built up in the person through repeated stimuli, or through a single vivid and deeply penetrating experience.

There is further organization of these acquired dispositions into habits, conventions, and traditions, which are much stronger and more subtle cultural factors in attitude and behaviour than we generally realize. Long ago Confucius observed: 'Men's natures are alike; it is their habits that carry them far apart.' And William James maintained that 'if we realized the extent to which we are mere walking bundles of habits, we would give more heed to their formation'.

We have considered the natural instinctive urges bound up in our heredity and constitution, and the many and complex environmental influences which interact with them to influence human attitude and behaviour. It is sometimes stated that all human behaviour is the

[1] *Psychology and Mental Health* (Allen & Unwin, 1950).

product of these two factors. This of course is the deterministic view of man. But as Dr Harry Emerson Fosdick [1] has pointed out there is a third and inescapable factor in human attitude and behaviour, personal response. 'Life consists not simply in what heredity and environment do to us but in what we make of what they do to us.' If man is not in the last resort a responsible being it is difficult to see how he could ever do anything much to improve the environment, particularly the social environment, in which he finds himself. Our whole society is built on the absolute conviction of personal responsibility, and it is certain that no democracy on the national scale, nor any ordered home life in freedom and dignity could exist without it.

In the growth and development of every one of us something important happens between childhood and adulthood: the gradual assumption of personal responsibility, the ability and determination to take a hand in the working out of our own lives and destinies, and in many cases to do something to improve our society. We learn much better by our mistakes when we accept responsibility for them instead of blaming other people or society for them.

Perhaps we can sum up the complex pattern of influences and motives behind human attitude and behaviour by saying that the instinctive urges from heredity and constitution, and the acquired dispositions built up and progressively organized throughout life from the total environment, provide the mental and bodily—and spiritual—equipment through which we can be the creators and not the victims of our circumstances. Human history is full of examples of great men and women who have shown that this is not an empty dream.

Jesus of Nazareth, more than anyone else in history, has demonstrated this personally and socially creative power, and no pastoral work in His name would be effective (as it has been throughout the Christian era) or even possible, unless there were something in man that could accept the challenge of life and rise up to become personally responsible and socially creative.

II. THE MAIN SCHOOLS OF PSYCHOLOGY

The richness and complexity of human nature and the different motivating factors in attitude and conduct may be more fully realized when we consider the different 'schools' into which the various

[1] *On Being a Real Person* (SCM Press, 1944).

insights and hypotheses about them have become organized. The most important of them seem to be the dynamic, the behaviourist, the social, and the philosophical and religious.

(a) The Dynamic School: Freud, Jung, and Adler

The dynamic school, represented by Freud, Jung, and Adler, and their adherents, considers human attitude and behaviour mainly from the point of view of the pressures and conflicts associated with the instinctive urges, and the interaction between these and the urges and goals that develop in the growing personality in its progressive adaptation to the total environment. Most of these pressures and conflicts appear to exist outside the range of awareness, although many of their effects may well be experienced consciously by the person.

Sigmund Freud of Vienna postulated two main biological instinctive urges in people, one of which works in the direction of preservation and carrying-on of life, and the other, 'the death instinct', presses for the destruction of life. These biological instincts are experienced in the mind by feelings of tension, and demands for action of a kind which will bring some degree of satisfaction or relief of the tension. The psychological components of these life and death instincts are sex and aggression respectively, which interact in all kinds of ways throughout life. Behind its destructive nature, aggression is also part of the mechanism for self-preservation.

In Freud's view the sex instinct includes many feelings and activities which have nothing to do with the genital organs. The manifestations of sexuality as he sees it begin at birth. For the first two years they are mainly associated with the baby's mouth, and particularly with sucking, the most necessary activity for the preservation of life and at the same time an experience associated with intense pleasure. Later the 'sex instinct' seems to become centred on the anus, and then on the genital organs, those of the male earlier than those of the female.

From the age of five until early adolescence the 'sexual feelings' lessen in intensity, after which they reawaken to play their part in the rapid sexual development characteristic of adolescence.

At the beginning the child gratifies his sexual desires by the enjoyment of the oral, anal, and genital sensations elicited from his own body, accompanied, in Freud's view, by various phantasies. This infantile sexuality may then be directed to other people, first to the mother, and then in girls to the father and in boys more intensely to the mother. This attachment to the parent of the opposite sex is often accompanied by hostility or jealousy toward the other parent, and to any brothers or sisters who may seem to take up the desired parent's attention. This is what Freud called 'the Oedipus Complex'.

The aggressive instinct is also very strong from birth onwards, and naturally brings the child into conflict with his personal and social environment. Its gradual adaptation to the pressures and restrictions of the environment brings many tensions and difficulties, and the future mental health of the child will depend to a large extent upon the manner in which the manifestations of this aggressive instinct, and the associated sex instinct, are handled by parents and others who may have any part in the upbringing of the child.

This primitive instinctive psychic mechanism, which Freud labelled 'The Id', is blind to any other requirement than the need for satisfaction: protection and promotion of instinctive needs. Of itself it ignores the interests and needs of other people or of reality, it is completely and unashamedly selfish. But reality cannot be evaded and satisfaction is not always possible without the co-operation of other people, and the child soon begins to develop a second psychic mechanism, which Freud labelled 'The Ego', to record and store in memory the various pleasurable and painful experiences gained from the environment, and to correlate them into a more or less coherent pattern. Gradually the ego assumes control of the child's attitudes and behaviour previously held by the id, but there may be occasional outbursts in which the primitive urges overwhelm the developing controlling mechanism for a time.

These primitive urges are generally unrecognized by the person. When they force their way into consciousness in the form of emotional tension, or burst forth in some kind of tantrum, they are mostly bewildering to the person. He may say, 'I am not myself', or 'I cannot understand what came over me'.

The whole process of education, in its broadest sense, is largely a matter of development of the ego. An important early change in the developing psyche is the evolution from the inexact pictorial dream-like thinking of infancy to the ability to think and express thought in words, first by speech, and later by writing. Through the child's growing awareness of his environment, made coherent through memory, his 'ego' can gradually take over the general control of his attitudes and behaviour, and harness the primitive urges of sex and aggression in the interests of safety as well as satisfaction.

c

A large part of the attainment of safety must depend upon the attitudes of the people with whom the child has to live, particularly his parents, on whom he is completely dependent for a long period. These parental and social attitudes are largely felt as restrictive by the child, and they become registered in his mind through the development of a third psychic mechanism, which Freud labelled 'The Super-ego'. These restrictive influences may become so deeply and strongly imbedded in the child's growing personality that when he grows up and becomes capable of deciding his own attitudes they may still dominate his scale of values, even though he may be mostly unaware of their real nature. When the restrictive influences have come strongly from one or two people, particularly parents, it may continue to be so powerful that it would almost seem that their personalities had been taken up by the child. Freud called this 'Introjection', and the strong unconscious influence may continue in a person long after the parents have died, even for the whole of his life.

This inner 'super-ego' may become more dictatorial than any external controlling agency in that it dominates the innermost thoughts and feelings of a person as well as his external behaviour. It is this which has made it possible for the Jesuit priest to make the well-known observation: 'Give me power to tutor the first seven years of any man's life, and he will not escape my influence although he live a thousand years.' When the super-ego has become overdeveloped through a very repressive upbringing the mere desire to do something out of harmony with it may bring a deep sense of guilt which seems quite beyond the control of reason. Conflicts between primitive unconscious instinctive urges represented by the id, and acquired unconscious 'instinctive' controls represented by the super-ego may be very painful, and they cannot be resolved until the person becomes aware of them—until they can be brought to the 'surface' into relationship with the conscious 'ego'.

The whole pattern of the Freudian concept is built on the existence and power of this deep unconscious part of the mind, without which the field of consciousness would be so cluttered up with useless material that the ego could not function properly. But however necessary the unconscious part of the mind may be for normal psychic function, it may provide some complex problems when psychic function is disturbed.

The ego or conscious self has therefore to deal with many and often conflicting urges and demands from the id, the external environment, and the super-ego. Some of these are threatening, or appear to be so, and others appear potentially humiliating, and any of them may produce extreme anxiety or guilt.

The ego seems to be protected from overwhelming stresses by some important automatic mechanisms. The first of these is Repression. Potentially injurious elements are either 'forgotten' or prevented in some way from being admitted into the conscious awareness of the person. The ego seems to create a plausible reason for many actions and attitudes which arise from repressed motives, a mechanism which is termed Rationalization. Repression and rationalization are not deliberate devices, they have nothing to do with the conscious self-control and the wish to be sincere which everyone experiences to some extent every day. They are unconscious and quite automatic processes of a protective nature, which may succeed for a time. But the most powerful urges cannot be held in check altogether, and they may produce still further discomfort.

Another common protective device may then come automatically and still unconsciously into action. The ego may blind itself still more to the unwelcome instinctive urge from id or super-ego by assuming the opposite feeling. A mother who has a feeling of hatred for her child may automatically repress it from a strong feeling of shame. When it continues to harass her she may, without being conscious of the hatred, become over-solicitous for the child's welfare. This is called Reaction Formation, and it is usually obvious to the trained observer because it appears in exaggerated form, as a compulsive need in this case for the mother to keep on convincing herself that she does not really hate the child.

Yet another automatic protective device against uncomfortable feelings is Projection, in which they are displaced on to other people. We tend to criticize most intensely the things in other people of which we are guilty ourselves but about which we have a convenient 'blind spot', and we sometimes impute such things to them without any real justification. This protective device tends to produce further difficulties when it stirs up resentment in the other people, or when it makes the 'critic' more and more suspicious and intolerant. In some cases it may even bring about destructive behaviour.

When the conflicts or tensions are persistently overwhelming the person may react automatically to them by remaining fixed at or by regressing to an infantile or immature stage of psychic development.

Many symptoms of mental illness can be explained by this hypothesis of fixation or regression.

When on the other hand instinctive urges can be accepted in consciousness they can be dealt with, either by suppression or self-control, which differ completely from repression. They may also be dealt with by deliberate redirection into constructive, socially acceptable channels. This is called Sublimation. The pugnacious aggressive urges may be directed and used constructively in fighting social injustice rather than in picking quarrels with other people.

There are many other aspects of Freud's conception of the working of the human mind, which are beyond the scope of this short summary. Freud began his attempts at making contact with the unconscious part of the mind by the use of hypnosis, but later he gave it up owing to the number of people in whom he failed to induce hypnosis. His method of psychoanalysis of bringing unconscious mental processes into consciousness, is that of free association. The patient is invited to lie quietly on a couch in a slightly darkened room, and to 'think aloud' without any attempt to direct his thoughts or to inhibit them. As time goes on (and this method involves about five interviews of about an hour each every week for up to three years), the repressed material begins to slip out, with considerable emotional reaction as it outwits the psychic 'censor'.

Many of the repressed loves and hates are projected on to the person who carries out the treatment, a phenomenon called Transference. By the correct handling and positive use of these occasions the patient may be helped to better insight into himself and his inner feelings and conflicts. The term 'Psychoanalysis' has now become reserved for the Freudian method of doing it. Psychoanalysis has also become a kind of philosophy: a way of interpreting life with many wider implications than the investigation and treatment of mental illness.

Freud was in the best sense a pioneer. He faithfully followed the gleams of truth as he saw them, and brought a brilliant courageous mind to their interpretation and correlation. His findings led him to the view that all mental processes are determined, which many people regard as one that goes beyond the facts. When Freud the scientist becomes Freud the philosopher and sees religion as an illusion he again lays himself open to the charge of unconscious emotional bias.

Freud never regarded his insights as final or complete. His ideas developed throughout his professional life, as any investigation of his works in chronological order will show. Many of his ideas have been modified since his last books, and many more changes will doubtless appear. But he is the undisputed founder of modern psychiatry.

The second great school of dynamic psychology is that associated with the name of Carl Gustav Jung. Born in Switzerland in 1875, Jung began his psychiatric work in 1900, since when he has travelled widely, and investigated a very wide range of human activities and ideas. He was one of Freud's early collaborators, but he eventually found his insights and methods differing so greatly from those of Freud that he cut adrift, and he has since followed his own psychiatric path.

Jung's psychological and philosophical insights are wider and more profound than those of any other psychiatrist. They link up psychology with religion, art, literature, and with the age-old heritage of alchemy and mythology, to build a growing synthesis of understanding of the deep complexities of the human soul. But Jung never ceases to remind us of the incompleteness of human knowledge of these profound mysteries, and of the great field of work still to be done in exploring them.

From his experience with the conscious attitudes of people Jung divided them into two main personality types, the extrovert and the introvert. He also recognized that all people of each type possess 'functions of personality', which they use to make their way through life and through their social environment. There are four of these functions: sensation, thinking, feeling, and intuition, which are present, or developed to varying degree, in different people. When one of these functions is or becomes habitual in a person it may be thought of as a personality type, so that there are really eight different types of human attitude: extrovert thinking, introvert feeling and so on. The understanding of these inevitable differences in habitual attitudes will help greatly to prevent destructive criticism and futile conflict between people.

But Jung's most important work has been in his exploration of the unconscious part of the 'psyche', which he has divided into two parts: the personal unconscious, and the supra-personal or collective unconscious.

He regards the personal unconscious as 'the precipitate of a man's experience of life',[1] which contains all his unpleasant and his trivial

---

[1] Hans Schaer, *Religion and the Cure of Souls in Jung's Psychology* (translated by R. F. C. Hull) (Routledge & Kegan Paul, 1951).

'memories', and many of his less primitive instinctive urges and infantile strivings.

Material from the personal unconscious finds its way into awareness in disguised symbolic form in dreams and phantasies, and in such phenomena as slips of the tongue, or abnormal emotional reaction to various experiences or even particular words. Jung used a series of selected words in an association test as one method of exploring the personal unconscious, and he regards the study of dreams as a very important and fruitful method of bringing unconscious material into awareness. His interpretations are more flexible than those of Freud, who also paid particular attention to the dreams of his patients.

The supra-personal or collective unconscious was discovered by Jung as an aspect of psychic activity that could not be accounted for in terms of personal experience and memory. It seemed to be infused by archaic and mythical concepts, and this led Jung to regard it as 'the precipitate of the experience of all mankind', a vestigial psychic pattern which has persisted from the mists of antiquity, when all men lived in the collective unconscious.

This ancient collective unconscious would be quite unknown but for the fact that some of its contents find their way into awareness in certain vivid dreams and phantasies of such a character as to suggest the most primitive archaic images and mythologies. These primordial images or 'archetypes' in Jung's view 'do not consist of inherited ideas, but of inherited predispositions to reaction'.[1] This of course makes them important factors in the consideration of the springs of human attitude and conduct. As Jung pointed out: 'They are to be found in all religions, in all esoteric doctrines, mythologies, legends, fable sagas; but they can also occur even when their mythological character is not recognized.'[2]

Many of Jung's best psychological insights can be seen in his description of the chief archetypes, which are represented to some extent in the personal as well as the collective unconscious; there are no watertight compartments in the psyche. Jung named the principal archetypes which affect human attitude and behaviour the persona, the shadow, the anima and animus, the old wise man, the earth mother, and the self.[3]

---

[1] *Two Essays in Analytical Psychology*, quoted by Schaer.
[2] *The Integration of the Personality*, quoted in *Two Essays*.
[3] Frieda Fordham, *An Introduction to Jung's Psychology* (Penguin Books, 1953).

The persona is the kind of psychic mask which we present to our society in conformity with what we believe is expected of us as parsons, doctors, artists, or whatever occupation or position we hold. Most people combine a degree of individuality with this kind of role-playing, but anyone who discards the social convention is regarded as eccentric and unreliable, out of harmony with his fellows. Such conventions make it easier for us to decide what to expect from other people and in this way they make for better organization of society. We tend to adopt the mask unconsciously and automatically as a response to the moulding of our society, and Jung regards it as part of the collective unconscious.

The shadow is the general pattern of our inferior qualities, the part of our personalities of which we are ashamed. It is largely repressed into the personal unconscious, but emerges into action at certain times when our emotions are sufficiently aroused to overcome our sense of propriety. Most people tend to project on other people these 'uncivilized' qualities, and criticize in them the very faults to which the critic is unconsciously prone. Even nations are not immune from the same tendency, which increases the complexity and tension of international relationships. For true mental health we must learn to live with this inconvenient self which we would generally like to forget. This is probably the main element in true humility, and when these elemental and uncivilized rebels in our personality are recognized and accepted they can more easily be brought under control.

The anima is the deeply laid female element in the personality of every man, which varies in its degree of influence on his personal attitudes. The underlying basis of this feminine soul is thought by Jung to be 'an inherited collective image of woman—with the help of which he can apprehend the nature of women'.[1] This unconscious image is made conscious and more specific by the man's progressive experience of women, from his mother onward. His actual feelings about women are greatly coloured by the primitive unconscious anima image, and this unreal composite image of woman tends to be projected unconsciously on to any woman who may attract him. If the image is greatly different from the reality of the woman he marries, it may result in a tragically unhappy situation, because the man is unaware of what he is doing and, being unconscious, the image is infused with a high potential of emotional energy.

The animus is the deeply laid male principle in the personality of

[1] *Two Essays . . .*, quoted in Fordham, ibid.

every woman. Like the anima it has its roots in the inherited collective image, this time of man, a psychic pattern of women's experience of men throughout the ages. This primordial image is modified by the progressive experience of men in the life of the woman, from her father onward. An unreal composite image of man tends to be projected unconsciously on to any man who may stir her emotions, with the same dangers as are associated with the anima.

The anima and animus then are dynamic powerful composite images of the opposite sex, made up of a 'precipitate of the experience of all mankind' in the collective unconscious, and a 'precipitate of the particular man's or woman's experience of the other sex', largely in the personal unconscious. Even if they are difficult to comprehend, some knowledge of their existence and power will help people in the understanding of themselves, and of the attitudes and actions of other people which may otherwise appear unreasonable and even aggressive.

The old wise man and the earth mother are archetypes in men and women respectively through which the personality tends to become 'inflated', possessed and blown up by something beyond its capacity and power. The man may feel a godlike wisdom and infallibility, which is still further inflated by the fact that such possession inspires others to follow him. After a short but often meteoric career the hollowness of his megalomania becomes apparent and the house of cards tumbles, leaving many disillusioned people to regret their allegiance to him. When a woman is possessed by the earth mother she may feel herself endowed with infinite love and understanding, and the desire to give herself to the point of sacrifice in helping other people. But here again she is carried beyond her natural capacity, and the 'love' tends to be possessive in the extreme. This characteristic in a mother may show itself vividly when her son becomes engaged or married, and may provide him and his bride with a most difficult and painful emotional situation.

The self is Jung's term for the centre of the total integrated personality, conscious and unconscious, as it is gradually developed in the progressive individuation: growth to wholeness and maturity. It differs from Freud's 'ego', which is mainly if not wholly concerned with consciousness. To be made whole we must learn to accept much that is not 'respectable' in our personalities, and also much that is inconsistent and irrational. This is very difficult for the Western mind with its passion for consistency and conventionality, and often involves great psychic conflict and suffering. But it brings the inner peace that can only come from an acceptance of all the facts of life.

Beyond these particular manifestations, Jung regards the unconscious as having an essential and significant part in the total life of every individual, compensatory at every point to the conscious part of the psyche. It often seems to come to the rescue of the conscious life of the person by preserving some necessary attributes neglected or allowed to lapse. In this it seems to represent a psychic '*vis medicatrix naturae*'. Some neglected qualities may suddenly assert themselves at a given point in life, and bring a complete change in personal attitudes.

This changing of something into its opposite has been observed for many centuries. As Jung observed: ' "Old Heraclitus", who was indeed a very great sage, discovered the most marvellous of all psychological laws, the regulative function of opposites. He called it enantiodromia, a running contrariwise, by which he meant that sooner or later, everything runs into its opposite.' [1] This inner endowment, so well clarified by Jung, may have much to do with many religious conversions, particularly those of an apparently dramatic nature.

The psyche then, in Jung's view, is characterized by constant dynamic interaction between its conscious and its unconscious parts, and the unconscious itself is in constant self-regulating movement between two opposing poles. This living tension is the basis of psychic energy or '*libido*', and the to-and-fro dynamic equilibrium in the psyche is comparable with that in such other parts of nature, such as the atomic structure itself, the tides, and the human cycles of heart-beating and respiration.

When the general movement of the dynamic equilibrium is 'forward', in harmony with the requirements of the conscious self, Jung calls it 'progression'. This is an active deliberate adaptation to external reality. When the general movement is 'backward', in response to the demands of the unconscious, he calls it 'regression'. This may include many normal activities of the unconscious as well as the abnormal, and in thinking of regression as the adaptation to our inner needs, normal and abnormal, Jung gives it a wider meaning than Freud, as he does with his conception of '*libido*'.

Jung set out to encourage and help the mentally ill to better insight into their unconscious mental processes through the practice of what he called 'analytical psychotherapy'. In the use of free association

[1] *Two Essays . . .*, quoted in Fordham, ibid.

and the interpretation of dreams it is generally similar to the Freudian method of 'psychoanalysis', but Jung's interpretations differ in many ways from those of Freud. He believes the Freudian and Adlerian view-points to be more applicable to younger people than to the middle-aged, and gives them due attention where they seem appropriate. But he goes beyond the elucidation of the factors which led up to the illness, and sets out to discover and use the constructive elements in the illness, so that he can help the person to a better and more satisfying integration of his personality. This particularly applies to middle-aged and older people who are finding life empty and meaningless, in spite of having achieved some personal standing and material success.

The third of the schools of dynamic psychology—the 'Individual Psychology' associated with the name of Alfred Adler of Vienna—is perhaps the most direct, and the least complicated of the three. Adler sets out to bring the science of human nature out of the exclusive domain of the experts and into the comprehension of all people. In his own words: 'Only the understanding of human nature by every human being can be its proper goal.' [1]

In common with many other authorities Adler believes that 'the most important determinants of the structure of the soul life are generated in the earliest days of childhood'.[2] Behind the unfolding sequence of attitudes and actions of each individual in sickness or health he sees a constant 'life style' or pattern, directed toward and determined by a fixed, and often unrecognized goal.

A person's life-style is partly determined by the particular impressions and experiences gained from his early domestic environment, and partly by the influence of the general social pattern in which he lives, and to which he must find some way of adapting himself.

The human infant is possibly more helpless and dependent than any other animal, and unlike other animals he is conscious of his own inferiority and insecurity. The main goal and motive of all his striving is in Adler's view the overcoming of this intolerable situation by the achievement of a sense of significance and power.

Adler thus sees the fundamental pattern of a person's life as the particular strategy—positive or negative—through which that goal would seem to be most readily attainable. The positive or affirmative strategies are those of compensatory personal development and of

[1] *Understanding Human Nature* (Garden City Publishing Co. Inc., New York).   [2] ibid.

service to mankind through what Adler calls a 'social feeling'. The negative strategies are those in which the person exploits his 'weakness' and uses it unconsciously to represent an inexorable demand for attention and help. This strategy of denial is the unconscious background of the neurotic personality.

Once the general pattern of psychic activity has become fixed in a person, any situation, experience, or attitude may be used in such a way as to fit in with the chosen strategy of life and with the person's ideas about the nature of life and of his world.

In helping the mentally ill or maladjusted it is the delicate task of the therapist to discover the person's fundamental life-pattern and strategy behind all his varying attitudes and actions, and then to help him gradually to gain insight into his evasions and self-deceptions in such a way that he is not driven deeper into his automatic psychic defences. It is clear that any suggestion of disparaging criticism by the therapist will tend to deepen the person's sense of inferiority, and mobilize all his defences, while the attitude of acceptance will encourage him to emerge from his psychic 'hide-out' and eventually to face the less acceptable elements in his life strategy. Until these things can be faced openly they are inaccessible to any effective modification, and the person will sink deeper into psychic despair.

(b) The Behaviourist School

The Behaviourist school of psychology, led by J. B. Watson of Chicago, has been built mainly upon the important researches of the Russian psychologist, I. P. Pavlov. In his investigation of the processes of digestion in dogs he noticed that saliva flowed into the dogs' mouths at the sight or smell of food as well as by its presence in the mouth. It also flowed when the dogs saw the dishes in which the food was generally placed, or when they heard the steps of persons who usually brought the food.

These responses were obviously conditioned by the dogs' previous experiences, and Pavlov called them 'Conditioned Reflexes'. He then set out to produce further conditioned reflexes by offering food to the dogs some fifteen to thirty seconds after he had started an electric bell ringing. After many frequent repetitions of this sequence he found that saliva began to flow in the dogs' mouths in response to the ringing of the bell before, and then without, the offering of any food. The dogs also turned their heads in the direction from which the food usually came.

From these initial experiments Pavlov went on to investigate the production of other conditioned reflexes, and also ways in which conditioned reflexes would decrease in intensity, or could be removed.

Many similar experiments in conditioning and de-conditioning have been carried out by psychologists during the half-century since Pavlov's foundation work, and it seems clear that many of our human attitudes and actions, especially those that are 'spontaneous' or habitual, are explainable by this interesting mechanism.

J. B. Watson and his followers have been so impressed with the importance of these phenomena that they have come to the belief that all human attitude and conduct can be accounted for in this mechanical deterministic manner, without the need to postulate any complex individual mental processes. Man in their view is a kind of living automaton, conditioned in every detail by the particular psychological influences to which he has been exposed. Any attitude or conduct that cannot be explained in this manner will become explainable, they believe, with increasing knowledge of the conditioning.

Watson undertook to accept any group of babies, selected at random, and by submitting them to the appropriate training produce in them any kind of personality, and any desired mental attributes and moral qualities. But the experiment has so far proved impracticable, and his views have never been confirmed.

While the experiments of the Behaviourists provide unquestionably accurate data within the boundaries of experimental facilities, the conclusions drawn from them are frequently open to serious criticism. It seems clear that Psychology is not yet the exact science that the Behaviourists assume it to be, and it is probable that it never will be an exact science. At present the Behaviourists are in an almost insignificant minority among Psychologists and Psychiatrists. Even the extreme determinists find it difficult to justify the relative disregard of the obvious influence of heredity that is essential to Behaviourism.

(c) The Social School

The 'Social' school of Psychology has arisen and developed mainly in Germany and America, and has become associated with the names of Erich Fromm, Otto Fenichel, Wilhelm Reich, Harry S. Sullivan, Karen Horney, Franz Alexander, Adolf Meyer, and others.

It sprang from the work of Cultural Anthropologists and other

Social Scientists, from which arose an increasing recognition of the influence of cultural and social factors on attitude and conduct. It freely acknowledges its foundation on the epoch-making work of Freud, but feels free to modify or discard any of his theories which appear to be invalidated by further experience and research.

Freud himself found his ideas continually developing and even changing throughout his professional life. After his death, however, there was a tendency among some of his loyal followers to regard his latest insights as fixed unchangeable dogma. A notable exception to this was the acceptance of the brilliant work of Melanie Klein, which revealed the strength and importance of aggressive urges in young children.

The social school has come to the belief that some at least of the feelings and attitudes which Freud regarded as biologically determined, inherent in human nature itself, are very largely determined by the kind of culture and the particular social atmosphere in which the person has grown up.

Karen Horney, one of the leading members of this school of thought, constantly applied Freud's theories for more than fifteen years, and was led to a critical review of them by her dissatisfaction with the results of Freudian Psychoanalysis. She soon came to the belief that 'Freud's disregard of cultural factors not only leads to false generalizations, but to a large extent blocks an understanding of the real forces which motivate our attitude and actions'. She believes further that 'this disregard is the main reason why psychoanalysis, inasmuch as it faithfully follows the theoretical paths beaten by Freud, seems in spite of its seemingly boundless possibilities to have come into a blind alley, manifesting itself in a rank growth of abstruse theories and the use of a shadowy terminology'.[1]

In her subsequent books [2] Karen Horney shows the progressive evolution of her insights and methods, based on this greater cultural and social orientation, as opposed to Freud's biological orientation. From a belief that a disturbance in human relations was the central factor in neurotic illness, she has come to realize the nature and importance of many complex intra-psychic processes. These processes are initiated and intensified by the social experience of the

[1] *The Neurotic Personality of Our Time* (Kegan Paul, Trench, Trubner & Co. Ltd., 1937).

[2] *New Ways in Psychoanalysis* (Kegan Paul, 1939), *Self Analysis* (Routledge & Kegan Paul, 1942), *Our Inner Conflicts* (Routledge & Kegan Paul, 1946), *Neurosis and Human Growth* (Routledge & Kegan Paul, 1951).

person, and also prevent his growth to personal maturity and the achievement of the capacity for creative work and for good personal relationships. There will probably be a steady development of this cultural and social orientation, and better integration between it and the enduring aspects of Freud's biological orientation.

(d) The Philosophical and Religious School

The Philosophical and Religious school of Psychology, while not denying the findings and general conclusions of the dynamic, behaviourist, and social schools, emphasizes the claims of Reason, Truth, Beauty, and Goodness, and an ultimate overriding purpose in the affairs of men. It has not become as well defined as the other schools in its leaders or in its insights, but it is actively alive and growing.

Freud's psychoanalysis came into being as a technique for the investigation and treatment of mentally disturbed people. It was probably inevitable, however, that the dynamically influential data, gradually accumulated from the intimate and rather artificial seclusion of the analyst's couch, should come to be applied to the wider canvas of Philosophy and Religion, not to mention Sociology and Politics.

Freud attempted to keep these social and philosophical applications of psychoanalysis distinct from the individual and therapeutic by labelling them 'metapsychology', but he did not altogether succeed in doing so. As a result of his adventures into philosophical and religious dogmatism, notably expounded in *Totem and Taboo, The Future of an Illusion,* and *Moses and Monotheism,* Freud the Philosopher and Prophet has failed to receive the recognition and respect accorded to Freud the Psychologist and Psychoanalyst.

But these philosophical and religious ideas have evoked an ever-expanding body of further thought and discussion among Freud's followers and opponents alike, from Jung to the present day. J. C. Flugel [1] has given considerable study and thought to the wider religious and social applications of psychoanalysis. Marjorie Brierley [2] in a later attempt to 'explain' religion by means of psychoanalytical concepts, maintains that, 'It is important for the psychologist to become fully informed of the archaic-infantile content of dogma and ritual, but this should not lead him to overlook the provision made

[1] *Man, Morals, and Society* (Duckworth, London, 1945).
[2] *Trends in Psychoanalysis* (Hogarth Press, 1951).

in ritual and prayer for the satisfaction of impulse and the recovery of otherwise lost instinctual energy in the believer.'

These and other similar approaches to religion from the findings of psychoanalysis do not really represent the Philosophical and Religious school of Psychology. They often seem to assume that there is little or nothing more in religion than what man has created, consciously or unconsciously, to meet his emotional and other psychic needs. But they point to the necessity for constant awareness of the subtle self-deceptions revealed by psychological research, and for willingness to allow for growth to greater maturity in religious as well as 'secular' attitudes.

The Philosophical and Religious school of Psychology is more fittingly represented by the growing band of men and women in many countries who see in religion the sincere but ever imperfect human response to the progressive and many sided revelation of God. They see this revelation as built on objective historical fact, and constantly enriched by all the unfolding experience of man and all that he finds in his asking, seeking, and knocking. They see in all human attempts at 'explanation' of facts and findings, the working of a divinely created and inspired intelligence which can only 'think God's thoughts after Him', in humility and objective open-mindedness.

The school believes that the ethical and moral principles and the scale of values by which men live are determined, not by the changing currents of expediency, but by the unfolding human insights into the nature and purpose of God, Man, and Society. All the findings of psychological and all other scientific research are then welcomed, and when confirmed they are built gradually into the growing structure of human understanding, to be still further moulded and enriched by further insights.

The general attitude of this school to other schools of modern psychology may be summed up in some words of W. B. Selbie: [1] 'There is no sort of antagonism between religion and psychology, though there may be between certain forms of religion and certain philosophical conclusions based on psychology.' It is becoming increasingly clear that no rational study of history, sociology, or of the human mind can fail to recognize the profound influence of religious attitudes and practices upon the thoughts, feelings, and actions of men; and this applies to every aspect and every department of human life.

[1] *The Psychology of Religion* (O.U.P., 1926).

(e) A Workable Synthesis

How are we to find our way through these complex and conflicting schools of psychology, and still more through the dense forest of psychological terms? If we believe that religion is an integrating influence in human attitude and behaviour it would seem to be an interesting and worth-while task to try to relate the relevant ideas of each of these schools to one another and to apply them to the understanding and helping of his people.

Much of the confusion is attributable to the infinite complexity of the human mind, and to the groping attempts of men and women to understand the complicated psychic processes and to formulate their concepts in understandable terms. It is certain that further experience and further research will help to clarify the confusion, and that the growing science of semantics, concerned with the meaning of words, will bring further progress.

At the risk of over-simplification and over-dogmatism, however, one might attempt to formulate a working synthesis. The ideas of each of these schools of psychology are backed by considerable factual evidence, and cannot be disregarded. They are fallacious only when they claim exclusiveness or attempt to elevate hypothesis into dogma. The 'higher' functions are superimposed upon the more primitive lower, and may drive some of them out of consciousness—but not out of existence. There is much evidence that they exert a very powerful and subtle influence as an 'underground movement' in normal mental processes, and still more in the various kinds of mental illness.

The existence and power of sub-conscious motives may be regarded as the most important and far-reaching fact established by scientific study of the mind. Its recognition is necessary for any understanding of human attitude and conduct, but it is seldom taken into account by people in general in their judgements of one another. This is an important factor in the causation of disparaging criticism, and its fruits of hatred and retaliation, and the poisoning of human relationships.

People are dominated far more than they generally realize by emotion, habit, social convention, and prejudice. They tend to rationalize, automatically to use their reason to provide an acceptable justification of their attitude and behaviour. They are thus blind to their own inconsistencies, and quickly see through those of other people. They tend to criticize the faults they see in others, particularly those to which they themselves are unconsciously (or semi-consciously) prone; and are quickly and vigorously on the defensive when criticized by others.

This finding emphasizes the profound wisdom of Jesus and His deep understanding of human nature, in His direction:

Judge not, that you be not judged. For with the judgement you pronounce you will be judged, and the measure you give will be the measure you get. Why do you see the speck that is in your brother's eye, but do not notice the log that is in your own eye? Or how can you say to your brother, 'Let me take the speck out of your eye', when there is the log in your own eye? You hypocrite, first take the log out of your own eye, and then you will see clearly to take the speck out of your brother's eye. (Matthew 7¹⁻⁵, *RSV*).

In our understanding of human attitude and conduct, then, we must begin with the basic instinctive biological urges in human nature as described by Freud (sex and aggression), Suttie (the need for the mother) and Jung (the personal and collective unconscious). We must then consider the vital influence of the total environment, particularly that of the earliest environment, in the moulding and conditioning of human personality. It exerts its influence through the child's perceptions which become organized into experiences, and their interactions with the biological urges, also through the child's reactions to these experiences and the counter-reactions of people around him. These again become organized into memories, sentiments, and complexes and attitudes, many of which are goal-seeking (Adler).

The growing personality or ego (Freud) then has to deal not only with the powerful urges from the 'id' (Freud) but also finds the restrictive influences of parents and others becoming 'introjected' to form an inner restrictive force, the super-ego (Freud), and the child's day-by-day methods of coping with his life situation become fairly well established as a set of habitual attitudes, or 'style of life' (Adler). It is made more complex by the inevitable conflicts at each 'level' of the personality, between different levels, and in his reaction to an often variable and inconsistent environment.

The sense of safety, originally felt in his close contact with his mother, is gradually modified and extended to a dependence on his society, and social acceptance becomes a powerful goal and a strong motivating influence, as emphasized by the social school.

D

Here, if he is fortunate, he comes into contact with the positive cementing influences in society, the products of the unfolding spiritual heritage of mankind, and there is that in man which can perceive and respond to the influence of faith, hope, and love.

In this way the child comes to develop his own religious attitudes which become synthesized into a philosophy of life, by which most of his impulses and urges can be regulated, and redirected to goals and purposes that seem worth-while and in keeping with what we can believe to be the will of God. This redirection is far more natural to a being who possesses intelligence and the capacity for value-judgements, and far more effective than any attempts at suppression and annihilation.

Man's animal nature is not in itself evil. It is, however, self-centred, disordered, and in need of control by the sense of right and wrong that we call conscience (knowing with). The first ideas of right and wrong come to a child from his experience of what is approved and disapproved by his parents, teachers, and others. It then seems largely restrictive and corresponds fairly well with Freud's 'super-ego'. But the super-ego is largely negative and restrictive, and seems to leave no room for the positive 'divine imperative' which inspires many people to acts of generosity, self-sacrifice, and devotion. This inner positive influence is an important element in the conscience.

Conscience has been described by the late G. A. Studdert Kennedy in these terms: 'Your conscience is only an eye which must have light to see with, and your creed is the light by which your conscience sees.' [1] Perhaps the most vital and far-reaching part of a child's growth to maturity is the gradual taking over from the early parental values of his own unfolding 'creed', or set of beliefs about God or life, man, and society. The pattern of that growth will depend far more upon the quality of the child's personal relationships and his personal experiences than upon the actual teaching to which he is exposed. That is not to deny the extreme importance of good teaching, but to emphasize its need for the whole-hearted backing of personal relationships.

The various controlling influences by which man's nature becomes regulated and ordered are not in any sense automatic, nor are they always clear or effective. 'The controls are not merely weak, in-effective and discordant. They are also not self-explanatory, and

[1] *Food for the Fed-up* (Hodder & Stoughton, 1921), p. 10.

therefore they are not ultimately authoritative.' [1] They need an ultimate authority, not imposed from without, but arising from within. To the Christian the most effective controlling influence is the Christian ethic, backed by Christian Theology, and by the Christian Gospel, embodied in and inspired by Jesus Christ Himself, 'Whose service is perfect freedom '.[2] This whole educational influence is kept alive and fresh in every age by its continued embodiment in the Christian Church, 'The Body of Christ', and brought to people by its whole living programme of preaching, teaching, shepherding, and worshipping, and through the ever-expanding pattern of its social service in the name of Christ.

One of the most important and far-reaching creative tasks of the pastor is therefore to be the main channel through which the Spirit and Personality of Jesus Christ can reach people with whom he can make contact, with such reality and power that they themselves can transmit it to others, especially the children committed to their care as parents or teachers, or in any other capacity. Only in this way can people receive the fullness of Christ's gift of abundant life.

[1] Balmforth, Dewar, Hudson and Sara, *An Introduction to Pastoral Theology* (Hodder & Stoughton, 1937).
[2] *The Book of Common Prayer*.

CHAPTER THREE

The Specific Psychological and Religious Background

THE PASTORAL function may be seen as the never-ending attempt to bring all the available resources of knowledge and inspiration to the fullest service of people, to help them to lay hold of the Christian gift of abundant life from the beginning or at any period of life, or to recover it when they have lost it. In this chapter, therefore, we shall attempt to consider some relevant aspects of the development and integration of personality, and the nature and meaning of abundant life: the essential manifestation of Christian personality.

Personality has been defined as 'That which distinguishes a person from a thing, or one person from another',[1] but there is no simple and yet adequate definition of this intangible entity. In all our discussions of personality we must use symbols to try to convey what we mean.

For example we talk of dimensions of personality, height, depth, and breadth; of levels of personality, and of such concepts as range of vision. We also describe the dynamics of personality, thinking of it as alive, endowed with and giving out energy, constantly developing, and capable of development and integration. We conceive it as organized about a centre: a master loyalty which is capable of changing with growth and experience from the infantile, self-centred, through the childish, gang-centred, and adolescent, sex- and community-centred, to the adult, life-work or God-centred.[2]

The degree of development of personality can be fairly simply assessed in terms that have been used by Henry C. Link as a definition of personality: 'The extent to which the individual has developed habits and skills which interest and serve other people.'[3]

In still further symbolism we think of stability and instability of personality, of conflicting energies which may be suppressed, repressed, discharged, or harnessed and directed.

Personality is therefore something rich, varied, and unique, and is

[1] Chambers's *Twentieth Century Dictionary*.
[2] D. Maurice Allan, *The Realm of Personality* (Abingdon Cokesbury, 1947).   [3] *The Rediscovery of Man* (Macmillan, 1939), p. 60.

seen as a most complex organization, continually changing, of many interdependent parts, at many different 'levels'. Any part is easier to comprehend than the whole, and many apparently contradictory ideas about the nature of man arise because human personality is viewed in part, often from one level only.

It is possible, for example, to take what we might call a 'dog's-eye view', and see man as nothing more than a clever animal, an idea that is still current in some quarters.

If we take a purely humanistic view man appears in addition as an intelligent, rational being: the master of his fate and the captain of his soul. This idea is also widely current, but it is wearing very thin in the face of man's obvious irrationality and his manifest inability to master himself. Modern psychology has allied itself with ancient religion in discarding this purely humanistic view of man.

If, on the other hand, we can venture to imagine a 'God's-eye view' of man, the animal and human components become raised to a new dignity and value. Man is then seen as the dwelling-place of eternal Spirit, through which he is given power to become the willing, co-operating instrument of a superhuman power and purpose. Man in this view is the bearer of values, he is a being whose effectiveness is lifted above his own stature, whose eternal destiny lies far beyond his own horizon.

It is obvious that the fundamental nature and scope of all pastoral work, and indeed of all human relationships, must depend upon which of these views of man that we take. If we regard men as little more than clever animals, then our medicine and our pastoral work will be largely veterinary in their nature and their limitations. If we accept the 'God's-eye view', on the other hand, we will seek to know and relate ourselves to the whole man, we will help to restore his broken spirit as well as his distracted mind and his pain-racked body.

In thinking of the living, growing, ever-changing human personality we must therefore use a wide canvas. We must think of the individual in terms of the constant dynamic interrelationship of body, mind (conscious and unconscious), the self-conscious soul, aware of itself as a person different from other persons and capable of personal relationships with them, and the God-conscious Spirit, the power that calls forth his noblest aspirations and actions, the divine imperative that summons from human clay the poet, the hero, and the saint.

Each of these interrelated parts of the human personality is always in reciprocal relationship with an appropriate part of the total environment, the body with the natural and biological environment, the mind with the cultural, the soul with the social, and the spirit with the spiritual. This of course is an over-simplification, but it is useful for the purpose of discussion. This two-way reciprocal relationship may be stable or unstable, and instability tends to bring a sense of discomfort, and a challenge, either to adaptation or radical change.

On the bodily plane Lecomte du Noüy has pointed out that 'whereas adaptation blindly tries to attain an equilibrium which will bring about its end, evolution can only continue through unstable systems or organisms. It only progresses from instability to instability and would perish if it only encountered perfectly adapted, stable systems'.[1]

What then do we mean by the term 'Abundant Life'? 'Abundant' is derived from the Latin word '*abundāre*', to overflow, and perhaps overflowing is the most appropriate characteristic of abundant life: a kind of radiance that shines out unselfconsciously in loving joyous friendship.

Behind this radiance there is always a good balance between the different aspects of life, which can be described simply as work, play, love, and worship. Such balanced living also shows out in what St John of the Cross once described as the combination of tranquillity, gentleness, and strength.

Another characteristic of abundant life, and indeed of life itself, is growth. Abundant life is different for the adult from what it is for the child. In later life there may be continued growth of soul and spirit even with some decline in body and mind. Abundant life means becoming as well as being.

Another important characteristic of abundant life is that all these qualities are present in spite of difficulties and setbacks, handicaps and temptations. In fact it has always been the unique genius of Christian abundant life to turn difficulties into opportunities, to be 'more than conquerors', in St Paul's arresting phrase. Abundant life will often mean being out of harmony with society to the extent that society is out of harmony with God. Jesus Himself, and many other great world leaders have found themselves so out of harmony with the social values and habits of their times that they had to endure persecution and even martyrdom for their faith.

[1] *Human Destiny* (Longmans Green, 1947).

Perhaps the most important of all facts about abundant life is that it is not something we make for ourselves at all. It is something given to those who follow God through Christ. The well-known words of Jesus, 'I am come that they might have life, and that they might have it more abundantly' (John 10¹⁰), come in the 'Shepherd' chapter, and St Paul maintains that we are 'more than conquerors through him that loved us' (Romans 8³⁷). And in the words of a modern authority: [1] 'We become saints, not by aiming self-consciously at sanctity, but by loving God and our neighbour with all our heart, mind, and strength.'

Abundant life, then, is the free gift of God through Jesus Christ, but it needs our deliberate acceptance if we are to have it, and that demands something important from us. We may see it more clearly if we consider five essential gifts of God through which we may find the answers to our needs, and the way to abundant life, through Jesus Christ.

We may think first of the satisfaction of our material needs. Jesus reminded mankind that God has endowed the earth with potential resources sufficient for everyone's need (Matthew 6²⁶⁻³²). He also pointed to the best way to make them available to the whole human race: 'Seek ye first the kingdom of God and his righteousness; and all these things shall be added unto you' (ibid., 6³³). The brotherhood of man under the loving Fatherhood of God, expressed in loving, self-giving service, in which our time, talents, energies, possessions and opportunities are used in the highest stewardship—that is our part in making the material gifts of God available for the promotion of the highest standards of life for all His children. Here is the Christian view of work as one of the great privileges of life, and a supreme opportunity of serving God.

The second great gift for abundant life is direction. We need to know how to live, and what to do to make the most of our opportunities. Some people think that they can find sufficient direction through certain ethical and moral principles, such as honesty, decency, and moderation, or through the unwritten laws of social convention. Others pin their faith on conscience, but this, as we have seen, is like an inner eye, which needs light to see with. All ethical and moral principles, and all commandments and virtues tend to be too abstract and even ambiguous to give the direction needed for abundant life. The clearest and surest direction surely comes from Jesus Himself,

[1] Balmforth and others, *An Introduction to Pastoral Theology.*

'the Light of the World', in whose life all these things are clearly embodied in unmistakable fashion, and in whose teaching the deep truths about life have been expressed for all time in terms that all men can grasp. Our part here is to come progressively to know Him and to follow Him in our lives.

The third great gift of God through Jesus Christ for abundant life is power, or inspiration. We may see the way clearly, but will fail unless we have the power to walk in it. Jesus went to the absolute limit of sacrificial devotion to win the love and loyalty of mankind, and His last words before His ascension included the promise, 'Ye shall receive power' (Acts 1[8]), a promise that has been abundantly fulfilled throughout the Christian era. This power of self-giving, outgoing Christian love is not natural to man. As Jesus told Nicodemus: 'Except a man be born of water and of the Spirit, he cannot enter into the kingdom of God. That which is born of the flesh is flesh; and that which is born of the Spirit is spirit' (John 3[5-6]). The power of Christian love (agape) is born in people through the spiritual experience of being loved in that way, by parents, pastors, or other human channels of the Spirit of God. As St John wrote, after a long and unique experience: 'We love, because He first loved us' (1 John 4[19]). Many a great military leader has awakened or given birth to the power of devotion in his men by his devotion to them. Our part in accepting this great gift of power is to remind ourselves of His devotion in our worship, to enlist whole-heartedly in His service, and to undergo the disciplined training for Christian living in company with other Christian people.

The fourth great gift is deliverance. With all his best efforts man is still a fallible being, prone to all kinds of stupid and even deliberate wrongdoing. No religion which fails to offer deliverance from repeated failures can ever help him to abundant life. In all His attitudes and all His dealings with men and women, and supremely at Calvary, Jesus showed in clear and unmistakable terms the forbearing and forgiving love of God, and the continual offer to man of a fresh start. He illustrated this utter forgiveness of God vividly in the well-known parable of the Prodigal Son, and it is interesting to recall that the Prodigal set out to find 'abundant life' in man's way, through possessions, popularity, and prestige, and ultimately found the truly abundant life in God's way, through humility, obedience, and service, which is the attitude by which we can best accept God's continual deliverance.

The fifth great gift is fellowship. The events in Palestine recorded in the Gospels are far away in space and time. Men and women need something visible and tangible (as the early disciples had) to grip their imaginations and inspire them to the highest level of life. Jesus provided for this by establishing the Christian Church, to be His continuing 'body', and to show Him afresh in every age, through the fellowship of His Holy Spirit. The Church is commissioned to carry on His work of proclaiming, exemplifying, and thus helping to build the Kingdom of God. As life can only come from life, personal life can only come from persons. Only the complete personality can speak adequately to the whole of man and lead him to abundant life. The most direct sources of abundant life in every age are people whose personalities have overflowed into human affairs in such a way as to awaken and mobilize the potential energies in their fellow men. It will always be so, and we might remind ourselves that the overflowing abundant life of all such people has come ultimately, through a kind of 'apostolic succession' of love, more from Jesus than from any other conceivable source. Our part here is in His own words: 'Love one another as I have loved you' (John 15[12]).

We have seen that abundant life shows itself as a combination of radiance, balance, growth, and overcoming; also that it is not something we can make for ourselves. Like health and happiness, with which it is related, it is given to us through following a particular standard and way of life in which we accept the great gifts of God in the right spirit and the proper co-operation. We have also described those gifts under five headings as material needs, direction, power or inspiration, deliverance, and fellowship.

But in thinking thus of abundant life we must face the very important fact that the vast majority of people live lives that could never be called abundant. Every pastor who knows his people soon comes to realize how many of them go through periods in their lives during which they find abundant life an elusive and apparently unattainable ideal. For some of them their whole lives appear to be far short of abundant life.

Behind a stolid or even gay façade many people courageously hide deeply bewildered minds, aching hearts, and despairing spirits. To help any large numbers of people to find or recover abundant life through Jesus Christ is no easy or superficial task. It demands a high standard of abundant life from the pastor, an unshakable faith and patience, and a sacrificial devotion that he will always recognize as beyond his unaided power.

An infectious cheerfulness, and a breezy good-natured optimism will play a useful part in all the pastor's encounters with people. But unless these are founded on a deep and overflowing understanding of the nature of human life in its sorrows and sufferings as well as its joys, and of the poignancy of human feelings, he will inevitably fail to reach the heart of his urgent pastoral opportunities, and to bring the creative and redemptive aspects of sorrow and suffering to people who are aching to find some meaning in their heavy experience. The pastor must be able and ready to 'launch out into the deep'.

There are two distinct but closely related aspects of the practical enterprise of helping people to abundant life. The ideal is of course that they should be helped to grow into it naturally from the beginning of their lives, and this is part of the personal and educational aspect of pastoral work. When this has not been achieved, or when people have lost the abundant quality of life that they once had, they need to be helped to recover it, and this is part of the therapeutic or healing, and of the evangelistic aspects of pastoral work.

For giving help in any of these situations it is necessary to have some understanding of the main outlines of the development and integration of personality, and particularly of the special needs of the growing child in infancy and during the unsettled period that we call adolescence, when he is awakening to the need and power of taking over the administration of his own life.

We shall therefore give some consideration to a few of the many important parts of this complex process of growth of personality.

In thinking about the development and integration of personality from the standpoint of Christian pastoral work we must consider the development and integration of the body, the mind, the soul, and the spirit of man, the integration of all these in the individual (the undivided personality); and then the integration between the individual and society (without which the personality cannot develop); and finally the integration between the individual and God, which sets the standard and gives the fullest power for all the rest. St Luke sees this pattern and hierarchy of integration in his account of the growth of the world's most fully developed and integrated personality, Jesus Christ—'And Jesus increased in wisdom and stature, and in favour with God and man' (2^{52}). And in more modern terms Dorothy Sayers [1] describes the purpose of Christian education as to help

---

[1] In Preface to *What is Christian Education?* by Marjorie Reeves and John Drewett (Sheldon Press).

the child to become 'a man, among men, in a world that makes sense'.

The newly-born child is possibly the most helpless of all animals, it has even to be lifted to its mother's breast. It possesses the potentials of personality, and is capable of learning, but it has everything (except the sucking and swallowing faculty) to learn. The principle of growth and integration seems to be inherent in man, as in some measure in all living things, but these great essentials can only be achieved by controlled living in the appropriate total environment.

The requirements for bodily development and integration are well known, and need little more than recalling. We can describe them as food (proteins, carbohydrates, and fats, water, minerals, and vitamins), fresh air, sufficient exercise and rest, and the appropriate stimulations and challenges. These have been and are still the subject of constant study and research by experts in various related fields.

It is now becoming more and more clear that for the proper development of the child's mind, soul and spirit he needs the right kind of love, security, and acceptance as a person, and that he needs them just as urgently and definitely as he needs protein carbohydrate and fat for the development of his body. The right kind of love can be described as an unconditional unquenchable demonstrative out-going affection, which is seen in its purest form in the best kind of mother love, which is in its turn a clear picture of Christian love (agape).

The clear findings of John Bowlby [1] from his painstaking and brilliant work for the World Health Organization, have established beyond reasonable doubt the absolute need of every child for a mother or a permanent mother substitute. Bowlby describes in broad outline the most important phases in the development of the child's capacity for human relationships:

(a) The phase during which the infant is in course of establishing a relation with a clearly identified person—his mother; this is normally achieved by five or six months of age.

(b) The phase during which he needs her as an ever-present companion; this usually continues until about his third birthday.

(c) The phase during which he is becoming able to maintain a relationship with her in her absence. During the fourth and fifth years such a relationship can only be maintained in favourable

[1] *Maternal Care and Mental Health* (World Health Organization Monograph, 1951), *Child Care and the Growth of Love* (Penguin Books, 1953).

circumstances and for a few days or weeks at a time; after seven or eight the relationship can be maintained, though not without strain, for periods of a year or more.

Bowlby goes on to say that

the ages by which these phases are completed no doubt vary greatly from child to child in the same way that the stages of physical maturity vary. [But] the evidence is fairly clear that if the first stage of development—that of establishing a relation with one particular person recognized as such—is not satisfactorily completed during the first twelve months or so, there is the greatest difficulty in making it good: the character of the psychic tissue has become fixed. (The limit for many children may well be a good deal earlier.) Similarly there appears to be a limit by which the second and third phases must be completed if further development is to proceed. Now it is these vital growth processes which are impaired by the experience of deprivation.

This is surely what would be expected by those who believe that man was created by a personal God as a member of a community of persons through whom, beginning with the pro-creator, the mother, the Spirit of God can reach him and give birth to the spirit within him.

It is interesting to remind ourselves that the sequence of events in the unfolding relationship between parents and child is the same as that between God and man. It begins naturally with creation, and this immediately merges into preservation: that of the mother and father for the child being typical of the loving preservation of God for man. Then comes one of the most wonderful episodes in the parent-child relationship: the mother and father setting out to reveal themselves progressively to their child, by smiling, handling, talking and singing, as well as feeding and caring in general, and looking anxiously for the first sign of recognition in the form of an answering smile in the child. Here again is a 'working model' of God's progressive personal revelation to man. It is well to remember that we can only know another person (as distinct from knowing about him) in so far as that person is willing to reveal himself to us, and the same is true of knowing God.

The sequence continues in each case with what we can describe as direction, inspiration, deliverance, and fellowship, which we have seen to be the main gifts that make for abundant life, and the ultimate goal in each case is to win the loving fellowship and freely-given co-operation of the 'child'.

It is clear then that the child's first ideas of the nature and character and attitudes of the heavenly Father will inevitably be derived from what the child sees and experiences in the human parent, and mother and father each have a part in this great and far-reaching project. The main qualities that parents need to show in their own relationship and in all their dealings with their child are love at the Christian level, dependability, and reverence for the child's personality, which show the main characteristics of God, and at the same time meet the great instinctive personal needs of the child for love, security, and acceptance respectively. These as we have seen are as necessary for the proper growth of the child's personality, as are protein carbohydrate and fat for the proper growth of his body; and the child is as hungry for them as for food.

It is important that these qualities should be expressed quite spontaneously in all the various parental attitudes and actions, particularly in feeding, the first intimate personal relationship in the experience of the newly-born child. A warm feeling of secure love is then absorbed into the child's growing soul while the appropriate food is being absorbed into his growing body. Here the child's first ideas, vague and instinctive, but none the less potent, are laid down about the new life into which he has been born. Here begin his feelings about the friendliness or unfriendliness of his environment, and these earliest feelings will colour all his subsequent insights.

The later parent-child relationships created by such homely matters as 'toilet training' and the parental attitudes to the child's early sexual interests (handling of his external genital organs), and his early aggressive attitudes, are also vital and far-reaching opportunities for showing and deepening the love dependability, and reverence for the child's personality. Later still the same loving acceptance can help the child very greatly in the inevitable episodes of anxiety and jealousy. At the same time the child is then being well prepared for the inevitable periods of separation from the mother and for the wider relationships into which he will gradually find his way.

There are some fairly definite early landmarks in the psychic development of young children which illustrate this gradual widening of their personal relationships.

During the first four years of life the child awakens to the gradual distinction between 'me' and 'not me'. He still has a strong emotional attachment to his mother, or mother-substitute, and separation from this person may bring serious and even irreversible harm. As he is unable to control his feelings at this stage the fullest maternal acceptance of them is very important. He is also capable of partaking in close personal relationships with his father, and with other regularly available people. It is most important that fathers particularly should set out to win the trust and confidence of their babies from the very beginning.

During the next three years there is a great expansion of all these social relationships, and particularly of those with the father if he has managed to build a good relationship from the beginning. If not the father may wonder why his child seems to be rather aloof to him. Disturbance or failure of the father-child relationship at this time may be very injurious to the child. He is still dependent on his mother, but more still on the mother-father relationship. In these three years he will also be making many other relationships in and outside the home, particularly at kindergarten, school, Sunday-school, and in the neighbourhood. The healthy friction with the desires, wills and rights of others will help greatly in his psycho-social development.

From 7 to 11 or more there is a gradual beginning of the growth of independence which goes on progressively through adolescence. He will begin to go about with and make his own relationships with 'the gang', and will come to deal with moderate frustrations and stresses through his own resources, often strengthened by parental or other encouragement.

We can realize, therefore, the immeasurable importance of a stable, happy home for the early stages of development and integration of personality; a home which provides the necessities for personal growth, enough challenges to stimulate his own efforts but not to demand what is beyond his capacity, and the deliverance from the troubles and fixes that form an inevitable part of the early experiments in the cultivation of skills and of relationships. The good mother possesses more than anyone the inexhaustible resources of love which absorb the childish crudities, the thoughtless ingratitudes, and the arrogant self-assertions that are so much a part of every normal child's early efforts at personality development.

At some time during the unsettled period known as adolescence, the rapid chemical and physical changes in the child's body are matched by an important change in his personal relationships, particularly those within the family. At some stage in the second decade of his life the child gradually becomes aware of his own individuality and power, and begins to take over the responsibility for the further development of his own personality. There is an awakening of idealism, and a tendency to think deeply and often impulsively, which may bring all kinds of conflicts within the adolescent, and with those among whom he lives and works, particularly with his parents.

During his childhood the parents will have had the upper hand, and the power to enforce their will, by punishment if necessary. The natural urge toward independence and freedom should normally lead to a gradual change in the parent-child relationship from a 'dictatorship' to a 'democracy', but that change is often difficult and painful unless the parents are endowed with the qualities already mentioned, and administer them with considerable wisdom and patience.

This and the further development of personality, will be considered in Chapter 10.

SECTION TWO

The Personal and Educational Ministry

E

CHAPTER FOUR

The Fine Art of Visiting and Interviewing People

I. IS PASTORAL VISITING STILL WORTH WHILE IN THESE DAYS?

THERE IS some difference of opinion about the worthwhileness of routine pastoral visiting. Those who doubt its value (except in special needs such as sickness or other trouble) point out that the whole situation has changed since the days in which it was found useful and beneficial. In those days families worked together as a unit in either agricultural or craft work, and there were no alternative means of communication. Wireless was unknown, the printing-press was not as widely used, and schools were not as well organized or as widely available. The routine visit of the pastor was then one of the few opportunities for personal contact with the family, and for educational work. And it was possible to see the whole family, sometimes two or three families or generations together.

In these days of industrial civilization, the husband is generally away at work during the day, and the wife often has to look after a small and very demanding toddler. With these difficulties, and also the intruding telephone and door-bell it is often difficult to obtain sufficient privacy for the kind of discussion that may be needed. In addition to these changes there are now many more methods of communication: wireless, newspapers, magazines, church papers, pamphlets, and last but not least the telephone. It is recognized that these generally fail to supply the personal touch to the extent to which it might be needed, but the questioning of the value of routine pastoral visiting still goes on, and some pastors have given it up except for people who deliberately ask for it.

II. THE REAL PURPOSE OF PASTORAL VISITING

This question can only be decided in terms of the real purpose of pastoral visiting, and the actual effectiveness of visiting will also depend on the pastor's general ideas of what he is trying to achieve.

If the pastor sees the main purpose of his visiting as to keep his people from feeling neglected, to stir up those who may be falling off in attendance at church, to enjoy a friendly chat with people he likes or with loyal church workers, or to collect money or goods for some worthy object, then it is very doubtful whether he is using his time, his ability and his opportunities to anything like the best advantage.

If on the other hand he sees and carries out all his visiting as an integral part of his total ministry to people, and an essential part of his pastoral vocation not fulfilled by anything else, then his visiting may provide unlimited short-term and long-term opportunities for good. Although we have included pastoral visiting for purposes of discussion in the 'Personal and Educational' section of this book, every good pastor knows that there are also great opportunities for healing and evangelistic service to people which may be missed if he neglects his routine pastoral visiting in any way.

The pastor is among people as one who serves in the Name of Jesus and in the power of the Holy Spirit. His purpose is to take into each home 'The grace of the Lord Jesus Christ, the love of God, and the fellowship of the Holy Spirit' (2 Corinthians 13[14], Weymouth), to offer them willingly, whether people seem to respond or not, and to leave people free to refuse without embarrassment. People hope to see in the pastor a natural, simple, sincere, loving man of God. Like the Greeks who came to Philip they are saying in their hearts, 'Sir, we would see Jesus' (John 12[21]). They look for a person who is one of them, but not quite the same as they are, a person who does not do many things which they do, but never looks down his nose at them, a person to whom they can safely entrust any confidences without risking rejection or being preached at.

The practical purpose of pastoral visiting is largely bound up in the fact that it offers the only available way of building and maintaining a pastoral relationship with his people, and of meeting many human needs before they are felt sufficiently for the people concerned to take any initiative about them.

From an educational point of view the well-equipped pastor will be sensitive to all kinds of apparently minor needs, and able to offer the kind of information and help that may well prevent many more critical difficulties in the future. Many such matters are concerned with personal and domestic relationships, and these, particularly when connected with children, may offer creative educational opportunities which would otherwise be missed altogether.

In his routine visiting the good pastor will sense an underlying personal difficulty or anxiety in many a person long before that person would even think of seeking help, certainly before he would take his courage in both hands and set out to get it. If the pastor is capable of creating the kind of relationship with his people that will encourage them to unburden such difficulties, he will be truly a physician of souls, and with this healing work he will also be doing invaluable service in preventive psychiatry.

The same is true of many specifically evangelistic opportunities, such as those provided by the religious difficulties and conflicts that people are diffident about confessing, and the periods of spiritual deadness that may so easily darken their personalities and poison all their personal relationships. A keen spiritual sensitivity born of Christian love, and a deep understanding of the dynamics of human attitude and behaviour, will enable the pastor to reach the bewildered soul of many a person with the reality of the love and power of God at the time of greatest need.

The influence of effective pastoral help given to any member of a family will spread in some degree to every member of the family, and often beyond it in widening circles in the community. Apart from this indirect influence it may well open up direct opportunities for pastoral contact with other people. The fact that husbands are generally away at work in visiting times is therefore less defeating than it may appear to the unthinking pastor.

The pastor will fulfil this unique purpose of visiting most effectively if in all his visiting and interviewing he is constantly on the qui vive for what feelings his people may be anxious to communicate to him, particularly when they may need some encouragement or 'putting at ease' before they feel they can do it. He will then be looking always for opportunities of understanding their deeper feelings and attitudes, and of responding in such a manner as to bring to them some at least of 'the unsearchable riches of Christ' (Ephesians 3⁸). It is most important that his interest should be in people all the time; and in problems, failures and conflicts only in terms of what they mean to the person concerned.

Apart from this practical purpose of visiting it is also a very good jumping-off place for all other pastoral work, and also for all preaching. Knowing people and their deeper needs, and being known by them will inevitably make preaching more vital and effective, and this will make the pastor's preaching lead to still further pastoral opportunities.

III. SOME PRACTICAL ASPECTS OF VISITING

In arranging his visiting, the pastor must first decide on some standard of priorities. It is important that he should continually ask to be informed about all who need comfort or help of any kind, and those in need must come before those who like to see him apart from any special need.

First of all will come the dying, the sick, the bereaved, the distressed, and those in any other trouble or adversity. Then the aged and 'shut in', who are unable to come to church. Then it is often most helpful to 'follow up' those people who have had some contact with the Church, relatives and friends who have attended a Baptism service, people whom he has met at a Wedding or a Funeral, and the parents of children who attend his Religious Instruction class at school. These are openings that may often lead to most effective contact with people who may be shy, or diffident about asking for a visit or coming to church after a long absence. After these people have been visited the routine visits can be planned, and all members of his church should be visited at least once in each year if possible.

When visiting church members, it is often possible to make house-to-house visits along the street to find out whether people belong to his denomination, and if not whether they would like the minister of their denomination to call on them. If the pastor is not invited in he should retire gracefully without pressing the matter, and he should ask whether the person would like him to call another day. It might have been inconvenient to admit him on that particular occasion.

An assistant minister will probably be given a list by his senior, of people to call on, so he will have no particular problems about who to visit. He should keep his eyes and ears open and always notify his senior of any situation that might warrant a special visit.

At the beginning of a new ministry there are many people who should be visited as soon as possible. A call at the home of each officer of the church will lead to better co-operation, to the benefit of all the work of the church, and may also help the pastor to become aware of some special needs. A call at the home of the leader of each of the societies associated with the church will often bring the same advantages.

The new minister should also call on those people who have suffered tragedies or have lost loved ones during the past year, so that he can show his sympathy and understanding, and find out how they are dealing with the trouble. This is a very useful opportunity for ensuring the continuity of pastoral help in spite of the potentially disrupting effect of a change of minister.

When these have been attended to, the new minister should call on ministers of all other denominations, to offer and ask for full co-operation. Then he should call on leaders of other community activities, and on people whose help may be invaluable, such as doctors, radio-station proprietors (in countries with commercial broadcasting), and also on hotel keepers.

All good pastors are awake to the value of calling on newcomers to the district, to welcome them in the name of the church, to offer any information they may need, or introductions to people. It is not such a general habit, but possibly a good one, to call on people without a Church, and also on people generally regarded as 'bad eggs', who are often not nearly as bad as they are painted. Jesus Himself remembered the publicans and sinners, and maintained that 'They that be whole need not a physician, but they that are sick' (Matthew 9¹²), and went on to say: 'I am not come to call the righteous, but sinners to repentance' (9¹³). Each of these different types of person may need a particular technique, a question which will be discussed in the account of interviewing later in this chapter.

A most important part of any pastoral visit is to make friends with the children. Children are naturally friendly people, and greatly appreciate the right kind of notice being taken of them. They are very loyal in their friendships, and can give great pleasure to the pastor in his work, and a great opportunity for him to be of future help to them. It has been said with much wisdom that 'a pat on a child's head touches its mother's heart'—and its grandmother's as well!

The other occupants of any home will also come under the good pastor's interest and care, as long as he refrains from forcing his attention on them.

It is a good plan to keep records of visits, including the names of the children and the other people in the house, and brief notes about the general attitudes of each person, and any particular problems or vulnerabilities they may have shown. Most of these records can be written up at home at the end of the round of visits, sometimes helped by brief notes made between houses.

It is also important for the pastor to put his mind into the right attitude for this important work by serious prayer before setting out, and possibly a short 'telegraphic prayer' at each door. It is well to have a definite plan, but to allow spontaneous visits on 'impulse'.

In all visiting it is essential for the pastor to keep his mind on the person's interests, and to keep his own rigidly in the background, to listen creatively and not to preach. He should be ready to have prayer with the person at the appropriate moment, and if in doubt about the person's feelings about it he should ask. The prayer should be short, simple, and fitting, expressing the main feelings conveyed by the person or persons visited, and relating them with the redemptive love of God as seen in Jesus Christ.

If a particular difficulty or strain is expressed or discovered, the pastor should offer further help, possibly in the form of deeper counselling. In any case these people should be followed up with further visits or interviews without too much delay.

IV. THE FINE ART OF INTERVIEWING

Interviewing may be carried out as part of pastoral visiting, or when people come to see the pastor in his study or vestry. More superficially it may happen in chance meetings in the street, at church or community functions, or by arrangement when the pastor and another person have lunch together. The principles are the same for all these occasions, modified only by the particular needs and limitations that may be present.

Interviewing is a universal activity. As Annette Garrett points out: 'Everyone engages in interviewing. Sometimes he interviews; sometimes he is interviewed.' [1] It is simpler and more superficial than counselling, to which it may sometimes lead. There are no set rules or techniques that will cover all types of interviewing and all purposes for which it is carried out, but some important principles have come from the experience of many interviewers, which will help to make any interview more effective, as long as they do not interfere with a natural spontaneity, flexibility and friendliness in the interviewer.

We should look for constant improvement with practice, and this will come if the 'technique' is based on knowledge, and constantly controlled by careful assessment of method and results, and frequent discussion with others.

---

[1] *Interviewing, Its Principles and Methods* (Family Service Assn. of America, 1942). (To whom grateful acknowledgement is given for many of the ideas expressed in this chapter.)

These are some of the underlying principles which are important for all effective interviewing.

First, it is a reciprocal personal relationship between two people, each with preconceived ideas and attitudes and purposes, each also with problems. All these inner personality attributes play their part in the relationship, but the more they are accepted and understood the less their influence will be, and this is particularly the responsibility of the interviewer.

Second, the feelings of people are generally much more important in interviewing than the objective facts. The ideas and attitudes of every person are influenced, far more than he ever realizes, by emotions, habits and prejudices, of most of which he is unaware, and some of which will appear inconsistent and even irrational to anyone else. People tend to think of their own attitudes as those which any sensible person must adopt, and to interpret other people's attitudes in terms of their own. The interviewer must therefore cultivate the attitude called Empathy, 'feeling into', and accept other people's feelings and attitudes, however inconsistent, inappropriate, or irrational they may appear. This does not mean that he condones (or approves) any such attitude or feeling; he simply accepts the other person's right to have it, and the first purpose of the interview is that he shall come to know and understand it. His interest in objective facts related by the person should be mainly in terms of what they mean to the person being interviewed. Any critical attitude on the part of the interviewer at this stage will be generally futile and may well be harmful.

The third principle is that in the interviewing relationship many of the person's intense loves or hates, or both in succession, may be brought to the surface and projected on to the interviewer. This phenomenon is known as Transference, and is found almost invariably at some point in all interviewing and counselling relationships. It is most important that the interviewer's acceptance of the person's feelings should include acceptance of those that are projected on to him, so that they are not allowed to stir up reactions of sentimentality or defensiveness in him. Such reactions will inevitably block, and may even ruin the whole interviewing process.

The fourth principle is that people are often dominated by two contradictory emotions at the same time, either consciously, or more commonly unconsciously. This ambivalence, as it is called, may account for much bewilderment and deep conflict. They may love and hate someone at the same time, or they may want help greatly, but be afraid to ask for it, or be unable to unburden themselves sufficiently for proper help to be possible. In some cases a person is unconsciously trying to be dependent and independent at the same time. People are often ashamed of this apparent inconsistency when they come to realize its presence, and sometimes think it must be a sign of something abnormal in their minds. It is important for the pastor to accept any ambivalence that appears as something quite natural, and to let the person know that he understands it as such.

The fifth principle is that there will practically always be some deeper troubles than those mentioned. People are often too ashamed or frightened, or too shy, to talk about them at the beginning. Many of their initial approaches are tentative, feeling their way, and trying out the pastor by watching his reactions to their early approaches. When the pastor understands this he will not be too quick to 'explain' or reassure, but will allow his quiet understanding and acceptance to encourage deeper unburdening.

V. SOME PRACTICAL ASPECTS OF INTERVIEWING

It goes without saying that all pastoral interviews should be kept strictly confidential, and no details ever divulged without the person's express permission. Even when somebody's experience well disguised could make a good sermon illustration, it is very important to obtain that person's permission (which will generally be given quite readily when the pastor has been helpful) before using it even in disguised form. People find it reassuring to be asked in this way, and appreciate it greatly. They are also reassured when they find out that not even the pastor's wife knows anything about the interview, even if she cannot help knowing that an interview has taken place. When she has won the confidence of people they will often tell her about it themselves.

It is most important that the interview should be 'client-centred' all through (to borrow a term from Social Case-work), that it should 'begin where the client is',[1] and take its pattern from how he feels, and what things mean to him. At the end of her book, Annette Garrett quotes two interviews from Phyllis Bottome's book, *London Pride*, which vividly illustrate the extreme importance of keeping the

[1] *Interviewing, Its Principles and Methods* (Family Service Assn. of America, 1942).

client's attitudes in the forefront of the whole interview. The whole process, in fact, is one of interviewing, of looking together at the client's situation as he comes to portray it, listening, understanding, and seeking ways of helping the client to help himself. The physical setting of the interview should be as appropriate to that purpose as the resources permit.

It is convenient for purposes of discussion to divide the interview into arbitrary stages, but in practice many of these will overlap greatly, and there may be variations in sequence according to the particular needs of the situation. With that proviso we can think in succession of observation, listening, questioning, talking, and concluding the interview. Each of these is a sufficiently delicate and skilled task to be regarded as an art.

The Art of Observation. The observant pastor will learn much of a person's real feelings by unobtrusively noticing the play of expression on his face, the tensions of his body and the movements of his hands, the way he sits or stands, the expression shown in his eyes, and the way he talks. These perceptions are kept in the pastor's mind, without being conveyed to the client, and linked up in due course with all the other information that emerges in the interview.

The Art of Creative Listening. The first essential is of course to pay full attention to everything the client says, but in doing this the pastor should be awake to certain things the client does not say, to significant gaps, inconsistencies and contradictions in the narrative. These again should be noted, but not pointed out at that time. They may possibly be referred to with profit during the later attempts at interpretation of the client's situation, when he has achieved better insight and there is firmer mutual confidence between him and the pastor. It is also helpful to notice any sudden pause or hold-up in the narrative and any sudden change in the subject. The client may suddenly be coming to feel that he is saying too much, or risking being disloyal to someone else, or he may be getting close to something painful or difficult to talk about. At such points it may be helpful to him for the pastor to make some understanding comment that summarizes the feelings expressed and shows acceptance of them. That will often give the client the little bit of encouragement that he needs.

A change in the subject may also point to a significant association of ideas, often unconscious, in the client's mind, and this can also be held quietly in the pastor's mind for use later if necessary.

Sometimes the client indulges in repetition, or 'talks in circles'. This again may point to a significant feeling, but is more often a device for avoiding facing something painful. After letting him go on in this way for a time that seems reasonable the pastor can sometimes bring him to the point by a suitable (and relatively harmless) question, such as 'What could you do about it?'

When the client criticizes or even abuses the pastor, the pastor should accept completely his right to feel that way, and avoid any defensive attitude or word. He should rather probe more deeply into what has offended the client and why it has done so.

Sometimes a client asks the pastor some personal question about the pastor's own life, or his attitudes or experiences. This may be an important part (to the client) of his 'testing out' of the pastor, or it may indicate the deepening of the reciprocal relationship. On the other hand the client may be trying to be polite and friendly. It is generally best for the pastor to give a brief, simple, and truthful answer in friendly fashion, and then to redirect the client to his own situation. To ignore or pass off the question may appear to the client as rejection or lack of friendliness.

The Art of Creative Questioning. We cannot begin the consideration of questioning more fittingly than by reminding ourselves of the very great use that Jesus made of questioning. A perusal of the Gospels with this in mind will show that in nearly every interview His main contribution was in that form. By this method He achieved far more than any categorical statement would have done, and often turned a vicious attack cleverly back on His attackers. At the same time His questions taught people much by making them think things out for themselves. Similarly the pastor can generally help his client very much more effectively by making his responses either in the form of recapitulation of the client's feelings as expressed, or of well designed questions. The art of creative questioning is well worth cultivating by any pastor.

He must be careful that his questions do not appear to indicate any desire to pry into the client's mind, or to cross-question him in any 'legal' fashion. They should invariably be expressions of real and genuine interest in the client as a free person, free to refrain from answering if he so desires, without any embarrassment.

It may be necessary to ask a question for further clarification of the client's narrative, and such questions will show interest and full attention on the part of the pastor. Further questioning may be necessary to secure some additional relevant, or possibly relevant, information, but this should be predominantly about the client's feelings and relationships. Information may be sought, if thought relevant, about his general feelings—happiness, anxieties, frustrations, regrets, doubts, and hopes—about his health, his domestic and social relationships, and his feelings about his work and any other aspect of his life. It is quite important for the pastor to be sensitive to any small details in the client's answers, and in the way they are given or the questions evaded. This may lead to much deeper understanding of the client's inner attitudes and feelings, and greater opportunities for help.

When the time comes for interpretation or clarification of the client's problem or situation there is again an important part for creative questioning to play. There is no better way for the pastor to relate the insights and values of the Christian Faith to any particular situation than by this method. People remember and profit greatly by the insights they work out for themselves, far more than by any that they receive passively. To a man dogged by a sense of guilt the question, 'Did Jesus ever withhold forgiveness from anyone who sincerely asked for it?', if asked at the right stage of the interview after the whole situation has been thoroughly explored, will do far more in the long run than any confident affirmation given by the pastor. Questioning will keep the client actively participating in the interview, and will help to mobilize and bring into action his own inner resources. This is the most effective kind of education or healing.

The Art of Creative Talking. Here again we most fittingly begin by remembering the superb artistry of Jesus in His expressions of the deepest insights in the simplest words. No wonder 'the common people heard him gladly' (Mark 12³⁷). Creative talking should be always controlled by the purpose of the interview, client-centred and not pastor-centred. The pastor is generally misusing the interview if he reminisces, gossips, or wanders off the subject. Creative talking is fittingly used to encourage the client, to clarify in his mind the things he is trying to express, to refocus his attention on the matter in hand when for any reason it has begun to drift away, and to give any needed information (more often than advice). In the later stages of an interview, or series of interviews, creative talking may be used to interpret and summarize all that has emerged. In all attempts at interpretation, either by statement or by question, the pastor should feel his way cautiously, watching for signs of defensiveness. When these are present he should desist from interpretation and encourage further unburdening by the client, until he is ready for interpretation.

The Art of Concluding an Interview. The interview should not be concluded too suddenly. The pastor can prepare for it by offering a short summary of what has emerged, and suggesting some further thought to be given to certain points, possibly in preparation for a further interview. He can sometimes encourage the client to formulate the next steps to be taken as a result of his new insights. It is generally wise to limit the duration of an interview to an hour or less, unless there are particular reasons for allowing it to take longer.

Keeping Records. If at all possible it is valuable for the pastor to make a summary of the main details of each interview soon after its conclusion. This will make his own thinking more explicit, and any further interviews will be carried out much more effectively if he has been able to glance over the previous records before beginning the new interview.

Finally, we may remind ourselves that we have no warrant for assuming that what we have to offer is all, or nearly all, that the client needs. He may need time, the experience of trouble, and many other types of influence or experience before many results happen. We must guard against the subtle tendency to 'try to play God', and not try to do too much. All results, or lack of them, are in God's good hand.

CHAPTER FIVE

Helping People in Worship, Prayer, and the Guidance of God

AN IMPORTANT and essential part of the personal and educational work of the pastor is to help his people to find the greatest practical reality in the main sources of spiritual nourishment provided by the Christian religion: worship, prayer, and the guidance of God in their daily lives. In this he is helping them to greater spiritual maturity, to greater spiritual intiative and creative power, and at the same time enabling them to become more directly dependent on the Holy Spirit within themselves, and less dependent on him. Only in this way can he ensure sufficient time and energy to be able to deal with the immature and needy, and train a reliable group of laymen to carry out some of the necessary pastoral work. Worship, prayer, and Divine Guidance are the greatest regulating and integrating influences, not only in the individual personality, but also in society, and only when they are reasonably understood and properly carried out by people. Otherwise it is all too easy for them to become devisive and even corrupting, as history has vividly demonstrated.

This important personal and educational work can be carried out in almost every kind of pastoral relationship. Some of it will take the form of direct exposition from the pulpit, discussions in the various church societies, letters and articles in church papers, articles in 'secular' papers and magazines, and possibly broadcast talks. A very effective part of it will take the form of simple appropriate comments or remarks in the ordinary day-by-day contacts with people, in visiting, interviewing, and in the various random social contacts when a suitable opening can be made. It is probable that any pastor who may take the trouble to find out the general ideas of a good cross-section of his regular Church members on these great themes would be astonished at their vagueness and their almost routine formalism. Conversely when there is in any congregation a group of people who have found abundant reality in worship, prayer, and the guidance of God, their overflowing spiritual vitality is quite unmistakable.

These profound subjects are worthy of, and have received, much

67

more adequate treatment than is possible within the confines of this book, or the spiritual limitations of the author. But an attempt must be made in any book on pastoral work to offer some basic ideas in as simple and direct terms as possible, from which, together with other sources of help, the pastor may work out his own personal attitudes in terms that his people can grasp.

The three subjects overlap to a very great extent, but for purposes of discussion they will be taken separately, at the risk of some repetition.

WORSHIP

The word 'worship' comes from an old Anglo-Saxon word '*Weordhscipe*', which could be translated 'Worthship', 'full of worth'. It has received many definitions, as would be expected from its many-sidedness.

From the etymological viewpoint Dr Howard E. Collier sees worship as 'any experience in which we ascribe value to the thing which we *do* value',[1] and Muriel Lester regards it as 'the practice of seeing deep down into the heart of things and finding their real worth'.[2]

From the more directly religious viewpoint Dr J. Alan Kay defines worship as 'man's response to the nature and action of God',[3] and Karl R. Stolz sees it as 'the awe-struck appreciation of God'.[4]

Why do men worship? Worship in one form or another has been practised wherever men have lived, and throughout recorded history. Such a universal practice must be based on some deeply fundamental fact about God and man, and this has been expressed by St Augustine in his *Confessions* in words which will live for all time: 'Thou hast made us for Thyself, and the heart of man is restless until it findeth rest in Thee.' Man is so made that he must worship something or someone, mammon or God, and he cannot sincerely worship mammon *and* God.

In all the attitudes, actions and teachings of Jesus Christ we see God as a loving Father who constantly seeks to reveal Himself to His children, and to win their freely given response of love and service in which their personalities are enriched. The discerning mind is left in no doubt that regular spiritual nourishment is just as necessary for

---

[1] *Towards a New Manner of Living*, Swarthmore Lecture, 1936 (Allen & Unwin, 1936), p. 37.   [2] *Why Worship?* (Independent Press, 1937).
[3] *The Nature of Christian Worship* (Epworth Press, 1953).
[4] *The Church and Psycho-therapy* (Abingdon Cokesbury Press, 1943).

the life and growth of the total personality as regular physical nourishment is for the life and growth of the body, and regular mental nourishment for the life and growth of the mind. We may go one step farther and affirm that some of the necessary spiritual nourishment for the life and growth of the total personality must be partaken in fellowship, for man needs his fellow men as well as God.

It is also clear to the discerning mind that every man must 'choose' his own spiritual 'diet' in terms of what he finds 'nourishing' in the same way as he must choose his physical diet; not always without competent help. The well-known proverb, 'One man's meat is another man's poison', can be applied in the spiritual life as well as the physical, and therefore men will always choose different forms and methods of worship. But in spite of this there are some universally valid principles on which all methods of worship are based.

Men worship therefore because God has endowed them with that which needs to worship, that which is unsatisfied without worship, and much of the worship of mammon may well be an indication of early spiritual malnutrition, of failure to realize or value the nature and action of God.

People are often told that they should worship because it is their duty, or God's due. While these statements are of course true, they do not generally succeed in stirring modern man to any effective worship. Among other practical motives suggested are those of stock-taking; considering where we are heading for in life, gaining release from anxiety, guilt, or conflict, or finding direction and power for everyday living. These are man-centred motives of expediency, out of harmony with the spirit of Christian worship, which in the words of Karl Stolz 'takes the individual out of himself, and focuses his attention on a Being greater than himself, to whom he gives himself'.[1] To elevate the beneficial results of worship to the status of motivation for worship is to devalue worship to something essentially selfish, and to transfer the worship from God to oneself.

The scope of worship ranges from the most deeply intimate private devotions and attitudes, carried out and formulated in the quiet places of the human soul, through the communal worship of small groups, such as that of the family, the local community prayer group, or the 'two or three gathered together' in the pastoral counselling relationship, to the largest congregation of people gathered together in public worship. In a very real sense it always goes beyond any

[1] ibid.

F

of these apparent limits to be linked up with all other worship on earth, and with the constant worship of 'angels and archangels and all the company of heaven'.[1] In another very real sense it is linked up with the worship that is offered in such ordinary day-by-day activities of mankind as work, play, and fellowship, in which the attitude of worship is needed to bind people in true community.

F. B. Welbourn has strongly emphasized this all-inclusive aspect of worship.

The devisive factors of age, sex, interest, employment, or individual likes and dislikes may form the basis of human *segregations*—men's clubs, girl guides, trade unions, hikers' associations or the like—from which their members derive much of enjoyment and of benefit both to themselves and to society at large: but whose constitution is deliberately exclusive of those who do not share the particular bond of union. The community is essentially a *congregation* of all inhabitants of a particular locality or kinship group, inevitably constituted into a distinct group by the accident of geography or physical relationships; but recognizing that their fulfilment as a community is only in the establishment of right relations with the whole human race.[2]

To the Christian understanding [he continues], personal development is dependent on right relations not only with human beings but with the universe as a whole. A true community is a *worshipping* community—recognizing every thing and event as sacramental—that is as the expression of personal will, on whom man is ultimately dependent, and only in personal relationship with whom fulfilment of human personality is to be found.

In this universal setting we shall now consider some of the essential components which combine to create the spirit of worship.

SOME ESSENTIAL COMPONENTS OF WORSHIP

The first essential is a deliberate remembrance of God, and in Christian worship we remember the nature and action of God mainly as seen in Jesus Christ. It is interesting for us to ask ourselves (and anyone with whom we may be discussing it): 'What more could Jesus have done than He did to win the devotion and service of mankind?' When it is realized that He went to the very limit of sustained

[1] *The Book of Common Prayer.*
[2] *Science and Humanity* (SCM Press, 1948).

devotion, the question then arises: 'Why then do not more people respond and follow Him?' The answer is probably that many are still ignorant or lacking in clear realization of the sheer magnitude of His sacrificial devotion, some know but are selfish and ungrateful, but most people are thoughtless, they carelessly allow many important things which they know to slip out of their active awareness. It is so easy to forget, unless we take steps regularly to remember or allow ourselves to be reminded of those things which have made and still make abundant personal and communal living possible. Kipling expressed this need in his 'Recessional':

> *Lord God of Hosts, be with us yet.*
> *Lest we forget—lest we forget;*

and in still more vivid terms in another verse of the hymn:

> *Judge of the Nations, spare us yet,*
> *Lest we forget—lest we forget.*

Jesus Himself, at the most intimate and solemn act of fellowship with His disciples, instituted the supreme act of worship of the Christian Church with the immortal words: 'This do in remembrance of me'. (Luke 22[19]).

All our commemorations are designed to promote remembrance, and in ceremonial and sacrament we act out together the commemoration. All religious symbols, and particularly the cross, are intended to ensure the necessary remembrance, and so are consecrated buildings and their furnishings, the special music played and sung, and the words that are spoken and sung. It is being more and more appreciated in these days that silence can also be a most potent help to remembrance when it is fittingly used.

For reality in worship it is most important that all these symbolic objects and actions are used with extreme care, artistry and naturalness, and that continual efforts are made to prevent formalism in actions that are essentially formal, or sterility in things that are essentially repetitive. Unless this can be done they will lose their power of bringing vivid and effective remembrance.

Along with the remembrance of the personal attributes of God as seen in Jesus Christ it is often helpful deliberately to open our minds to the remembrance of the infinite majesty of God, and the immensities and eternities associated with His vast universe and His great unfolding creative enterprise. We shall then come to see many of our frettings and fussings in much truer perspective, and a new steadiness will take hold of our restless and unsettled souls.

The nature and action of God are such that any adequate perception or remembrance of them will naturally lead to adoration. 'We love, because He first loved us' (1 John 4¹⁹). Adoration is described by Dr Kay as 'reverence raised to its highest point, . . . a complex state of mind compounded of wonder, fear, and love'.[1] It ascribes the highest value to God, and expresses the deep thankfulness of His children. This response of loving gratitude is the main source of power for Christian living. Having given men the great gift of free will God will not force them to respond. Having made them to be persons He will neither bribe nor bluff them into His service. He can only seek to win the response of His children, which He has done by His progressive self-revelation, culminating in Jesus Christ. The faculty in man which can perceive and respond to this self-revelation is that of adoration or loving gratitude, which has been called 'the seed-bed of all the virtues'. But this, like every other worth-while faculty in man, needs constant cultivation; gratitude will not come naturally, nor will it deepen naturally, of itself. St Paul thought enough of the importance of this cultivation to say about it: 'In every circumstance of life be thankful, for this is God's will in Christ Jesus respecting you' (Thessalonians 5¹⁸, Weymouth). Without this constantly renewed power of gratitude, Christianity would appear as little more than a vague and relatively sterile humanism.

Any adoration or gratitude that is sincere will naturally lead to the third great component of worship, self-giving. True Christian self-giving is not a matter of mere self-renunciation, which may be a morbid neurotic escape-mechanism; nor is it rightly performed with any idea of future reward, or any fear of consequences of failure. It is a glad, spontaneous, whole-hearted response of continually re-awakened gratitude and love: the offering of a loving and intelligent obedience to the will of God.

Self-giving in this spirit is of the greatest importance in preventing worship from becoming a purely subjective emotional or intellectual experience, in which case it would soon degenerate to something comparable with drug-addiction: sterile and even harmful. This is a danger which cannot be too greatly stressed.

God-directed thought and feeling, awakened and inspired by the

[1] op. cit.

beauty and relevance of all the chosen words and music, and all the appropriate symbols, have an essential part in worship. But the very essence of worship is in the realization that it extends beyond thought and feeling to action. The central act of worship of the Christian Church was instituted by Jesus in the universally cherished words: 'This do in remembrance of me' (Luke 22[19]).

Worship at its best is therefore a corporate action of the whole Christian Church—minister and congregation—deliberate, intelligent, grateful, self-giving action. It should be recognized and carried out in any particular church as the expression in time and place of the unceasing and universal action of the whole Church, visible and invisible, and of the progressive spontaneous self-giving of every member of it.

This aspect of worship tends to be overlooked when the members of any congregation are discouraged in any way from taking their fullest part in the corporate action, when they are allowed to drift into passive listening to beautiful singing by the choir and reading and preaching by the minister. When they find themselves merely spectators and listeners, they may well feel themselves deprived of the unique gift of spiritual re-creation which active corporate worship can supply. They may even feel that they can listen more adequately and with better concentration to a wireless service in their own homes.

It seems certain that the early Christians thought of worship in this way. They could have set aside times for remembrance and thanksgiving and for reading, meditation, and discussion, in their own homes, and thus avoided most of the dangers to which they were exposed in their public worship. But they accepted the risks, even of martyrdom, and gathered together to participate in the corporate action of worship, to re-enact together their communion with God and with one another in the loving remembrance of the death and passion, and the resurrection, of Jesus Christ, through which this sacred communion was for all time made possible.

For adequate and sustained Christian self-giving, then, we need communion with God and with one another in active worship, in which our total self-giving is focused down and re-enacted as a loving response to the sacrificial love of God in Jesus Christ. In this act of worship we can find the direction and power for everyday living. We can seek guidance for the best use and further development of our talents and our opportunities, the constantly needed forgiveness and humility, and the better understanding and acceptance in fellowship of all whom we would serve. All our petitions in the name of Jesus Christ will find their greatest reality and effectiveness when they are conceived and offered in the framework of Christian self-giving, and any petitions that we cannot honestly offer in His name can well be re-examined to see whether or not they are selfish and therefore out of harmony with the spirit of worship.

These requirements for self-giving Christian service are listed in the ancient exhortation at the beginning of the Morning and Evening Services in the *Book of Common Prayer*:

Although we ought at all times humbly to acknowledge our sins before God; yet ought we most chiefly so to do, when we assemble and meet together to render thanks for the great benefits that we have received at his hands, to set forth his most worthy praise, to hear his most holy Word, and to ask those things which are requisite and necessary, as well for the body as the soul.

Another essential component of worship is habit. We have recalled the fact that it is all too easy to allow the important things that we know to slip out of our vivid awareness, and so to lose their power to move us. If therefore we are to 'maintain the spiritual glow' (Romans 12[11], Moffatt), it is necessary to cultivate the habit of full regular private and public worship, and particularly worship in Christian Fellowship, with its unique mutual challenge, support, encouragement and help. This regular giving and receiving in worship seems to constitute the essential spiritual nourishment, by which our spiritual stamina, or 'second wind' is received and main- tained. The famous prayer of Sir Francis Drake lays due emphasis on this aspect of worship. 'O Lord God, when thou givest to thy servants to endeavour any great matter, grant us to know that it is not the beginning but the continuing of the same until it be thoroughly finished, which yieldest the true glory. Through Him that for the finishing of thy work laid down His life.'

Here then are four essential components of worship: remembrance, which is an activity of the intellect; adoration and gratitude, which are offerings of the emotions; self-giving with the necessary petitions for ourselves and others, which is an offering of the will; and the cultivation of proper habits of worship, without which even the most whole-hearted and sincere worship tends to lose its power. 'Fine art', said John Ruskin, 'is that in which the hand, the head, and the heart of man go together.' [1] The fine art of worship needs the habit of man as well as the response of the whole man among men to the nature and action of God.

An inescapable duty of the pastor in his work of educating and training his people in the art of worship, and helping them to find increasing reality in it, is to help them to feel its application to the whole of life. There are many indications that people often fail to find any adequate link between their worship and the ebbing and flowing of their everyday lives. And many if not all of their attitudes and actions are deprived of the relevance, the power, and the coherence that they could otherwise have. Any act of worship could be compared with the ceremonial parade in the armed services, in which the men and women come into the presence of the Commanding Officer for a short time, and receive the inspiration which they carry into their everyday tasks.

With the inspiration received in Christian worship all other activities and attitudes can be seen and carried out as opportunities of worship, and they become greatly enriched by the all-embracing spirit of worship.

Any creative or healing work, however modest, which is thought of and carried out in the Christian spirit of service and the Christian fellowship of team-work is an act of worship. '*Laborare est orare*' is the very fitting motto of the Benedictine monks.

Play, like work, can be made into an act of worship when it is carried out in the Christian fellowship of sportsmanship and team-work, and is limited to creative (especially in children) and re-creative activities, and not made an end in itself.

Friendship, fellowship and social intercourse and co-operation can also be made into occasions for worship when infused with the Christian spirit awakened and sustained in the more formal acts of worship. A very important consequence of the linking of worship with fellowship is that it will help to keep love itself in its proper perspective, and put the love of God before that of any person, even one's husband or wife. In more simple terms it will help people to do what they really believe to be right, even when it conflicts with what any other person expects or demands from them. Of course they will take every possible care to make sure that they have had all available help in deciding what they believe to be right in such cases.

[1] *The Two Paths*, quoted in *The Oxford Dictionary of Quotations* (Oxford University Press, 1942).

Finally, worship, as a spontaneous outpouring of the human soul, is a living activity. Has the time come for much more exploration into further ways of worship?

PRAYER

If a number of different people, selected at random, could be induced to give a completely candid account of their attitudes to the activity we call prayer, their responses would probably fit into one of four groups. Some of them would express open disbelief in it, or would even ridicule the idea of prayer, regarding it as a self-deluding childish superstition. Others would confess to serious doubts about it, but would admit that they sometimes practise it on chance, or when they are in trouble. Many soldiers have felt this way about it in times of great danger or hardship. Others again practise it in a kind of blind faith; they regard it as quite beyond understanding, but pray instinctively and naturally. And there are some who have come to a strong rational faith in prayer, which grows and deepens steadily with time, and who find it increasingly effective in the whole of their everyday lives.

Many people would find themselves fitting into more than one of these groups at different periods of their lives. In many cases, too, a person's attitude to prayer will depend largely on his conception of what prayer is, which may vary considerably from person to person.

Anyone who has the opportunity to find out the attitudes of a good cross-section of the community to prayer will have no doubt that very many people are in a real fog about it, and because of their lack of understanding of the nature of prayer, or of God to whom prayer is addressed, they fail to tap even a fraction of the power available. In this respect the average person's use of prayer is comparable with our grandparents' use of electricity.

It is one of the great personal and educational privileges—and duties—of the pastor to help as many people as possible to find much more reality and power in prayer than they have previously experienced, and in the attempt to help him do so, some of the practical aspects of prayer will be considered briefly.

One of the most common questions asked about prayer is: 'Why should I pray?' Here, for example, is an honest, sober, kind, and generous man, a good husband and father, industrious and public spirited, who never goes to Church and never says his prayers. There are many such people in the community. When he asks frankly and seriously, 'Why should I pray?', what kind of convincing answer can we give him?

The first answer, which will probably surprise him, is that he *does* pray, over and over again, and that much of his steadiness as a citizen and as a husband and father depends on it. Every time he asks 'himself' what he should do, or what attitude he should take about anything, every time he makes a moral choice (and he does so repeatedly) he is praying. This is not the highest form of prayer, unless he is consciously looking to Jesus Christ as the ultimate leader, but he is certainly acknowledging and trying to follow a moral leadership, he is accepting a moral obligation to something—or someone—beyond himself.

He had probably been regarding prayer as little more than a series of selfish requests, which had quite rightly offended his logical mind. The realization that prayer is something which he has always been doing quite naturally and with great profit to his character, will probably open up a new and fascinating vista of thought, and a new stage of spiritual growth.

From this beginning we could then look with him at the kind of moral authority he has been accepting—ethical or moral principles such as honesty, generosity, decency, moderation, or the unwritten laws of social convention, or the condensation of any or all of these in his 'conscience'. As we saw in the chapter on abundant life all these tend to be too abstract and ambiguous and even conflicting, to give the direction required for the most effective living. At the same time they are lacking in power, deliverance, and fellowship, all of which are available with the clearest direction through a personal loyalty to the Person of Jesus Christ and His Holy Spirit.

In some such way as this our good non-churchgoer may be led to a much more vivid interest in Jesus Christ as Teacher, Leader, Lord, Saviour, and Friend, and at the same time to a more vital appreciation of the meaning and power of prayer in his life.

Before leaving this important question, 'Why should I pray?', we might face the fact that Jesus Himself, and many of the greatest men and women in history and contemporary life have openly admitted their need of it. To give just one example, Abraham Lincoln confessed: "I have been driven many times to my knees by the overwhelming conviction that there was nowhere else to go; my own wisdom, and that of those around us, seemed insufficient for the day.'

Thomas Carlyle once described prayer as 'the native and deepest instinct in the soul of man'. People pray, even without thinking of it as prayer, because of a spiritual hunger with which God has endowed human nature. As the poet James Montgomery has expressed it in some famous lines:

> *Prayer is the soul's sincere desire,*
> *Uttered or unexpressed,*
> *The motion of a hidden fire*
> *That trembles in the breast.*

But prayer still has to be learnt and practised if we are to make the best use of it. Neglect of prayer will lead to a kind of spiritual mal-nutrition, and if this continues too long it may reach a point at which (as with physical malnutrition) it produces lack of appetite, and then any help becomes much more difficult.

For any consideration of the true meaning of prayer, and still more the practice of it, the supreme and ultimate authority is Jesus Himself. He regarded prayer as intimate communion with God, whom He portrayed and described as 'Our Father'. Here at once He shows up many current false ideas of prayer. We so often take the One who ought to be acknowledged as the Head of the household, and put Him down in the servants' quarters! Such a 'spoilt-child' religious attitude to prayer will rightly offend the reasonable intelligent non-churchgoer, and it has no support in the teaching or the practice of Jesus, whose whole life was dominated by the desire to know and do the will of His Father.

The twelve disciples of Jesus were obviously impressed by the great value of prayer in His life, and it was natural for them to ask Him: 'Lord, teach us to pray' (Luke 11[1]). From that simple request came the perfect model for all prayers, which has been known throughout the Christian era as the Lord's Prayer. This great prayer shows in about seventy words the clearest way to an understanding of the nature and the practice of prayer. Even the great French soldier, Napoleon, was so impressed by it that he once said: 'Do you wish to find out the really sublime? Repeat the Lord's Prayer.'

The first two words, 'Our Father', set the whole standard of true prayer, and we can apply the well-known characteristics of the human father-children relationship at its highest standard to the better understanding of prayer. The good human father takes the initiative and sets the standard in his family in the fullest union with the good mother. As we saw in Chapter 3 the sequence of events in the parent-child relationship—creation, preservation, revelation, direction, inspiration, deliverance, and fellowship form a working model of the unfolding relationship between God and man.

We know too that the good human parent offers a diversity of gifts freely and lovingly to his children, but the best of those gifts need the co-operation of the child before they become really available to him. For example, a boy may ask his father for a good education, but it cannot be accepted fully without the boy's willingness to do the appropriate studying. To ask, seek, and knock in the sense in which Jesus used the terms, includes this readiness to do our part in the acceptance of the gift. And 'If ye then, being evil, know how to give good gifts unto your children, how much more shall your Father which is in heaven give things to them that ask him?' (Matthew 7[11]). Of course the kind of father to whom we are likening God is good, and that means that He sometimes says No; for the good parent knows better than the child what he needs, and does not give all he wants.

Above and beyond all gifts, parent and child are always in one another's thoughts, and also enjoy special times of fellowship together. These great facts of human experience point the way to the intimate communion with our heavenly Father which is the very nature of prayer. As Oswald Chambers has suggested, we should be 'unconsciously conscious of God, as a child is of its mother'.

What reasonably simple ideas can we adopt for ourselves, and offer to other people, about the practice of prayer? Prayer is an art which is mainly learnt by practice, and there is always more to be learnt. Each individual will gradually work out his own natural methods according to his unfolding experience. The Bible itself records an infinitely rich variety of attitudes to prayer and methods of praying. As H. E. Fosdick points out: 'Nothing could be more intensely individual than the prayers of the Bible. Nobody tries to commune with God in anyone else's way. . . . There are as many different ways of praying as there are different individuals.' [1] But there are some general principles which are helpful and appear to be valid.

For convenience in discussion, and for orderliness in praying, prayer may be considered under successive headings.

Like worship, of which it is a part, intelligent prayer must begin with remembrance of the One to whom we pray. It may range from a brief 'staccato' remembrance to a deep and prolonged contemplation

[1] *The Meaning of Prayer* (SCM Press, 1915).

of God in which the soul is uplifted to the ecstasy of adoration. Without remembrance there can be no conscious communion. But Jesus guards against any danger of thinking of God in selfish terms in the first two words of His prayer, in which, as in the two great commandments, our relationship with our fellow men is inseparably linked with our relationship with God. This two-fold remembrance provides a necessary safeguard against the all too common tendency to make our prayers, and our religion in general, too individualistic. The words, 'Hallowed be thy name. Thy kingdom come. Thy will be done, as in heaven, so in earth' (Luke 11²), emphasize the God-centredness of prayer, and the constant use of the word 'us' in the rest of the prayer carries on the 'social'-consciousness characteristic of Christian prayer.

The most vivid contemplation of God will naturally be through the remembrance of the Person of Jesus Christ and of all His dealings with men, women and children. The remembrance of great men in history and contemporary life may also be of help, and some people will find a sense of reality in the contemplation of God in Nature, and in such eternal realities as truth, beauty, goodness, and love.

As in worship, remembrance will naturally bring the sense of loving gratitude, a positive creative attitude of mind which will be strengthened as we go on to count our blessings. Many people endure depression and self-pity far beyond what is justifiable because they take many of their blessings for granted. If we made a 'balance sheet' with life, and put on the left side all the bad things that we have not deserved, and on the right side all the undeserved good things, there are few if any people in a civilized country who could honestly say that the bad outweighed the good. This is even more obvious if we remember the heritage of knowledge, skill, beauty and goodwill handed down to us independently of our deserving. We may reflect on what our situation would be if every new generation had to rediscover fire, electricity, medicine and surgery, social organization and tradition, and the many other humanitarian resources for human life. Such reflections as these will bring the sense of gratitude to life, and to God the Author of life, and put our thinking into much truer perspective.

If we are sincere in our remembrance and gratitude it is entirely natural for these thoughts and feelings to lead to an equally sincere desire to become day by day more worthy of the love and goodness of God. This will begin by the attempt to face our real selves in the light of what we know of Jesus Christ, and an honest admission, which we call confession, of the many ways in which we have fallen short of our obligations. It is important for balanced thinking that we should face our sins of omission, as well as those of commission. Jesus Himself took far more notice of sins of omission than the more obvious acts of wrongdoing, and a few direct questions regarding the things we have left undone that we might have done will straighten out our perspectives very quickly. In this we may well ask, with blind Bartimeus: 'Lord, that I might receive my sight' (Mark 10[51]).

But Christian prayer, communion with God as shown in Jesus Christ, brings the certainty of forgiveness as well as the conviction of sin. We have only to remind ourselves of the constant readiness of Jesus to forgive all who were penitent, of all His teaching in precept and parable about God's forgiveness, and above all of His supreme demonstration at Calvary of the lengths to which the loving forgiveness of God will go. From the facing of our real selves in the light of Christ we can therefore accept with humble gratitude the utterly gracious gift of forgiveness and a fresh start, and rededicate ourselves enlightened and enriched by the experience of deliverance, to better service.

People sometimes wonder why a single act of dedication should not be sufficient, and regard the need for repeated fresh starts as evidence of serious failure. But it seems that this is the way that we fallible human beings are given the opportunity to learn and to grow. As our physical nourishment requires a return regularly to the meal table, so our spiritual nourishment and nurture requires a return regularly to the Throne of Grace in prayer and worship.

In this atmosphere of rededication to better service we can most fittingly come to ask for 'those things which are requisite and necessary, as well for the body as the soul'.[1] In St John's priceless record of the intimate and loving words of Jesus to His disciples in the upper room 'in the same night that he was betrayed',[2] we have the very essence of His teaching about what we should ask, and about some of the conditions under which our requests can be granted. 'If ye abide in me, and my words abide in you, ye shall ask what ye will, and it shall be done unto you' (John 15[7]), and 'Ye have not chosen me, but I have chosen you, and ordained you, that ye should go and bring forth fruit, and that your fruit should remain: that whatsoever ye shall ask of the Father in my name, he may give it you' (John 15[16]).

[1] *The Book of Common Prayer.* [2] ibid.

To ask in a person's name means to ask the kind of things that person might have asked, and to ask in the name of Jesus will therefore eliminate all purely selfish petitions. It will mean that we should look at all our plans and desires, fears and dilemmas, in the light of what we know or can discover of the attitude of Jesus Christ.

Here is where prayer will link up with Bible study. When we look at these things in this way we immediately begin to see them in a new perspective. Some of them will fade in importance, and others will gain new strength and confidence. This attempt to know and fit in with the purpose of God as shown in Jesus Christ is far more rational than the childish superstition that tries to make prayer into a kind of spiritual 'Aladdin's lamp', however much we may be tempted to do so at times.

The poet Milton expressed the necessity of seeking and fitting in with the purpose of God in some eloquent lines in his *Paradise Lost*:

> *If by prayer*
> *Incessant I could hope to change the will*
> *Of him who all things can, I would not cease*
> *To weary him with my assiduous cries:*
> *But prayer against his absolute decree*
> *No more avails than breath against the wind*
> *Blown stifling back on him who breathes it forth:*
> *Therefore to his great bidding I submit.*

In all sincere prayer, intercession for others will go hand in hand with petition for ourselves and our work, and the experience of all kinds of people through the ages leaves no doubt of its effectiveness. Apart altogether from the good that may come to the people prayed for, multitudes of people have found it to be of great help to the person who prays. In the ancient epic poem known as the Book of Job we are told that 'The Lord turned the captivity of Job when he prayed for his friends' (Job 42¹⁰). It is quite in harmony with what we know of human nature that the diversion of our thoughts from ourselves to the welfare of other people is beneficial to the personality.

If in addition we can find some clue to the way in which intercessory prayer works in the general plan and purpose of God, we can then co-operate more intelligently with it. There is a possible clue in what the scientists have discovered about thought transference, and it may well be that the deliberate positive thoughts that we give out in intercessory prayer radiate like wireless waves around the globe, and in some way alter the spiritual pattern in other people.

If this is true, there are two quite obvious consequences which must affect our praying. The first is that any negative thoughts or feelings that are in our minds, such as fear or hatred or destructive criticism, will radiate with the positive ones, and will probably neutralize their good effects. As St James pointed out long ago: 'The prayer of *faith* shall save the sick . . . and if he have committed sins, they shall be forgiven him. . . . The effectual fervent prayer of a righteous man availeth much' (5¹⁵, ¹⁶).

The second consequence is that when many people join in 'effectual fervent prayer' for others, we should expect greater results than would come from solitary prayer. There are many indications in the practical experience of Christian people that this is so, and there is a great need for much further careful research into the inner dynamics of intercessory prayer, and indeed of all aspects of prayer.

Intercessory prayer is not something formal, nor is it to be regarded lightly or carelessly. For full effectiveness it demands intense, almost sacrificial concentration of attention, and for that reason it is probably better to pray for not too many people or causes at a time. Many people organize their prayers so that certain specific persons, organizations, and causes are prayed for each day over a period of time.

An essential, but often overlooked part of prayer is a period of silent meditation, in which 'the still, small voice' may have a chance to be heard in the quiet places of the human soul, and the whole personality is opened to the inflowing Grace, Love, and Fellowship, which we so often pass over quickly in our Benedictions. In this period of silence, all our seeking for the guidance of God will become rewarded and we shall find all that we are willing to find of direction and power, and at the same time the true peace of mind and soul—and even some health of body.

The unique beneficial effects of prayer are not in any way limited to those who pray and those for whom they pray. They issue in new attitudes, and in all kinds of soundly conceived creative action, the beneficial consequences of which are beyond our measuring, and unlimited by space or time. For all true Christian prayer must lead to some kind of dedicated, self-giving service.

It is probable that we are still only on the fringe of the possibilities of Christian prayer, and there is need for many more well-conducted prayer fellowships for research and for the fulfilment of more and more of the possibilities of prayer for people and for the nations of the world.

THE GUIDANCE OF GOD

The need for clear direction of human life, over and above the fumbling conflicting devices of human wisdom, is being increasingly realized as the world comes closer to the edge of the abyss of total destruction of human civilization. The vast power in the hand of fallible and short-sighted man, and the infinite possibilities for good as well as the urgent danger of world catastrophe, have brought the question of Divine guidance into the very forefront of human thinking.

It is becoming crystal clear in these days that, as it was put by a psychologist, not a theologian: 'There is really only one virtue— humble volitional conformity to the will of God—and only one sin— defiance of God's will.' [1] Or as Tennyson expressed it in his *In Memoriam*:

> *Our wills are ours, we know not how;*
> *Our wills are ours, to make them thine.*

Apart altogether from the fact that the guidance of God has been experienced by people of all kinds in all kinds of situations throughout human history, it is entirely logical and reasonable that men and women should be able to discern the will of God with sufficient clarity for their everyday lives. As Lionel Curtis puts it: [2]

I cannot conceive of a creative God not inspired by a purpose, with no plan in His mind. If He calls into being creatures to join in His work of creation, I think He means that these creatures should grasp *enough* of His purpose to join in His work. Could they see the whole of it, from first to last, it is hard to see what power of intiative would remain to them. To me it seems He assigns us the task of divining the meaning of things with faculties which cannot indeed grasp the whole of an infinite purpose, but are yet sufficient to join in the work.

We may begin our consideration of the guidance of God by reminding ourselves that everybody is guided by many and often conflicting influences, some of which are out of the range of awareness. Emotion,

---

[1] Rudolf Allers, *The Psychology of Character*.
[2] *Civitas Dei* (Macmillan, 1938), p. 846.

habit, prejudice, social convention, suggestion, conscience, and certain ethical and moral principles, such as 'the golden rule' can all play an important part. Reason has been found to exert a rather smaller influence than most people like to think. We often use it unwittingly to provide a 'logical' and satisfying 'reason' for what our emotions, habits or prejudices have induced us to do.

We have seen in the consideration of Abundant Life in Chapter 3 that these guiding principles are too abstract and ambiguous unless they are backed up and clarified—and inspired—by the knowledge of Jesus Christ, in whom all effective guiding principles are embodied. As an example of the limitations of the golden rule we may remind ourselves that a drunkard who helps another man to the over-consumption of alcohol is carrying out the golden rule, and so is the schemer who tells lies to get his colleague out of trouble.

We need the guidance of God, not only for single decisions and actions, but still more for the whole of life, for what we should be more than for what we should do. The good human father tries to bring up his child to be the kind of person who will know what to do in most ordinary situations, but will seek his special help in difficult or complicated matters; and we may confidently assume that God's guidance will also leave some room for human intelligence and initiative.

Our conception of what we should be will depend on our ultimate loyalty and our goal of life, which will determine our priorities, our sense of worthship. Guidance is therefore linked up at the very centre with worship. Our inner instinctive urges are not to be choked back and suppressed; they are to be harnessed, controlled, and directed in harmony with our highest goals and loyalties. For example, to be a Christian does not mean to try to suppress, let us say, our instincts of pugnacity; men and women will always be angry. But instead of allowing it to lead us into useless quarrels with our fellow-men, we can direct it to the fighting of social injustice and the other common enemies of mankind, to overcoming evil with good.

The essential channel through which guidance comes is of course the mind, the whole mind—intellect, emotion, and will—through which we can seek, love, and do the will of God. We are told to seek first (not 'only') the Kingdom of God; the 'other things' which are added to us demand some of our time and effort.

We may assume that the faculty of reason and intelligence which we call our intellect was given to us by the Creator so that it could

G

be cultivated and developed for making the necessary decisions and moral judgements for everyday living. One of the most important channels of divine guidance is therefore the surrendered reason and intelligence—surrendered to the Kingdom, or Kingship of God. We come to know our Personal God through coming to know Jesus Christ as a real Person, and when we know a person we know what his attitude is likely to be in most things.

We come to know Jesus mainly through what we are shown and taught about Him from childhood onward, by good parents, ministers, and teachers, through Bible study, worship, and fellowship. Then, and only then will such 'absolutes' as honesty, purity, unselfishness and love emerge from the fog of abstractness and ambiguity and become vivid and compelling because the Word is then made flesh.

In this atmosphere of personal loyalty we can think seriously of how we can best use our time, talents, possessions, energies and opportunities in accordance with our unfolding knowledge of the mind of Jesus Christ and in obedience to His specific commandments.

We ought to think of the mind of Christ in the perspective of the Old Testament prophets and their insistence on Righteousness. Jesus came to fulfil, not to destroy the Law, and assumes His hearers' knowledge and acceptance of this in all His teaching.

With this progressive enlightenment our conscience and our moral perception and judgement can become as reliable as the perception and judgement of our physical senses.

But Divine guidance is by no means always a solitary matter. The influence of other people may constitute a most important channel, because we do not always know enough either of external realities or of the subtle self-deceptions of our own minds. As the great theologian Baron von Hugel once wrote: 'God works horizontally as well as vertically.' We can profit greatly by the help of parents, teachers, people with special knowledge or experience, and in some cases by the special help of pastoral or psychiatric counsellors. Through any or all of these avenues of help we can come to better insight into external and internal reality, and overcome the distortions of partial knowledge and of unconscious defences and motives.

Some people are acutely sensitive to what is called the direct inner voice. Many such inner leadings seem to come from the unconscious part of the mind and we may assume that they would be most dependable when the person's unconscious mind is 'saturated' with

God, by a long life of Christian discipline and worship. All the great authorities warn us that these inner leadings need to be tested by what we know of God, and discarded when they do not seem to be in harmony with the mind and attitude of Jesus. But such inner convictions may be of great importance and, thus safeguarded, may lead to much greater sensitivity to the guidance of God. They may sometimes be accepted as a signal to be ready for some further opportunity to come. Some of them may be the inner perception of someone else's intercessory prayer, and lead to an important positive answer to it. There is a need for much greater study of this whole problem, with careful safeguards against wishful thinking.

Our emotions have an important part in the perception of Divine guidance, in that unless we love God and our fellow-men enough we are not likely to be sensitive to the 'still, small voice' or to take the trouble to think out the right thing to do. Emotion can also distort our judgement to an alarming extent, as everyone with an experience of 'crowd psychology' knows well. The common saying, '*Vox populi, vox Dei*', is simply not true and in fact is a distortion of the original observation made by Alcuin, an early English theologian and man of letters, in a letter to Charlemagne *circa* A.D. 800. The original reads: 'We would not listen to those who were wont to say the voice of the people is the voice of God, for the voice of the mob is near akin to madness.' [1]

Our emotions can be turned to good effect in seeking Divine guidance through acts of worship, in which we remember the utter devotion of Jesus to mankind, and that of all kinds of other people in His name. They can also be inspired through the Christian fellowship, if we open our souls to perceive and appreciate the many acts of friendship around us.

The enlightenment of our intellect and the awakening of our emotions will reach their natural and essential fulfilment in the deliberate exercise of the will in some kind of creative action. Like all other faculties the will is strengthened and brought under control by constant disciplined training, and tends to atrophy with neglect. The very essence of Christian living as practised and taught by Jesus is to do the will of God, and this is also one of the most effective ways of coming to know it better (John 7[16-17]).

There are two special applications of the general principles through which we seek Divine guidance, which seem to be worth some

[1] *Stevenson's Book of Quotations* (Cassell, 1943), p. 1480.

particular consideration. The first is in the very common situation known as a dilemma, in which every alternative solution involves some undesirable consequences. It may be possible to find the best way through such problems by putting motive at a higher level than deed, by seeking the solution which involves and expresses the highest motives as judged by the Christian scale of values. In many such cases the clearest insight will come in the course of frank discussion with some trusted friend or a trained Christian counsellor, when the different aspects of the situation can be seen more objectively.

It may help in some dilemmas to remember the difference between compromise and toleration. Jesus faced the situation of slavery, which was quite contrary to everything He stood for. He also had to face the fact that He could not change it immediately without the use of force or compulsion, a temptation to which He had refused to yield. He never compromised with it, but tolerated it while planting in the heart of man the kind of respect for human personality which eventually cast it out. Even in St Paul's time we can see by his letter to Philemon that this new respect for human personality had begun to make itself felt. It often helps to remember that there are times and tactical factors in most situations, and that God is often more patient than we are.

The second special application is when we feel 'guided' about what someone else should be or do. Here we can take Jesus at His word: 'Let your light so shine before men, that they may see your good works, and glorify your Father which is in heaven' (Matthew 5^16). This would seem to suggest that we should offer our 'light', our ideas and reasons, and leave it to the other person to decide freely what he should do about it. We are to let our light shine out of us, and that is quite different from trying to make it shine into the other person. If what the other person is doing still appears to be harmful it may help to suggest talking it over with someone else.

Many people find it much easier to decide what other people should be doing than to recognize their own inconsistencies and shortcomings. This is often an unconscious defence-mechanism against a deep sense of inferiority or failure, and it needs good counselling if it is to become recognized by the person.

Guidance can generally be tested by asking ourselves a few straight questions about it. Does it fit in with what I know of God through my knowledge of Jesus Christ? Is there a 'cross': any real sacrifice, in it? (If not it may still be right, but if there is it is more certainly so.) Does it make for abundant life? Does it show the fruit of the Spirit? (Galatians 5$^{22-3}$).

No human decision is infallible, and we are not expected to be all-wise. We are expected to give the fullest and deepest thought and to make use of all necessary help in making our decisions, and to act in good faith, leaving the results—or apparent lack of result —in God's hands. A final test of our guidance is often found in the results of our action, and we should be always willing to admit it when we find that we were mistaken, to do what we can to remedy it, and to learn by experience.

The results of Divine guidance are incalculable and unlimited. It will often enable people to turn difficulties into opportunities, a unique power that has always been part of the Christian endowment. It will lift people above the domination of habit, prejudice, and of social convention; and free them from the domination of time, because Divine guidance is in the setting of eternity. More important still in everyday practical terms, it frees them from the heavy burden of possible mistakes through their certain conviction of the redemptive love of God, and their reassuring feeling that they are but imperfect and fallible instruments in His dependable hand.

CHAPTER SIX

Educating People for Christian Marriage and Parenthood

I. AN URGENT AND UNIVERSAL NEED

THE INESCAPABLE need for sound, stable, and permanent marriage is being increasingly realized in every community. We are continually being confronted with the tragic frequency of divorce, and with the even greater frequency of separation, and of marriages hanging uncomfortably together for the sake of the children or for mere expediency. We can imagine some of the associated disillusionment, bewilderment, misery, despair and cynicism, and the frequent extreme hardship affecting the people concerned, and even more the innocent children.

It is now becoming clear that there are many far-reaching and tragic personal and social consequences of failure in marriage and parenthood, which are less obvious, but no less important.

To begin with, the most potent known and controllable causative factor in mental illness is the deprivation of love, security (physical and psychic) and significance (the sense of being wanted and valued) in early childhood in the home—in other words the failure of marriage and parenthood. And when we consider the extent and the sheer weight of the burden of mental illness, on the community as well as on the sufferers and their loved ones, we can see the vital importance of any measures that will help to reduce it.

It is also becoming clearer that disturbed home life is a very potent factor in the causation and the progression of many physical illnesses. The greater speed and higher tension of our modern competitive society have increased the frequency and the severity of what are now called 'stress diseases' and 'psychosomatic disorders', and the effects of these stresses are much greater when people have not a restful happy home in which the balance and poise of their lives can be 're-created'. It is probable that many very able men, leaders in various walks of life, die of coronary occlusion or some other degenerative disease at a substantially earlier age when their home life is unsettled and turbulent than they would otherwise do; and this often happens at the very time when they are ready to ease up on their special work, and give their experience and ability to various humanitarian social services.

In addition to the burdens of mental and physical illness already mentioned, it is now generally agreed that a most potent causative factor in many other social disorders, such as delinquency, vandalism, and crime, is a broken or deficient home—a failure in marriage and parenthood. The same may be said of many destructive social conflicts, which undermine and frustrate our industrial and political organizations, and of much of the 'accident-proneness' which constantly reduces productive efficiency.

It is very illuminating to attempt to work out the total cost of all these things to the community. There is the more obvious cost, in public and private money, in trained and devoted man and woman-power, in buildings and equipment, and not least in the crushing burden of misery.

Above and beyond all this there is the hidden cost, in loss of productive power—the sick and the delinquent are consumers only and seldom produce anything, and the 'contagion' is often passed on to other people, and to the next generation—and the next!

Society has of course attempted to deal with these troubles, and the attempts have generally followed a fairly uniform pattern of evolution. At the beginning the main method of handling all these 'social problems' was penal in character. The mentally ill and the criminal were simply put away out of sight—and often out of mind. Then people began to think of ways of helping some of these people back into society, by devising remedial treatment for the mentally ill and considering methods of reforming the criminal. The difficulties of this remedial and reformatory treatment led to many attempts at earlier recognition, through various mental hygiene services and clinics, and this in turn led to more and more attempts at prevention, through kindergartens, child guidance clinics, and through all the other mental hygiene services. But so far there has been no co-ordinated large-scale attempt to prevent these personal and social problems at the place where they really begin: by setting out to give all people the fullest training for home and family living.[1]

[1] The recently published Report of the Royal Commission on Marriage and Divorce, 1951–3 (London: H.M.S.O., 1956), has strongly recommended that 'the Government should at an early date set up a suitably qualified body to review the Marriage law and the existing arrangements for pre-marital education and training' (p. 94).

It is true of course that many efforts have been and are being made to educate young people for the most important work of their lives: marriage and parenthood. But most of the efforts are limited to certain sections of the community, and are generally not availed of by those who may need the education most.

These progressive insights into the social importance of and the necessity for sound stable marriage and parenthood have gradually come over the last half-century. During that same period there have been many decisive changes in society itself, which have made sound stable marriage and parenthood much more difficult.

The most important of these is perhaps the social and financial emancipation of women, which has constituted a major social revolution. Practically all women are now able to earn their living, and can live alone in a 'bachelor flat' in the middle of a large city without exciting any social disapproval. Women are socially and financially independent. Marriage in consequence has changed from a male-dominated relationship to an equal partnership between free independent people. This is nearer than we have ever been to the Christian ideal of the sacredness of human personality and the freedom and equality of all persons before God. But marriage has come to demand much more from both partners if it is to remain stable and permanent. People are not held miserably together by social or financial necessity as they often were in the days of our grandfathers. The only real bonds today are love, and the sense of duty toward the children—until they are independent. Marriage has therefore reached a much higher standard than ever before, and has become more difficult and demanding. This is one of the most potent causes of the high divorce rate in any community.

The last century, and particularly the last half-century, have also brought vast changes associated with the emergence of industrial civilization, which have greatly affected marriage and parenthood, and home and family living. Large numbers of people have crammed together in cities, with often inadequate housing and playing space. Families have become smaller, which has largely done away with the situation in which an older brother or sister cares for the child, and thrown all the domestic responsibility on to the parents, particularly the mother. In other words the parent-child relationship is much less often balanced by the older-younger child relationship, and if the parent is emotionally unstable there is more risk of emotional tensions in the children.

In addition to all this, the husband's work is generally away from home, and it is often dull and monotonous. The wife is generally unable to share in her husband's work, which is a large part of his life, and her children spend much of their waking time away from home at kindergarten, school, and later whatever work they come to do. She cannot obtain much domestic help, and is often much lonelier than she was in the job that she did before marriage.

The marriage partnership has also to cope with the much greater noise, speed, and competitive tension of modern life, and with the fact that children are exposed to all kinds of subtle and powerful influences outside the home, such as the cinema and high-pressure sport, and inside the home, such as the wireless and television, before they are sufficiently mature to deal with them. The children do not get the opportunity to do as many things with their parents as they used to do, at the very time when, because of the greater moral laxity in the community they need to do more things with them. Because of better transport the children often make their friends, and later choose their marriage partners, from families at a distance, and the families may know little of each other's background, which sometimes makes for later instability in the children's marriages.

All these modern difficulties are intensified to a variable extent by the general insecurity of our time. Some countries go through periods of inflation, there are depressions and industrial conflicts, and over all the constant threat of war.

These strains and tensions of modern life make stable permanent marriage and sound parenthood much more difficult, but large numbers of young people are proving their ability to build good sound homes and families in spite of them. But if the partners are in any way unstable or immature, or untrained in the delicate 'give and take' of human relationships, any of these modern difficulties may well strain the marriage beyond their capacity and precipitate a far-reaching disaster.

There is an inescapable consequence of these great social changes which have made modern marriage and parenthood so much more difficult, and of the new realization of the great social importance of sound stable home and family life. It is that a new and urgent need has forced itself into human affairs—the need for universal first-class education and training of a most comprehensive kind for marriage and parenthood. This will involve all parts of the mind—the intellect, the emotions, and the will—which need teaching, training, and in-spiration respectively. It will also involve counselling for those who are immature or emotionally unstable, and psychotherapy for 'sick homes' and for people in conflict or difficulty. In some cases it will also involve material help.

This kind of educational and remedial programme is not beyond the capacity of the great majority of people to receive, nor of the educational and therapeutic resources of most communities to offer. It is clear that it demands a high level of team work and professional organization, and therefore first-class leadership.

There are many reasons for believing that the Church, more than any other organization, could and should assume this leadership, and sponsor and co-ordinate the whole programme. The Church has a particular interest and concern regarding Christian marriage and parenthood, and the great majority of weddings take place in churches. The Church also has the vocation, and the best resources, for the whole task.

This responsibility has to some extent been accepted by some branches of the Christian Church. In 1930 the Lambeth Conference of Anglican Bishops made a statement about it, and in the same year it was referred to in a Papal Encyclical. Since then the work has generally developed very slowly, and in many cases more under the sponsorship of other organizations with the support and encourage-ment of the Church than by the Church itself.

Universal and comprehensive education for marriage and parent-hood, and the necessary counselling and healing services for the pro-motion and preservation of sound creative home and family life therefore constitute one of the most important and far-reaching programmes of pastoral work available to the Church. Properly carried out it will have incalculable results for good on the mental and social health of the community for our own time, and for genera-tions to come. It will prove to be a most productive field for evange-listic work, possibly the most logical and effective of all, because the spirit of home and family living radiates outward into every part of human community life.

II. A COMPREHENSIVE PLAN TO MEET IT

The unfolding sequence of human life presents itself as an ever-recurring cycle, from birth and babyhood, through childhood, adolescence and young adulthood, with friendship, courtship, choice of mate, engagement, marriage, parenthood, 'parent-in-law-hood', and grandparenthood; and with parenthood the cycle begins again in another generation. The 'recurring cycle' has tended to become a 'descending spiral' with the increasing frequency of divorce, and the urgent need of our day is to try to convert it into a steadily ascending spiral. To do this any practical coherent programme of education for marriage and parenthood will need to deal with every stage in the recurring cycle, and also to offer some practical help to the unmarried, who will generally fill important roles in relation to many stages of the process.

CHAPTER SEVEN

Pre-Marital Preparation: Medical and Pastoral Aspects

FOR PURPOSES of discussion we may begin at any point in the recurring cycle, and perhaps the best starting-point on this occasion is that from which many attempts are initiated in these days —the coming of two young people, we shall call them John and Mary, to a minister to make arrangements for their marriage. It is understood of course that it would be much better if they had been given the kind of earlier preparation later to be described from birth onwards, or even throughout their engagement period. If the minister knows of their engagement it provides a good opportunity to invite them for an interview as an expression of the Church's interest in their fullest welfare and happiness.

At the first interview the pastor can find out how they are feeling and planning about such general matters as housing, finance, the question of Mary's going on working for a time after marriage, and possibly about the attitudes of the respective parents and families to the marriage. In this interview he will be able to gain some idea of the general maturity of John and Mary, and of their attitudes to each other and to their marriage. He may also ask whether they intend to seek help from their family doctors on the many medical aspects of their marriage.

I. THE MEDICAL PART IN PRE-MARITAL PREPARATION

It is very helpful for the pastor to have the co-operation of one or more doctors in all pre-marital preparation. This can usually be obtained by a personal approach in which the pastor informs the doctor of his interest in good preparation of people for marriage and of the general lines on which he is trying to carry out the work. If he then asks the doctor's permission to refer any young people to him for specific help, the doctor will generally be glad to do what he can.

It is generally desirable that people should have a good medical overhaul before marriage, and some review of their family histories to make sure that any obvious hereditary disorders are known to the two people before they finally commit themselves. This is obviously best carried out when possible by their respective family doctors, who are most likely to know or find out about these things.

Another part of the medical preparation for marriage is the specific instruction of the two people in the various sexual factors in the marriage union as they apply to the husband and wife. This will include some information about the anatomical and physiological, and probably the psychological factors in sexual intercourse, and about its technique. If they desire it there may also be given some definite help regarding the technique of contraception. It is suggested that whatever the personal views of any doctor on this subject may be he has no right to impose them on anyone else. He may state them, and even refuse to give any help on conscientious grounds, but should then leave them quite free to consult anyone else for the necessary help if they so desire.

This educational aspect of the medical preparation for marriage may be given by the family doctor in conjunction with the medical examination of the two people, or it may be given by any doctor who has fitted himself to do it. The more the education can be given in the form of a discussion between all three, rather than a lecture by the doctor, the better it will generally succeed. In some cases specific information may be given to groups of engaged couples, again in the form of a discussion in which all are encouraged to take part. These discussions may be part of a series in which there are also discussions about the many other aspects of marriage and parenthood, led by marriage counsellors or other specially qualified teachers.

In some cases it may be most valuable for a doctor to have the opportunity of talking over some aspects of the medical preparation with each partner separately. This is most likely when one or both partners show any evidence of emotional immaturity or emotional tension or conflict. In such cases, which often prove to be complicated by undue possessiveness or undue parental domination, a few counselling sessions with each partner separately will bring greater insight and maturity than any attempt to deal with them together. In general it may be said that instruction is generally best given to the partners together, while counselling is far more applicable to each partner separately.

II. THE PASTORAL PART IN PRE-MARITAL PREPARATION

This principle also applies to all the help attempted by ministers and marriage counsellors in preparation for marriage and parenthood. The pastor should try to arrange an interview with each one separately as early as possible in the preparation. If possible it may be wisest to do this before seeing them together at all. If he knows one of them he can invite that one for an interview, and then ask for the opportunity of a talk with the other one at some suitable time. In these interviews he may encourage the person to talk about many things that would not be mentioned in the presence of the other one, and he may be able to find and help them to deal with some deep personal anxieties, conflicts and dilemmas, and immature and insecure personal relationships.

If the pastor sees them together on the first occasion he will be guided by his general impressions of their attitudes to each other and to the marriage, and will decide whether to interview each of them separately. It is generally easy to arrange separate interviews by saying that he wants to talk over some particular things with each of them separately. There is of course no fixed or stereotyped pattern of pre-marital interviewing. Each pastor will inevitably develop his own individual approach, and as long as certain valid principles already described are observed it will prove effective. A simple natural friendliness is far more helpful than any rigid adherence to someone else's approach.

'What Every Engaged Couple Should Know'

An attempt will now be made to give an account of the kind of instruction that the pastor might offer to engaged couples. For completeness some things will be included that would normally have been given to them as they grew up and before their engagement. Many people are still coming to marriage without adequate knowledge or emotional acceptance of important facts that have a vital influence upon the working-out of their whole partnership and union.

(a) What is Marriage?

The first essential is a discussion on the nature and purpose of marriage itself. Many people marry without any discussion about this, and find to their bewildered disappointment that they disagree on the fundamental basis of their marriage. It may be that Mary thinks of it in its modern form, as an equal partnership between two free and responsible people, while John cannot accept any other view than that in which the husband is the 'boss', whose commands are to be obeyed implicitly and without question. A proper hammering-out of this question before marriage would have saved them many hurtful disagreements and quarrels, and would probably have helped John to clearer insight into the unconscious causes of his obsolete attitude to marriage to be found in his own upbringing.

A good definition of marriage is contained in the statement that 'Marriage should be the fulfilment of human love in the life-long companionship of a home and the complete intertwining of two lives.' [1] The prevalence of divorce, and the publicity associated with it, have combined to encourage many young people to think of marriage as a partnership that could be broken or discarded by mutual consent if it ceased to work out satisfactorily. Such a view constitutes a real danger to the continuing stability of society, as well as to the preservation of the sanctity of marriage. As *The Times* [2] stated in 1952:

The governing principle of civil and canon law on marriage is that the union of man and wife is life-long. Just as the Church in its pastoral work has to take account of cases in which the principle has been broken, so the State must acknowledge that it has not the power to impose on every one the standard to which it is publicly committed, and must try to ensure that those who depart from it are treated fairly by the standards of secular justice. The problem is to reconcile the maintenance of a principle with the regulation of inevitable breaches of it. . . . No community, whatever its religious or ethical basis, can, without disaster, consider its marriage customs as empirical rules of convenience to be modified repeatedly without any regard to their place in the general structure of society.

Without necessarily discussing such supporting details as these, marriage must be seen clearly by both partners as an equal democratic partnership of mutual obedience to God and loving co-operation with one another for life. Its purpose must be seen as something far greater than 'the devices and desires of our own hearts'.[3] Its threefold purpose is expressed in 'The Form of Solemnization of

[1] F. R. Barry, Claude Mullins, and Douglas White, *Right Marriage* (SCM Press, 1936).
[2] *The Times Weekly Review*, 29th May 1952, Sub-Leader: 'The Church and Marriage.'   [3] *The Book of Common Prayer*.

Matrimony' [1] as the procreation, nurture, and education (in its highest sense) of children, the fulfilment and ordering of the sex instinct, and 'the mutual society, help, and comfort, that the one ought to have of the other, both in prosperity and adversity'.

(b) What do we mean by 'Love'?

Having described marriage as 'the fulfilment of human love', the next essential question to be discussed is 'What is human love?' It is necessary to take some trouble with this because current ideas about it are generally vague and superficial.

For purposes of description we may divide this complex emotion into three parts, which correspond roughly with the three main 'levels' of the human personality—physical, mental, and spiritual—and which can be expressed by the three Greek words, '*eros*', '*philia*', and '*agape*'.

At the most primitive level love exists as a strong and widely diffused physical attraction and desire between the two sexes. Its basic foundation seems to be in the biological endowment of people, in which it is comparable with the sexual attraction between male and female animals, though not identical with it. As with animals it is excited and intensified by a variety of stimuli through the various senses, but beyond anything we know of in animals it is also influenced very greatly by many social and cultural factors in the environment of the growing person. When these social and cultural factors are unbalanced, distorted, or inconsistent some abnormal sexual attitudes and feelings may result.

The second 'level' of love may be described as a personal attraction which enriches the physical or sexual urge, and narrows it down to a great extent to those of similar intellectual and cultural interests, and particularly to the person who may be chosen as a life partner. Without this intellectual and personal bond even the strongest physical attraction would be a very poor basis for any lasting marriage. It is quite sufficient for animal mating because temporary mating is all that is needed for animals whose young are 'self-supporting' very early in their lives. Physical attraction alone has no 'staying power', as those who depend on it almost inevitably find out to their great disappointment—and to their cost and that of their children.

These two aspects of love are 'natural' to man—they are bound up with his physical and intellectual endowment; they are present in

[1] *The Book of Common Prayer.*

some degree in all human beings, even in primitive and savage tribes. They have in them a strong element of desire and demand, often partially regulated by some outgoing devotion. This 'demanding' love, however, is vulnerable; when it is rejected or frustrated it may well turn to hate. When it is the basis of marriage it may hold the partners together quite well as long as there is no great stress from the environment or from failures in either partner.

But human beings are essentially fallible, prone to all kinds of stupid mistakes, impulsive ill-considered words, attitudes and actions, and even deliberate wrongdoing. If we believe that marriage is meant to be a happy life-long union of two fallible people, in spite of all their differences of attitude and outlook and all kinds of internal stresses and external interferences, it is clear that the bond that holds them must be very much stronger than any possessive demanding love can be.

For life-long union of two free reasonably independent fallible people their physical and personal bond must be ruled, sustained and strengthened by a still higher quality of love: a third level of love, which we may call Christian love because it has been more clearly shown and taught by Jesus than by anyone else. It has been eloquently described by St Paul in 1 Corinthians 13. Unlike the other two aspects of love Christian love is not 'natural' to man: it is not generally present in savages or in very young children, although man has in him the capacity for it. This kind of love is generated, or 'born' in him and then cultivated in him through the experience of being loved in that way, by parents, teachers, ministers, and others. As Jesus told Nicodemus, flesh can only give birth to flesh, it takes spirit to give birth to spirit. Christian missionaries frequently have the joy of seeing this kind of love born in people who had never previously come into contact with it; and it is born in them far more from the love that the missionaries offer than from anything they may teach, however essential their teaching may be.

Part of the strength of Christian love is in the fact that it has in it the unique grace of Christian forgiveness—an essential need in all lasting human relationships, and particularly in marriage, the most intimate, delicate, and far-reaching of them all. Christian forgiveness is based on the realities of life. We do, in fact, receive far more from life (or from God the author and director of life) than we can ever earn or deserve, and it ill becomes any of us to withhold the same generosity, which includes forgiveness, from others.

H

Jesus Himself gave a vivid illustration of this important principle in His parable of the unmerciful servant (Matthew 18²³⁻³⁵). Forgiveness then is not something we do by sheer will-power, we are inspired to forgive by the consciousness that we are loved and forgiven by God far beyond any of our possible deserving, and can therefore do no less than forgive our 'fellow-servant' of God, even though he can do nothing fully to deserve it.

The 'priorities' of Christian love were laid down for all time by Jesus in His enunciation of 'The Two Great Commandments' (Matthew 22³⁷⁻⁴⁰). Christian love is inspired and directed throughout by the love of God first in response to the awareness of His loving nature and action. Each partner in Christian marriage sets out first to be loyal to God: to what he or she honestly believes to be right, whether the other appears to be loyal or not. Their total love of one another, the appropriate blending of physical, personal and Christian love, can only live and grow in the creative and healing power of a common devotion to God. And when two people are joined together by that total blending love we can believe that they are in fact joined together by God, for God is Love. Then no man can put them asunder, and they grow from an intimate partnership to a deep indissoluble union.

(c) Love is Alive!

In all our thinking about love we have been seeing it as something that lives. It is 'born', nurtured through a vigorous but unstable 'childhood and adolescence', and eventually should come to a rich and stable maturity. The early 'glitter and glamour' stages have a delightful, but unreal sentimentality about them, which cannot stand up for long to the realities of everyday life, but hold the partners together while they are forging the deeper and stronger bond of mature, well-founded love.

Like every living thing love needs constant adequate nourishment if it is to live and grow to the necessary stable maturity. It is nourished by being expressed to one another; by 'worship' of one another in the atmosphere of worship of God; by the steady continuation and deepening of courtship. There are three main ways of expressing love, by word, by attitude and action, and by sacramental action.

It helps greatly to be told, over and over again, what we know in our hearts, that we are loved; but if words are not supported by attitudes and spontaneous thoughtful kindly actions they soon lose their power. But people generally realize that their love is 'too deep for words to express', and they would generally agree that love is too deep even for kindly actions to convey. We can do many kindly things for our neighbours and friends. Of themselves, therefore, words and actions do not generally go deep enough to express adequately the profound holy mystery of total love, and the 'one-fleshness' on which true marriage revolves. Some kind of sacrament, or 'sacred action' is needed: a regular enacting together and realizing (making real) of this holy 'one-flesh-ness'.

(d) The Meaning of Human Sex Intercourse

When it is thought of in this way the act of sexual intercourse between husband and wife can become a most fitting expression of total love: love of body, mind, and spirit; a channel of the Love of God for the enrichment and sustaining of the bond of love between the husband and wife. This sacred action takes the most intimate and complete union there is between two people, and expresses through it the utter, abandoned, self-giving of each to the other as part of their self-giving to God. It can be seen how this will find its greatest reality when it is linked up more specifically with God and with the wider family of God in the regular participation of husband and wife, and later their children as well, in the sacrament of Holy Communion.

This view of sexual intercourse is not generally found in the 'secular' literature about sex and marriage. The Christian minister more than anyone has the duty and privilege of offering it to all those who are about to enter 'the holy estate of Matrimony', to be linked up with all the more 'scientific' and technical instruction they may receive from books, or at the hands of doctors. It would make sexual intercourse a hollow sham when there is not real, devoted, self-giving love to be expressed, or when the inner feelings of the two people are not lived out fully 'in the life-long companionship of a home, and the complete intertwining of two lives'.

People who think of a man as little more than a clever animal find it difficult or impossible to think of sexual intercourse in any deeper way than as the gratification of desire, and there may be profound emotional conflicts between them when the desire at any time is not mutual. It is also difficult or impossible for such people to keep the Christian standard in human relationships in and outside marriage. It needs to be emphasized that Christian morality is essentially for

Christian people, in whom it can be sustained by the power of their Christian loyalty.

There is an important practical consideration about sexual intercourse which the pastor ought to bring to the attention of his engaged couples because it is not generally realized. It is the difference between the common attitudes of men and women to sexual intercourse when it is sought after a quarrel. Men tend to think of it as a gesture of reconciliation, but women are more apt to regard this as an affront to their self-respect, an act of condescension, which in many respects it is. When John seeks it as a way to reconciliation and finds that Mary 'refuses' to co-operate, he may well misjudge her and feel more deeply aggrieved and hurt, all for the want of a little understanding. If he waits until a full reconciliation has been established, the wounds healed, and emotional tranquillity re-established, he will generally find that it fulfils all the highest expectations of both of them.

(e) The Personal Relationship in Marriage

The pastor may take the opportunity of his discussion with John and Mary to tell them some very practical things about their personal relationship as it unfolds in their marriage. The first is about what is often called 'letting off steam'. Love is never quite 'one hundred per cent'. The aggressive instinct is part of the fundamental endowment of human beings as it is of all animals. It is always present to some degree, and will be sometimes provoked to bursting-point, particularly in impulsive, excitable people. John and Mary should therefore be ready to accept occasional outbursts from each other, and then they will not be so deeply hurt when they happen, when many things are said that may well be regretted afterwards.

Such occasional outbursts appear to have some considerable value for many people in the preservation of mental health, and it is the privilege and genius of mature self-giving love to accept and absorb them without allowing them to hurt unduly. When they are frequent, or when they come from apparently trivial causes, it suggests an emotional immaturity or even the possibility of neurotic illness. When the recipient feels deeply hurt it may suggest undue vulnerability, either from a neurotic perfectionism, or some other kind of emotional immaturity. Many people marry in the belief that they will find another indulgent 'parent'. They are not aware of the unreality of such an attitude to marriage, and become disillusioned and upset when they discover that they only have a husband or wife! Situations of this kind need some counselling.

Above all John and Mary should be warned of the futility and even harm of retaliating when outbursts come. The other person is desperately in need of love and acceptance at such times, however much it is pushed away when offered. They should also be warned of the danger of bringing up old grievances, whatever the provocation.

Some guidance may also be given regarding the most helpful attitude to differences of opinion and tensions of any kind within the family. It may be said that they will inevitably happen among any two or more people with ideas of their own, that they are seldom what they seem, and that they can be productive if handled with loving tolerance.

There are two different kinds of argument: productive and unproductive. The productive kind is about the things on which people differ. Each puts his own feelings and ideas with supporting facts, and allows the other one to do the same. Even if eventually they must 'agree to differ', each has learnt that there is another point of view which is strongly held, and that has widened both minds a little.

The unproductive kind of argument is one in which the discussion is switched from the things about which people differ to mutual criticism. When personalities are dragged in- in this way the main subject is displaced by the personal battle, reason by emotion, and each is deeply hurt without any progress toward the solution of the problem. In most cases it is even made more difficult to solve. People need to see the absolute relevance of the teaching of Jesus about removing the beam from their own eye before attempting to deal with the splinter in their 'brother's' eye (Matthew 7$^{1-5}$).

When people find it difficult to come to any reasonable agreement on some important questions, such as the disciplining of children, it is often helpful to seek further illumination from a counsellor or from someone with special knowledge who is trusted by each of them. But the essential attitude between them is readiness to accept the other one's right to hold his views. These and other underlying principles of human relationships could well be taught to people from childhood, in home, school, and church to a greater extent than they are at present.

Finally, John and Mary may be reminded of the desirability and value of living out their partnership in everything, especially in matters of finance, in the many things to be done, and in decisions to be made in their married life.

CHAPTER EIGHT

The Wedding and the Early Years of Marriage

I. MAKING THE MOST OF THE MARRIAGE SERVICE

THE MARRIAGE SERVICE is possibly the most important and far-reaching event in the lives of John and Mary, and of all the 'Johns and Marys' in any community. It is the culmination of a joyous succession of deeply significant experiences in each of their lives: growing mutual interest, gesture and response, increasingly close companionship, mutual idealization ripening into love, with some painful but testing and strengthening misunderstandings and conflicts, and then the tacit understanding, later made public and symbolized by the engagement ring.

And now, after a much wider and more intimate mutual revelation, and a wealth of planning and arranging, they come into the consecrated house of God before His ordained minister and their own relatives and friends to ratify all their private undertakings and to commit themselves to each other utterly and for life by the most solemn vows, 'to have and to hold from this day forward, for better for worse, for richer for poorer, in sickness and in health, to love and to cherish, till death us do part, according to God's holy ordinance'.

This public committal is also the foundation and beginning of an entirely new creative social unit, the stability and fruitfulness of which will be of the greatest importance for the welfare of the whole community.

How can the pastor prepare for and conduct this important ceremony so that John and Mary will find in it the deepest reality and meaning as they commit themselves to the greatest and most far-reaching enterprise of their lives? How can he make the most of what may be a rare opportunity to bring a spiritual impact on the lives and thoughts of many people who seldom attend Church or read or listen to any specifically religious teaching?

These questions demand much thought and discussion on the part of the pastor, and possibly some careful experimenting with different methods of approach. The actual pattern and structure of the Marriage Service is fairly uniform, with some variations appropriate to different denominations and to the personal attitudes of the minister. He will choose the degree of solemnity, the finer points of ritual, the loudness and inflexion of his voice, and the kind of exhortations, if any, to the bride and bridegroom and to the assembled company apart from those laid down in the actual liturgy.

He will have seen to it that the participants in the ceremony know what they are to do and when they are to do it, and he will also have satisfied himself as far as possible that the bride and bridegroom have given the fullest consideration to the seriousness of the step they are undertaking and of the vows they are about to make. He will then be able to think of each part of the service in terms of its reality to all those present, and particularly to John and Mary.

John and Mary will find much greater reality in the service if the pastor has rounded off his preliminary talks with some explanation of the symbolic significance of the main elements of the ceremonial. This has been clearly described by Paul E. Johnson,[1] and may be summarized briefly as follows:

The flower girls and bridesmaids who precede the bride from the church door to the altar represent her steady growth from childhood to maturity. The bride is conducted by her father to symbolize her dependence on her parents until he 'gives her' to the bridegroom to begin the new relationship of marriage, and steps back into the congregation.

The groomsmen and the best man represent the dependence of the bridegroom on his friends. He shares the dependence of all people upon society but is expressing his independence of his parents by standing at the altar without his father. In these days when many girls are almost equally independent of their parents at the time of marriage the 'giving away' has lost some of its symbolism.

Behind the wedding party as they face the altar is the loving and well-wishing congregation, with the families of bride and groom in the front pews on either side backed by row upon row of their friends, married and unmarried, expressing their loving support and witnessing to the social value of marriage. The families and friends of the bride are seated behind the bride on the left-hand side of the aisle, and those of the bridegroom on the right. After the ceremony the families and friends mingle and join into one company as an expression of the union of bride and groom.

[1] *Christian Love* (Abingdon Cokesbury Press, 1951).

The minister standing at the altar and facing the bride and groom and all the assembled company, is the ordained representative of the Church and of the Divine spirit of Christian Love in which the bride and groom are pledging life-long union. He is also the authorized representative of the State—the organized community of citizens, responsible for seeing that there is no legal impediment to their marriage, and for establishing the legal rights of each of the partners in marriage.

The solemn vows made first by the bridegroom and then by the bride, are made to the minister as representative of God, Church, and State, and they specifically include the many difficulties and dangers to which all marriages may be exposed. The vows are 'embodied' in the giving and receiving of a ring: the unbroken endless tie which is to bind their lives together.

Having come separately to the church, the newly married walk down the aisle together—the straight and narrow road of life, with the love and good wishes of all their friends, tangibly expressed through the rich variety of wedding presents, and through the 'ceremonial' of the wedding reception. They then withdraw from the society of their friends for a short 'honeymoon' so that they can deepen and strengthen their union, after which they re-enter society as a new social unit, the beginning of a new family and a new generation.

These are some of the many symbolisms of this deeply significant and far-reaching ceremony. Properly understood, and fittingly conducted, it may gather up all the different elements in the pre-marital preparation and weld them into an unbreakable foundation of Godly union. Then they will find their Christian Love enriched day by day as they open their hearts and lives to God and to one another, and build up the infinite resources of the parental love that they will later give to their children.

A wedding is therefore a very great pastoral opportunity, particularly for establishing or deepening the pastoral relationship with the two people most concerned and their future family, but also with many other people with whom it brings close contact. A wedding reception is one of the best opportunities for friendly and spontaneous fellowship with many people, and the pastor's natural friendliness on such occasions may win the confidence of many people in him and in the One unto whom he is seeking to be a good witness.

II. EDUCATION AFTER MARRIAGE AND FOR PARENTHOOD

All our growing understandings of the importance of the parent-child relationships from the very beginning, and our experience of the increasing difficulties of modern family living, have underlined the urgent and inescapable need for very much better education and preparation of all our young people for the far-reaching responsibilities of parenthood. It has become clear that however strong the parental instinct may be, it needs to be directed and helped by some knowledge of the principles and methods of child care, and some awareness of the subtle dangers of faulty attitudes within and between parents themselves.

An increasing amount of information is becoming available to parents in books, articles, and broadcast talks, and more and more personal guidance is being offered through child guidance clinics, kindergarten and other parents' associations. The Church is also offering increasing help through mothers' clubs of various kinds, and through 'fellowships of marriage'. These are all valuable as far as they go, but the needs of the situation will not be adequately met until a much more fully integrated programme can be built up, and applied much more widely in the community.

By its very nature the necessary education must combine fully adequate information in simple terms with the promotion of fitting attitudes. In other words it must have within itself a full blending of technical, intellectual and cultural, emotional, and spiritual elements. This will demand a high quality of team work between many different professional callings, but it would seem that the Church more than any other organization is fitted (potentially at least) to take the lead in this great educational enterprise.

An attempt will therefore be made to suggest the main requirements in an adequate programme of education after marriage and for parenthood without trying strictly to define the pastor's part in it. If the pastor knows what is needed he is in a better position to decide how much he can do in his own educational work, and what he should try to organize through Church clubs and through the available or potentially available community agencies. If pastors are fully awake to these needs the Church will regain the position of leadership in which its heritage of Divine wisdom can be of greatest service to the community.

When the pre-marital preparation as previously described has been well done a good personal relationship will have been established with the two young people, and their confidence in the pastor will make it easier for him to get them to join with other young married people in some kind of 'fellowship of marriage' or at least to keep in touch with him and to read selected booklets and pamphlets that may be of help. It may be that there are good opportunities for this further education in existence apart from the actual Church organization, and in such cases the pastor may feel that he can give the fullest service by taking an interest in what such bodies are offering, by giving his own active co-operation to them, and by encouraging his people to make the greatest possible use of them and to give their practical support to them. The attempt at 'spiritual enrichment' of such educational and remedial services outside the actual Church organization is showing itself as one of the most creative and productive functions of the Church.

There may be some early difficulties and fears in marriage, which are generally part of the delicate process of mutual adjustment to one another, to 'in-laws', to friends, and to housing, finance, the demands of work, and the many other matters that may arise. Sometimes there may be unexpected illness or calamity, which may bring severe strains to the partnership before the two people are ready to meet them. Some of the difficulties and fears will come under the scope of medical, or even specialist gynaecological or psychiatric help, but many of them can be greatly relieved by the help of a wise and understanding pastor before they have been intensified by misunderstandings and by impulsive words and actions which wound rather than help the other person. If the pastor has built up a good co-operative relationship with the doctors in the district he may be able to use it to good effect in securing help.

During these early months of marriage the partners are building up the essential resources for good parenthood, the mutual love and understanding out of which they can forge a united front in the care of their children and from which they can give the outgoing mature Christian Love their children will need. They can also set out to gain the fullest information and cultivate the most helpful attitudes for the carrying out of the vital responsibilities of parenthood.

'What Every Parent should Know—Beforehand!'

(*a*) *The main facts about Reproduction.* Many of these will have been given to the partners already if their pre-marital preparation has been well done. The medical details of conception and the management of pregnancy and the confinement will generally be given by the doctor, but there are some personal matters that may come into the field of the pastor. Many husbands need to know more about what we may term 'the fine art of expectant fatherhood', and they could probably be helped greatly in this through a 'fellowship of marriage' in which are some young couples who have learnt many things by the experience of having one or more children.

(b) *Babies and children are People!* They are persons in their own right and not things, ends in themselves and not means of inflating parental pride or releasing parental emotions, or otherwise satisfying parental needs. These are very subtle dangers in that parents are generally unaware of such injurious attitudes when they are present, and need careful loving handling in a good counselling relationship if they are to be helped beyond their emotional defences to a rational insight. All the 'modern' discoveries about the handling of babies and young children are bringing us back to the recognition of the infinite value and necessity of outgoing, unconditional, demonstrative Christian Love, expressed in all contacts: in words, attitudes, and actions.

(c) *The expression of love through breast or bottle feeding.* The taking in of food is the first really intimate experience of the newly-born baby, and it probably colours all his later relationships. It is now believed that the baby has no sense of the future, and that when his hunger is not immediately satisfied he is gripped by an intense, if indiscriminate, anxiety, as if he were never going to be fed. The modern conduct of feeding is therefore not altogether dominated by the clock, nor by what amount per feed the 'average baby' of that age takes. As far as humanly possible feeding is given 'on demand', and in quantity sufficient to satisfy his demand. Any tendency to overfeeding can be corrected by giving more water between or before the feeds.

Above all, each feeding, whether by breast or bottle, should be given with warm loving cuddling by the mother, who should be as far as possible in a tranquil relaxed frame of mind. Such feeding is a deep experience of 'love, joy, and peace', the three first fruits of the Spirit, to the baby. Throughout life, affection, goodwill, and friendship are associated with feeding. For example the good salesman entertains his prospective client at a meal before putting his proposition. The family meal-time should always be kept as a time of love, joy, and peace as far as possible. Apart from feeding-times the baby should be handled as often as may be possible without interfering with his resting, and always gently, confidently, and lovingly.

(d) *The expression of love through toilet training.* Bowel and bladder control represent the most personal disciplines of the young baby, disciplines in which the social requirements differ from the baby's instinctive attitudes and behaviour. This represents an adaptation from the 'pleasure principle' to the 'reality principle', and there will generally be a better response to the mother's efforts when the initial feeding has been well handled.

The essential nerve tracts for proper bowel and bladder control are not developed until at least one year of age. It is therefore essential to allow time, and not to try to 'keep up with the Joneses', which would be trying to boost up maternal pride at the expense of the baby. It is quite normal for bowel control to be established at some time between 1½ and 2 years of age, and bladder control to come at about 3 years of age, but they are often delayed when the baby is exposed to emotional strains. Established control may also be temporarily lost in the face of strain or anxiety or jealousy.

It is most important for the parent to avoid any ideas or attitudes which could convey the impression of 'dirtiness', shame or disgust to the child. The excretions appear to be regarded by the child as a 'gift', and simple approval may encourage the evolution of this sense into the more socially acceptable impulses of generosity.

It is possible that a number of later neurotic troubles may be attributable, partly at least, to faulty toilet training.

(e) *The expression of love through management of infantile sexuality.* It is probable that infantile sexuality is characterized by curiosity and pleasure rather than 'hunger' or awareness of maleness or femaleness. This pleasure sensation appears first to be centred round the mouth, and gratified by suckling, thumb-sucking, and later by biting. Later the baby becomes more conscious of its anal region and gains some apparent pleasure from the expulsion of motions. Occasionally the retention of motions appears to give a pleasurable sensation. These early manifestations of infantile sexuality are generally seen in the first three years of life. During the next four years the male baby finds pleasure in handling his penis.

It is important for the parent to regard all these as normal, and not to interfere or show disapproval in any way. A child tends to repeat any experience or action from which he is restrained, and to become more interested in it. Attempted interference will also impose conflicts, while ignoring it will generally allow the impulse to wane in due course.

If the child seems to be unduly interested in his genital organs it is right to look for an emotional problem, to see that he has no reason to feel rejected, and to offer other attractive playthings.

(*f*) *Preparation for necessary maternal absences.* Where possible the mother should prepare the child for any forthcoming absence of more than a day or so by arranging for a suitable person to look after the child, and making it possible for the child to get to know and trust her and accept her as 'mother'. The child's routine should be disturbed as little as possible during the mother's absence, and above all he should be given plenty of demonstrative affection. The longer the absence is likely to be the more important it is to allow a close relationship to be built up with the mother-substitute. One or two special new toys will often be of help at this time, especially if they come to the child as 'from mummy'.

(*g*) *The handling of 'behaviour problems'.* Most 'behaviour problems' are amateurish and futile ways of solving a problem faced by the child. If the parent simply deals with the behaviour itself, with 'appropriate' scolding or punishment, it will generally have disappointing results, and the child will feel still more bewildered and even rejected. If the parent accepts the child's feelings and sets out to discover the problem as the child sees it; and then joins with the child in loving fellowship to help him deal properly with it, the experience will deepen the child's sense of loving confidence in the parent, and often overcome the 'behaviour problem'. Recognizing the child as a person means accepting his right to his own feelings, even if the parent cannot see the 'sense' in them, but not necessarily accepting his behaviour. But if the inner feelings behind the behaviour are accepted most children can be helped to more co-operative behaviour with reasonable patience.

The handling of *jealousy in children* may be taken as a specific example of the way in which parents can accept the feelings of a child. Jealousy is inevitable in all children—they will always tend to see things in a different light from that of their parents and to make their own comparisons. Even an only child will sometimes feel jealous of the amount of his mother's time and affection given to his father, and the attention given to other people and things.

Needless to say jealousy should be reduced as far as possible by treating all children, not so much equally, as fairly. Any attempt to treat children of different ages equally is bound to raise insuperable problems, and may well increase the tendency to jealousy. The older child, for example, must have some of the privileges of his age, and so in other ways must the younger; and in each case the responsibilities that go with them. Each child, of course, should be offered the same demonstrative affection and acceptance, and should know how far he can go and what he can expect from his parents. When there is to be a change in the domestic arrangements, such as the arrival of a new baby, it is important for the parents to prepare for it very completely in advance, by making any changes that will affect the other child or children.

For example, if the new arrival will mean a change in the older child's bedroom, or the sending of the older child to kindergarten or school these should be done a few weeks before the new baby's appearance so that they will not be too closely connected with it. The older child should be told about the forthcoming arrival, and in some cases even allowed to feel its parts and movements by putting a hand on the mother's abdomen. After the new arrival the older child should be given all possible attention and affection so that he will not feel displaced in any way. A common cause for jealousy can be avoided if the visitors who may come 'to see the new baby' are asked particularly to pay a lot of attention to the older child, which they may otherwise not think of doing, and even to bring a small present to him rather than to the baby.

When a child shows any evidence of jealousy the parent should not show any disapproval or defensive reaction. The mother should take him on her knee and tell him that she knows how he feels and that she doesn't mind his feeling jealous. Also that she loves him and wants him to be happy; and that she is trying to treat him fairly. She can then go on to say that she wants him to help her by telling her whenever he thinks he is being treated unfairly, and that she will always listen to him and try to understand. She might point out that she cannot promise always to do what he wants, and that he must learn to trust her love and her judgement of what is right.

It is of the greatest importance that the child should always feel really at home, and able to be his real self with his mother of all people; and feel free to express any of his real feelings with the confidence that they will be accepted without ridicule or hostility. Acceptance of the child's feelings does not necessarily mean acceptance of his behaviour. But it is the application of Jesus Christ's attitude and direction: 'Judge not, that ye be not judged' (Matthew 7[1]). As a matter of practical realism we have no right or power to dictate the feelings of anyone else, adult or child, and especially the young child, whose self-control has not yet had time to become fully established.

In the same way *a child's anxieties* are best handled, not by the common attitude of 'there's nothing to be frightened about', but rather by taking the child on one's knee and saying: 'Tell me all about it and then we shall have a look at it together to see what it is all about.' It is generally not wise to attempt to shield children too much from family anxieties. They sense the atmosphere, and if not allowed to participate in the situation they often feel bewildered and anxious, and even troubled by a sense of guilt, that they must have done something to bring the trouble about. When loved and accepted they can take a surprising amount of stress, especially if treated as people, and given a part to play, however small.

In all these family matters it is vital that the two parents should present a united front to their children, and to all other people. The child's father can have the same part as his mother in all the foregoing methods of handling situations.

These are some of the important things that every parent should have the opportunity of knowing before their children come. Many of them, and many other things may be offered to them by doctors, nurses, and other authorities, or discovered by reading suitable books. Two comprehensive, reliable, and reasonably priced books on the subject, which can be safely recommended to any young parent, are those by Benjamin Spock [1] and by Florence Powdermaker and Louise Grimes.[2] If the pastor has a good working knowledge of the general principles and practice of good parenthood, it will be of great help in the bringing up of his own children, and enable him to give much good help to the young married people with whom he comes into contact. This is a far-reaching pastoral educational opportunity, and one which, if well carried out, will lead to many more pastoral relationships.

[1] *Pocket Book of Baby and Child Care* (Pocket Books Inc., New York).
[2] *The Intelligent Parents' Manual* (Penguin Books in assn. with William Heinemann Medical Books Ltd., 1953).

CHAPTER NINE

Equipping Parents to give Religious and Sex Education to Young Children in the Home

ONE OF the greatest privileges and duties of parenthood is that of giving the most effective early religious and sex education in the home. Linked up with and carrying on from the early handling of babies this is the essential beginning of all efforts to help children to become good husbands and wives and parents, and good citizens in any walk of life. The home, in fact, is the first and greatest school of personal character and social relationships: the two prime necessities for good living. We learn these things, not so much by hearing about them, as by seeing them in other people, and by working them out by trial and error in company with other people in a reasonably favourable atmosphere.

Parents who imagine that they can allow children to grow up 'with an open mind in matters of religion, able to choose their own faith if they want to', are bluffing themselves. They cannot help giving some kind of religious education, good or bad. Every decision they make, every attitude they adopt, and many things they say and do express their religion, whether they like it or not. Children are keen observers, and 'see through' their parents far more than is generally realized. They are also born imitators, and pick up most of their early religious education from what they see and hear in the everyday life of those nearest to them.

Religious education in its true sense is not the indoctrination of a child with adult religious conceptions, which are often not suited to the child's immature personality. It is rather the steady continuous process of leading the child to his own progressive discovery of God, within and around him, so that he can make his own natural spontaneous responses, and work out his own individual attitudes to God, to life, and to people. It is clear from the last three thousand years of human history that knowledge of moral principles is not nearly enough. We need to care enough for them to want to make the necessary sacrifices for living by them.

Sex education is also concerned with much more than the giving

116

of information to children about 'the facts of life'. Sex is a vital force in men and women which demands a particular attitude to it, and to life, as well as knowledge about it. What we might call the religious and sex instincts are inseparable from the whole of life, and consequently from one another. Sex and religious education are therefore best given together, at least in the early stages, and given, not on 'special occasions' but intimately woven into the very warp and woof of everyday life. By their very nature they are most fittingly given at the beginning in the intimate atmosphere of the home by the parents. In any case when the child is old enough even for Kindergarten Sunday-school, some of the most important opportunities have already gone.

It seems to be a fairly general experience that parents are given insufficient help to carry out this very important responsibility and consequently many first-class opportunities for creative education are either missed or unwittingly mishandled. It is sobering to remember that the home can be as powerful an influence for evil as it can for good, and that early failures in the home may be very difficult to overcome by any later efforts. A good pastor can exert an incalculable influence for good if he sets out as part of his educational work to give as many parents as possible the best kind of help in this great work. If we remember that Christianity is open to all people, illiterate as well as educated, children as well as adults, it will be clear that in essence it must be simple enough for all to grasp.

There are four important 'channels' through which people can be educated; the example of others, their experience of life, their experiments in living, and the teaching they take in from picture, instruction, and the answering of questions. Parents should therefore be helped to give the necessary religious and sex education to their children in the home through these four channels, which may be described as 'the character of the parents', 'the parents' control of the early environment', 'project and practice', and 'direct teaching'.

I. EXAMPLE: THE CHARACTER OF THE PARENTS

Under this heading are included the attitudes of the parents to each other, to the children, and to people in general. It is inevitable that the child's first and most deeply imbedded ideas about the character of the heavenly Father will be built on what he sees in the human parents. Also that his basic views about life, its friendliness or

I

unfriendliness, its practical 'livableness' or otherwise, will depend on his experience of his parents' attitudes.

As we have seen in Chapter 3 the main qualities which Christian parents ought to show to their children are Christian Love (*agape*), dependability, and reverence for their personalities, qualities which can meet the essential needs of children for love, security, and significance or acceptance respectively.

(*a*) The kind of love that Christian parents ought to show to each other and to all their children has also been described as unconditional, unquenchable, demonstrative, outgoing affection. It is the kind of love that was lived out in its highest quality by Jesus Christ, and eloquently described by St Paul (1 Corinthians 13).

Christian love is to be distinguished from sentimentality, a debilitating idolatry, which rests on the 'fairy-tale' assumption that the 'idolized' one can neither do nor suffer any wrong. Such worshipping of one's children will tend to give them the erroneous idea that life exists to serve them, that God is like an over-indulgent 'good fairy', ready to gratify all their desires. When they come inevitably to meet the realities of life they find themselves unprepared to cope with them. They quickly become disillusioned and discontented, because they have grown up in the 'hot house' climate of sentimentality instead of the invigorating climate of love.

Christian love is also to be distinguished from possessiveness, another false quality which often masquerades in its place. Possessiveness is a clutching, cramping self-love, which will inevitably bring agonizing destructive conflicts in the growing personality of the victim. Parents are entrusted by the Creator with the power to bring new lives into being and with the privilege of caring for them, but children are persons in their own right: they belong to God alone. Any child with character will rebel against possessiveness, for which the parents may accuse him of ingratitude, and make the agonizing conflict still greater.

In contrast with sentimentality and possessiveness Christian love has a robust dependable reality in it. The love of Christian parent for his child, like that of God for man, sees beyond preservation of his skin and possession of his personality to the establishment of the warm steady background of loving care that will encourage the most healthy growth of the child's own unique personality. As part of this purpose it may allow him to endure suffering or to learn by experience, but in doing so it shares in the suffering.

Love at this level is given freely and unconditionally to all children without favouritism: it is not dependent in any way upon the child's character or attainments. Every child is loved for himself alone, even when, as sometimes happens, the love is apparently rejected. Christian love is an unquenchable passion for the other person's welfare and it is willing, if necessary, to be a 'one-way-traffic'.

When parents offer such love to their children they are showing them an unmistakable picture of what God is like. In this they are laying the strongest possible foundation for their children's religious education in the home, and beyond it to every part of their children's future lives. If, on the other hand, parents fail at this point, all their children's future religious education will be seriously handicapped, however much 'religious teaching' may subsequently be given to them.

But we can only offer such love to anyone when we have developed the capacity to love, as well as the knowledge of the nature of love. This involves the realization and acceptance of the love of God as seen in Jesus Christ, in the deepest places of our own souls. Education for parenthood therefore includes evangelism and may involve healing as well as instruction, and the living, constantly outgoing love needs constantly to be nourished and cultivated in worship and service. The true Christian love is then given to children as the expression of the parents' love of God, with heart, soul, and strength, which comes ultimately from the realization that He first loved mankind.

(b) Dependability, the second quality of character to be offered by parents for the religious education of their children, is essential for the growth of a sense of security in any child. It includes a degree of strength and emotional stability, and also consistency in attitude and behaviour. The human parent who punishes on one occasion what he tolerates on another is failing to show his child one of the most outstanding characteristics of the heavenly Father. He is also creating a deep moral confusion in the mind of the growing child, because our earliest and deepest ideas about right and wrong are mostly based on what brings parental approval and disapproval. Without the physical and psychic security built on dependable parents, children may easily develop emotional instability or become anti-social 'problem-children'—and later 'problem-adults', 'problem-citizens', and still worse, 'problem-parents'.

If parents are to offer this double characteristic of strength and consistency to their children they will need to conquer rather than to deny or repress their own fears and inconsistencies. They will also need to reconcile their own differences regarding the handling of their children, and indeed regarding most other important matters. Few people realize the deep insecurity produced in the personality of the young child when the two people on whom he depends come into serious conflict or dissension. It goes beyond a conflict of loyalties, which is bad enough, to appear as a threat to his ultimate security. This may not be formulated in definite terms at the time, but it will often be expressed then or and later in abnormalities of attitude and conduct superficially unrelated to the earlier domestic discord.

Parents who disagree on vital matters cannot hide the fact from their children, however much they may imagine they can do so. It is vital therefore that they should try at all costs and with all available help to reconcile their differences.

(c) Reverence for the child's personality, the third of the good parental characteristics that we are considering, is the exact opposite of possessiveness. It allows and encourages the child's growing initiative and creativeness. It seeks to lead forth all his unique aptitudes, and constantly to inspire him to the highest standards of character. It never seeks to push this new personal creation into the parental, or any other conventional mould. It never claims, but rather seeks to win, the child's affection, trust, and willing spontaneous co-operation. It preserves and encourages his proper self-respect—based on usefulness rather than on adulation—and his individuality as a person among persons.

Reverence for the child's personality is quite different from the licence which is often permitted under the doubtful label of 'self-expression'. This comes from a perverted doctrine of individualism, which tends to think almost entirely of the individual child and to overlook the group or society to which he belongs, and to which he largely owes his ability to live at all.

The balanced attitude of reverence for personality in the proper perspective of reverence for other personalities is an essential basis of democracy, in which there is a kind of living dynamic equilibrium between individual and community welfare, each being continually limited by the needs of the other. It is also the basis of all good religion, and the birthright of every child.

Love, dependability, and reverence for personality—these then are the three facets of the nature of God that parents need to show in their own characters, as the foundation of all attempts at the religious education of their children in the home. They are doubly important, because children are incurable imitators as well as keen observers. They tend to become 'infected' with their parents' scale of values, not that to which parents give 'lip-service', but that which determines their everyday choices and decisions, their real sense of 'worth-ship'.

The child who grows up in a sensibly and naturally disciplined home, seeing his parents devoted to something—or Someone—far greater than themselves, will tend to accept sensible discipline as the normal way of life when it is directed and controlled by love, dependability, and reverence for his personality. We do not learn morality or discipline from those for whom we have no respect or love, and children, as a French writer has pointed out, 'have more need of models than of critics'.

Example is thus the basis of all good authority, and much of the lack of reverence for authority in children is probably due to a similar lack of reverence in their parents. The far-reaching influence of the character and influence of parents is therefore a great challenge to the quality of parenthood in our society. When the religious education of children is founded on the visible and tangible reality of parental example as we have considered it, it will become ingrained in the very 'stuff' of the children's everyday lives, as of course it should be. It will then be deepened and strengthened by the proper use of the parents' control of the early environment of their children, about which we must now think.

II. EXPERIENCE: THE PARENTS' CONTROL OF THE CHILD'S ENVIRONMENT

Immediately after birth all children begin a new and rapidly growing experience of their physical and personal environment. Their early environment is almost completely under the control of their parents, who thus have at their disposal a vital channel for the early religious education in the home, from birth onwards.

When the newly-born baby is bathed, given his mother's breast, and put to rest in his warm cot, he begins to learn, instinctively rather than 'intellectually', his first lesson about life and about God, the Creator and Director of life, and that he is given comfort, nourishment, warmth, and protection. This is the very beginning of his realization of God as the Giver and Protector-in-chief. When his mother uses the feeding and other relationships to express the right kind of love it will dawn more and more clearly on his awakening mind that the world is friendly, that, as Browning so vividly expressed it, 'a heart beats here', that 'God is love' (1 John 4[16]).

When the newly-born child cries for something and does not get it at once he begins to learn his second instinctive lesson: that he cannot always have what he wants from life. This is the dawning of the realization that God is not our Servant: a lesson that some people never quite succeed in learning.

Before he is very old he learns that something is required from him in life. This begins with the training in various habits of regularity and cleanliness, the forerunners of all kinds of discipline in every part of life.

A fourth early lesson is that he cannot depend on things always remaining the same. At some time he has to be weaned from his mother's breast, and there are many other necessary changes to which he is compelled to make some adaptation. This is the beginning of a long process of education in self-dependence and in adaptability to 'the changes and chances of this mortal life'.[1]

These four basic homely lessons about life make up an important part of a child's early religious education, even though they are commonly regarded as matters of 'secular' routine. As we have seen, they can only be learnt properly in the domestic 'atmosphere' of love, dependability, and reverence for personality. They then become woven into the child's earliest personal relationships to form a further part of the foundation of his attitude to life and to God. Religious education ought to be woven into the warp and woof of everyday life, and when it is so linked up from the beginning it will never be forgotten or separated from life in the mind of the child.

As the child's mind begins to awaken, the parents can offer more and more good religious education through their control of the child's environment. They can allow him to learn many lessons through experience and experiment, some of which may be painful when he disregards repeated warnings.

The parental response to various experiments in behaviour may greatly help or hinder the child's religious education. Most children look for attention, and any kind of attention seems to be regarded as better than none. When the parents are busy their children may get 'attention' when they are 'naughty', and not so much when they are

---

[1] *The Book of Common Prayer.*

good, which only tends to encourage 'naughtiness'. If children could be given more attention when they are good and perhaps less when they are 'naughty' they would probably learn more about reality.

Reward and punishment, if wisely and lovingly handled, can be used to teach some important lessons about life, if the reward is made to fit the deed and the punishment to fit the 'crime'; if in home life as in Nature, there are really no rewards or punishments, but only consequences. In this way we can represent an environment which expresses truth and reality, not a 'fairy-tale' over-indulgence or a 'fairy-tale' 'dragon'.

In all their management of the child's early environment the parents ought to do all in their power to ensure that it represents clearly to the child the three great realities of truth, beauty, and goodness. These are ultimate and eternal values, which exist whether or not we respond to them, and offer three great aspects of the nature of God.

Many people appear to overlook the great importance of strict devotion to truth in all their dealings with children. Children have an extraordinary ability to find them out, and it is then difficult to imagine how they could be expected to have any reverence for truth. When such parents punish the child for being untruthful one can imagine the confusion that will be produced in his questioning mind. It would seem impossible to give a child any real conception of the heavenly Father when the earthly parent is so obviously inconsistent.

There are many ways in which parents can surround their children with beauty. The beauties of Nature will generally come first and any child will gradually awaken to them if given the opportunity of seeing them in gardens, parks, mountains and valleys, river, lake, and sea, orchard, pasture, and field of grain, sunsets, cloud effects, and moon and stars. They should also be exposed to beauty of colour in pictures and in the toys they handle, to beauty of form and structure in animals and plants, insects and birds. Their ears may be filled with beauty of sound in the song of birds and in good music, open in these days to every home, and beauty of speech and language, gesture, deportment and dress. All these and other manifestations of beauty have a contribution to make to the child's religious education.

To surround children with goodness, the third great aspect of Reality, or God, is not as easy as it may sound. It involves for the parents the willing acceptance of a moral authority that may best be described as the will of God. The proper motive for goodness is not fear, the avoidance of punishment here or in the hereafter; that makes people clever and crafty rather than good. Neither is it the hope of reward here or in the hereafter; that leaves them greedy.

The one adequate motive for goodness is love: a grateful response to a loving and self-giving Father, who has taken the initiative with His children, set the standard, and seeks to win their devoted allegiance for their own good: their obedience as sons, not as slaves.

Goodness then should be seen by the child as something of immense value for its own sake and in its own right—as a positive adventure—something which, if not practised for its own sake, is really not goodness at all, but a thinly disguised selfish expediency.

This inner meaning of goodness provides the one adequate basis for parental authority, and for obedience on the part of the child. Parental authority should only be exerted in matters that are morally imperative in their own right, and then explicitly and consistently. This is implied by St Paul (Ephesians 6[1]), 'Children, obey your parents in the Lord', and in his similar words in his letter to the Colossians (3[20]). If parents insist strongly in matters that are simply for their own convenience they will tend to become petty dictators, and stir up an increasing sense of injustice and rebellion in the minds of their children.

If, on the other hand, parents lovingly administer the moral authority to which they also give their obedience, there may still be some resistance, but their authority, backed by the laws of life itself, will generally prevail, especially if it is sweetened by understanding love and a sense of humour.

The child who grows up in this kind of atmosphere will generally come to see that sensible discipline is necessary for true freedom, a lesson badly needed in these days when people think so much more of rights than of obligations.

III. EXPERIMENT: PROJECT AND PRACTICE

One of the most important channels of learning is practice—we learn many of our most important lessons in life by doing things, both alone and in company with other people. Before he is very old the child begins to feel and respond to the domestic 'atmosphere', to fit in, comfortably or uncomfortably, with the most practical and inevitable project of all: the everyday life of the family. Whether this project will help or hinder the child's religious education will depend very greatly on the character and example of the parents, and the kind of control they exert on the child's earliest environment, which have already been considered.

An important early stage of any child's social development is achieved through playing with other children, in and around the home, and in nursery schools and kindergartens, which are doing vital work in this regard. The first deliberate project activity to be encouraged in the home may therefore be in the form of play, in which all kinds of life situations are dramatized, acted, and in this way woven into the child's personal experience and character.

Bismarck is reputed to have said, 'You can do anything with children if you only play with them', and any kindergarten teacher would confirm his words. Apart from its effect on personal character, play also enables children to work out the principles of team-work and mutual co-operation in a manner that would be impossible without it.

It is a common experience in nursery schools that at the beginning there is little or no attempt at co-operation among children in their play—every child wants to be the 'tram conductor' or the 'engine driver'. But with intelligently supervised play the co-operative spirit gradually develops, and the various projects, working models of communal life, begin to be carried out smoothly and happily.

In such communal projects we learn to give and take, to lead or follow according to the needs of the situation rather than our own will to power, and to respect the capacities and the views and feelings of other people. We learn these things far better in this way than through any kind of verbal teaching or exhortation.

These are all very important parts of our religious education, and there are many adults who show little evidence of having learnt them. Quiet observation of children at play will often afford some surprises in the depth of insight and the capacity for team-work they show. It may also provide an opportunity for discovering some faulty tendencies in time to correct them without undue conflict. It may be said, however, that a reasonable amount of 'letting off steam' by children is probably healthy, and generally harmless as long as it is kept within bounds.

In addition to allowing and encouraging the play of children with one another it is important that both parents should make as many opportunities as possible to play with their children in the spontaneous, light-hearted spirit of childhood. If entered into in this spirit such play will provide something of infinite value for the personalities of the parents and for their whole personal relationships with their children. Many a man is saved from becoming a dull pompous bore among people by the saving influence of his children through the wholesome relationship of play.

From this initial project of play, children may gradually be led to simple acts of social service. To experience the joy that comes from 'being of use' to people will do more to teach the child about service to his fellows than any words can ever do. If the service is conceived and carried out by parent and child in the spirit of Jesus Christ they will gain an experience of the practical expression of religion without which the more abstract qualities of goodness will tend to remain sterile.

This living expression of the brotherhood of man will provide the real experience of which corporate worship is a symbol. And if the noble sentiments expressed in our corporate worship are not carried out into our corporate lives they rapidly become unreal, and even hypocritical.

In the setting of acts of friendliness and service, however, all kinds of corporate worship become full of meaning and power, and provide a constant inspiration to further practical expression of the Christian spirit. Worship, as we have seen, means worth-ship. When this 'worth-ship' is expressed in social action as well as in word and ceremonial it provides the best means for steady growth of personal character and social ability.

There is no limit to the opportunities of creative service, and such service may be carried out in ever-widening circles as the child grows up—from the home (the smallest society) to the world (the largest). When more young children are encouraged in the performance of acts of loving creative social service the general standards of community life will soon begin to improve.

There are many other simple projects that can be undertaken in the home, particularly in the form of family celebrations and commemorations. Some useful and effective teaching can be given through the commemoration of important events in history and in the lives of past and present members of the family. These commemorations can be used to bring home any lessons and truths, and any reasons for thanksgiving that may be enshrined in the events. For children, of course, the lessons of Christmas are particularly helpful—and for adults too—and they underline the various acts of friendliness and service carried out at this and other times through the years. Family birthdays, wedding anniversaries, and other events of domestic significance can be used in the same way. All these commemorations can well be linked up with the regular observance of Sunday with its own special projects of corporate worship, and with private and family worship.

Grace before meals, and family prayers and Bible readings will preserve the reality and perspective of spiritual values in the minds of children and adults if they are intelligently and thoughtfully performed, and not allowed to degenerate into mere repetition and formality. We are better with no ritual than with superficial and careless worship.

It is often helpful to commemorate the lives of some great people, and to remind ourselves from time to time of their devoted service, and of their influence on mankind. This will provide a splendid subject for family conversation at meal-times. An interesting and valuable piece of project work that could well begin during adolescence when the 'collecting fever' makes itself felt, is the collection of biographies of great people in a kind of 'scrap book' or loose-leaf binder. From time to time new names can be added, or further details included, by pasting into the book any available newspaper cuttings or pages from 'digests'. These biographies will have great value later in life, and their collection would involve much less trouble and expense than many more fashionable 'collections'.

Children will provide many projects for themselves if parents encourage their creative initiative, regarding it as part of the Divine nature planted in them. When a child's initiative is discouraged or laughed at great harm may be done to his sensitive personality, which is almost certain to be cast in a different mould from that of his parents. There may have been many 'mute inglorious Miltons' because of parental discouragements of children's crude initial ventures into poetry, and the same applies to many other human activities.

At all costs, then, and at whatever inconvenience, parents should try to encourage the creative initiative of their children as something of priceless value. Many of their experiments and 'crazes' will die a natural death, but the parents will have provided an environment favourable to the growth and fruition of whatever talents may be locked up in the unpredictable personality which they have brought into being.

Every child should be given projects calculated to develop in him a sense of responsibility and trustworthiness. This may involve willingness to risk the consequences of much initial clumsiness and carelessness, but the results will generally be more than worth while. To lead forth his talents and skills in relationship with the part of our heritage of knowledge and wisdom, culture and inspiration that parents can offer is a far-reaching part of religious education. And anything that will increase the number of dependable people in a community will be of great value to our national life.

All these types of project and practice, and there are many more, will tend to help the child to develop a widening vision, an active initiative and spontaneity, a sturdy self-reliance, and a growing influence for good. They will counteract his natural self-centredness and help to lead him into the best kind of Christian fellowship, which is based on co-operation in active service. Through this linkage of worship, fellowship, and service his religion will be geared into the whole of his future life and will infuse it with purpose and power.

Much of our corporate worship has become too formal, and thus tended to lose some of its living reality and relevance for the everyday life of men and women. With the rush and bustle of modern life we need more than ever the regular spiritual nourishment that comes from worshipping in spirit and in truth rather than in formalism and convention. Corporate worship at its best is a first-class piece of 'project work', for it provides the continuing inspiration for all other projects: the regular communion with the firm steady realities which underpin all aspects of life and offer the quietness and confidence in which men and women find strength. Children may not see the full significance of these things, but they will absorb the atmosphere and spirit of good worship if they are exposed to it in company with their parents.

Even if parents fail to find a fully satisfying spiritual atmosphere in any particular church, some good use can generally be made of what is at hand if they are keen to give themselves to it rather than to get everything from it; if they will offer their own special contribution to its improvement. If they think of it in this way they will find themselves more tolerant of the essential diversities in methods of worship, and of those who practice them. Good religious education in the home will then make itself felt to greater advantage in the church, and it will provide an active leaven throughout the community.

Perhaps we can sum up these ideas regarding the value of project and practice in religious education by quoting some words of Karl R. Stolz: 'Children acquire desirable character qualities, not by listening to exhortations to be industrious, courageous and kind, but by being involved in situations in which these virtues are called for, and may be exercised.' [1]

IV. DIRECT TEACHING BY PICTURE, WORD, AND THE ANSWERING OF QUESTIONS

Direct teaching, commonly regarded as the only kind of religious education, is put last in these headings, not because it is regarded as the least important, but because it gains greatly when it is given in the setting of example, experience, and experiment. We may remind ourselves that the main objective in all Christian religious education is to lead children to the fullest knowledge of Jesus—His character, His teaching, and His work—so that they can make their own responses to His loving leadership.

All our teaching about His character will be much more real to a child if he has seen it reflected, sincerely if imperfectly, in the character of his parents. The truths about life that we offer from His teaching will be seen more clearly when related to the child's unfolding experience of life through the parents' control of his early environment. And the work of One who 'went about doing good' will find a responsive chord in the heart of a child who has done a little of the same kind of good in His name in his projects.

On this triple foundation, therefore, we can most fittingly carry out the simple yet profound direction of Jesus Himself, 'Suffer the little children to come unto me', and it is right that we should build upon it such teaching as will help children to know and love Him as well as they do their best friend, and to trust Him as their guide and leader.

This teaching may begin with suitable pictures, interesting and revealing to all children, and with stories related to the pictures. It is best to begin with pictures and stories which convey the wonder of the love of Jesus for little children and for the sick, and which may generate some feeling of thanksgiving in the mind of the child. These will naturally be followed by pictures and stories illustrating His courage and strength, His great kindness, His power to heal the sick,

[1] *The Church and Psycho-therapy.*

His attractiveness, which led people to follow Him, and above all His devotion to what he believed to be right whatever the cost.

In all this the child should be helped to visualize something of the childhood of Jesus, His home life, and His work at the carpenter's bench, all of which can be made absorbingly interesting to the vivid imagination of a child. Among the books that may prove helpful in this are *A Little Life of Jesus* by Basil Mathews (Oxford University Press), and *A Boys' and Girls' Life of Christ* by J. Paterson Smyth (Hodder & Stoughton).

As the child comes to know something of the character of Jesus the simpler aspects of His teaching may be gradually introduced, and later still the mysteries of His birth, death, and resurrection. It is altogether wrong at this stage to use this great lover of little children as a weapon for the coercion of children to be 'good'. The blasphemous lie, 'Jesus doesn't love naughty children', should by now have been properly killed and buried, and with it the implication that He is like a kind of super-spy peeping round the corner at the children's 'naughtiness'.

If we present Jesus faithfully to children as a strong, healthy, vigorous young man, who spent His life doing good and helping people to live better, and had the supreme courage to go even to His death rather than go back on what He believed right, it will find a ready response in their hero-worshipping minds. In most of them it will tend to awaken a sense of thanksgiving, which may be the foundation of natural spontaneous prayer, the only kind really worthy of the name.

'A single grateful thought toward heaven', said one writer, 'is the most perfect prayer', and children should be led to see prayer as something far greater than saying prayers. We think of prayer as 'communion with God', but we can present it fittingly to children as 'remembering Jesus'. Remembering His character will awaken humility, gratitude, and loyalty; remembering His life and teaching can illuminate and direct their lives; and His revelation of God as 'our Father' will bring faith in God's love and forgiveness.

Much of our customary prayer is made up of praising God, giving thanks to Him, confessing to Him and asking for things from Him, all of which are essential and helpful aspects of prayer. Sometimes we even go on to advise Him, which is neither essential nor helpful. But we do not generally listen to Him nearly enough as our Father, in whose will, as Dante observed, 'is our peace'. 'Thy will be done', a ringing call to personal dedication and co-operative action, is quietly toned down into a pious hope.

If parents can be helped to learn themselves and to teach their children to accept the leadership of Jesus Christ as the most reliable interpreter of the will of God, then prayer would soon become the central activity of their lives. Family prayer would become much more real and effective if the main family conferences and discussions thought of and accepted Christ as the real head of the family, and asked the right questions about specific problems and situations. Some productive questions are, 'What would He want me (or us) to be, or to do?', and 'How would He want us to use our time, abilities, possessions, and opportunities?' The same questions, and others like them, would then find an increasingly prominent place in children's private prayers as they grow older.

To use prayer in this way means of course that parents and children must learn all they can about Jesus Christ, so that they come to know His mind as well as they know their own. Asking the right questions will help greatly to keep their thinking positive and practical, and the influence of Jesus will then become much greater in their lives, their homes, and consequently in society. Children growing up in such homes will learn to know Christ as easily as they learn to know their parents, and they will learn to pray as easily as they learn to think. Their minds are much clearer, and their insight deeper than we generally imagine.

It is possible that much of the unreality of prayer in people's minds is attributable to lack of naturalness and spontaneity at the beginning, for example the 'ready made' prayers that children are made to repeat 'parrot fashion' without much real thought or encouragement of their own spontaneous feelings. Such prayers may have an important place for children and adults alike when the person can make them his own, when they reflect his real feelings and aspirations. But it seems important that some at least of children's prayers should arise spontaneously from their dawning awareness of God through all that their parents and others offer about Jesus, in attitude and example as well as teaching. Prayer is inevitably woven into the pattern of life, and the 'spoilt' child will think of God as his convenient servant because his parents have been over-indulgent. He will then find it virtually impossible to pray 'in spirit and in truth'.

From the pictures and stories about Jesus Christ the parents can go on to tell their children other stories from the Bible in simple language, avoiding those which present any difficulties until the children are older. When parents find it impossible to give adequate explanation to difficult stories children may come to put 'religion' into a separate compartment of their minds—among the 'fairy stories' —and regard it as unrelated to their everyday lives. This may be one of the reasons for the fact that religion seems to have grown away from the day-by-day living of many people. The Bible is full of stories that are rich in human interest, in vivid drama, and in lessons for life in any age. But many of them need to be presented in simpli-fied terms if they are to be of the fullest interest and value to children, and the fact that a story is in the Bible does not automatically make it suitable for to-day's growing children.

Stories about great men and women in history and in contemporary life provide another useful part of parents' direct teaching in the home. Children are always interested in what other people do, and are inveterate hero-worshippers and imitators. Stories about great people, given in simple terms, will provide a potent stimulus for children to try in their own way to emulate their heroes. Particular emphasis should be given to the sterling qualities of the selected people, their persistence in the face of all kinds of difficulty and frustration, even persecution and suffering. Where possible their characters should be related with that of Jesus, using Him as the 'measuring rod', and seeing Him as their greatest ultimate inspiration, even though that inspiration may have come through many human 'channels'. This is a procedure that could most profitably become the general rule in the teaching of history in schools.

There is a much-quoted remark of Professor Whitehead's that 'Moral education is impossible without the habitual vision of great-ness', and Jesus, more than anyone else in human history, can offer such 'habitual vision', and the inspiration and power for abundant victorious living.

Another important part of parents' direct teaching should be about the nature and significance of the Church—the world Christian com-munity, whose mission is to carry on the work of Jesus in the world. As they become aware of the divisions of the Church children should be helped to see that in spite of these divisions the Church is still the greatest hope of the world. Also that the Church needs the active love and service of all Christian people, young and old, to be of the greatest service in a needy world. These lessons are only given adequately when they are backed up by the example of the parents in their own love and service of the Church.

Children may be introduced to the meaning of symbols, which are so much used in worship, by being taken to Church, with care at the beginning to avoid long sessions of little direct interest to them. This is helped further by the use of symbolism at home, such as kneeling for prayers.

Some good direct teaching may also be given through the appropriate use of children's own experiences, applying any lessons at times when they are most open to profit by them, but taking care to do it in love and understanding, and not to 'rub it in' too vigorously. It helps also to remember that children often take in much more than they feel disposed to admit at the time. There is generally no need to labour any points about which parents desire children to be convinced.

Finally, children may be taught in a very effective manner by the answering of questions. The normal healthy child is insatiably, and sometimes uncomfortably, curious, but he provides in this a golden opportunity for teaching. When the parents take the trouble to answer his many questions simply, briefly, and naturally, their teaching is directed to his exact need at the time, and it is carried deeply into his mind through the close bond of mutual confidence and fellowship. Would that parents could more often realize the priceless value of such opportunities, and the harm that may result from evasion or untruth.

If the answer is not known it is generally best for the parents to admit the fact to the child, who does not expect them to know everything. Then they can either go with the child to look it up, a very worth-while domestic project in itself, or undertake to find out and to tell him on another occasion. Children often want to work things out clearly in their own minds and may ask the same questions more than once. They will be quite happy to hear the same answer over and over again for a time, and it is generally a mistake for the parent to try to put them off with the statement that the question has been answered before and the child could not have been paying attention.

V. THE SEXUAL PART OF RELIGIOUS EDUCATION IN THE HOME

This method of teaching is particularly important in the early sex education of children in the home. This is a vital part of religious education, and any separation of one from the other is to their mutual

K

disadvantage. As we have seen, the early sex-education is most fittingly given in the home by the parents, not as a special occasion or a series of special occasions, but woven into the everyday affairs and conversations of the family. Archbishop Temple once observed that 'the most influential of all educational factors is the conversation in a child's home'.[1]

If parents delegate these most intimate bonds of companionship to anyone else they remain parents in little more than the reproductive sense. Their children, finding that their natural questions are evaded, will hesitate to confide in them regarding other intimate concerns, and the parents may then come to wonder why their children seem to be so reserved with them.

The attitude of people to sex and to love tends to reflect their total attitude to life and to society, and the early sex-education of children is greatly dependent on what their parents feel and what they do in everyday living as well as on what they say.

With the gradual awakening of awareness of his environment, physical and personal, a baby soon begins to absorb the general emotional 'atmosphere' which comes from the attitudes and behaviour of the parents and all other members of the household. This absorption goes on all through childhood, and indeed all through life; and what we absorb unconsciously or unintentionally generally becomes most deeply imbedded in our minds, and most influential for good or ill.

During these earliest years the parents are also building the growing bond of love, understanding, and confidence, which will make it easy for the child to ask them all kinds of intimate questions. They should be helped to understand the importance of the child's bodily sensations, and to welcome his natural spontaneous pleasure in his unfolding experience of them. This understanding will help them to a positive attitude to the child's enjoyment of suckling, urinating, the movement of his bowels, and the handling of his genital organs and of other parts of his body. Such attitudes will help greatly in the parental training of the child during this important period.

During the third year of life many boys and girls begin to investigate, think about, and compare their bodily structures, and to ask all kinds of questions about their origin and function. It is generally best for the parents to answer the questions when and where they are asked, at meal-time, bath-time, bed-time, or while their parents are

[1] *The Hope of a New World* (SCM Press, 1941).

doing some work around or within the home. The answer should be as brief and simple as possible and should not go beyond the scope of the question. It should also be truthful and reverent, and when possible it should convey a simple reverence for life and gratitude to God.

It is sometimes necessary to make sure that the questions are really expressions of curiosity and not merely devices for getting the parents' attention. In most cases this will be fairly obvious, because the attention-getting questions will generally come in rapid succession and the same questions will be repeated. The best way to handle this kind of situation is to try to give plenty of attention without waiting for the child to seek it. The answering of questions should be kept in healthy perspective in the child's life by the encouragement of plenty of play, outdoor exercise, and other occupation, and where possible by the discipline of a group, such as a kindergarten or 'play-group'.

Here is a brief sample of answers which can be given to the most common early questions:

Where do babies come from? (or Where did I come from?) Out of Mummy's body.

Why was I there? To keep you safe until you were big enough. God's wonderful provision can be emphasized in this.

Where did I come out? Through a passage near where the urine comes out.

Could I see a baby being born? When a baby is being born only the doctors and nurses are generally there.

Why do little boys do their stream standing up? (or some other question about the differences between the sexes). Boys have a penis so that they can be daddies later, and girls have a different arrangement so that they can have babies later.

How did I get inside mummy? Daddy planted a little seed which joined with one inside mummy to make you. When daddies and mummies love each other God sometimes gives them children in this way. Such answers can be linked up with the child's knowledge of domestic animals and later with facts about pollination of plants. It is generally much less effective to begin with animals and birds and plants than with human beings, the child is much earlier and much more interested in his own nature and origin than in other living things.

During this childhood period (roughly from 6 to 10 years) there should also be some training in elementary hygiene and cleanliness. There will probably be some furtive investigating of the many interesting objects and sensations, and much secret discussion between children. If the emotional atmosphere of the home is open and natural, and the child has plenty of healthy open-air exercise and a rich variety of other interests this will generally be a passing phase, like all the other 'novelties' that come and go.

Ideas of self-respect and respect for others will also be offered by example, project, and teaching during this childhood period. 'Self-respect' can be made to include the general attitude that playing with one's own body is normal for babies but becomes cheap and childish when it persists.

At some time between the ages of 10 and 12 the child should be told about the forthcoming signs of puberty, preferably by the parent of the same sex, but not necessarily. This age period is most suitable because the information is then given before these signs appear and generally before there has been much discussion about them by other children at school; and also before the child's emotions begin to awaken to the point of self-consciousness. Boys should be told about the appearance of nocturnal emissions and the possibility of similar experiences when performing such actions as climbing trees which press the thighs inwards on something. Girls should be told about the forthcoming periods. The naturalness and normality of these events should be affirmed, together with their significance and meaning.

If the previous stages in sex education have been neglected by the parents there may be some opportunities for them to 'catch up' during this period. Some co-operative project may be utilized to initiate the discussion if it seems difficult for the parent to 'break the ice', or to find out how much the child already knows. It is often possible for a pastor, or a Marriage Guidance Council to arrange to show a series of carefully selected films accompanied by a commentary, and to invite fathers with their sons, or mothers with their daughters. By going with the child a parent is acknowledging his or her previous omissions, and a readiness to do something about them. Such occasions have almost invariably proved to be starting-points for the development of new and spontaneous intimacy between parent and child in this important aspect of education.

When the early sex education has been given in some such manner as this in the natural intimate atmosphere of a good home and in full relationship with good religious education, the child is ready to gain the greatest advantage from any further available opportunities for sex and religious education in schools and clubs as well as in the home. The intimate personal teaching will then be widened by progressive instruction in elementary Biology and Nature Study, assisted by all available resources of visual education. At the same time the closely related questions of sexual morality will be discussed, and related with morality in general, and the whole subject can be given in the perspective of the positive religious attitudes already suggested.

These moral aspects will be greatly clarified and vitalized if the child's loyalty and 'hero-worship' can be won by example and by the outgoing interest and devotion of his teachers. In this atmosphere it may be possible to awaken in him a deep conviction of the value of healthy discipline and self-control in every department of his life. He may also come to see beyond his human 'heroes' the ultimate Hero: Jesus Christ, who may then go on being his Hero long after the human heroes of his childhood have passed beyond his ken.

An essential part of the intimate parental sex education during the 'teen age' period is the giving of clear and definite information to boys and girls about the possible effects on the opposite sex of too enthusiastic 'petting', even when there is mutual desire. A girl may be awakened in the depths of her being to such an extent as to leave her with a difficult emotional problem, and a boy may be stirred to such a pitch that his emotions may without warning get beyond his control and lead to tragedy, all because the young people were not warned of the danger.

In all this teaching boys and girls may be enabled to see the priceless value of clean, open, healthy comradeship, working and playing together and learning to get on naturally with one another.

CHAPTER TEN

Equipping Parents and Others to Understand and Help the Adolescent

MANY PARENTS who find little difficulty in handling their children through the first decade of life become bewildered and even despairing in the face of the many problems they provide in passing through the second decade. At the same time many pastors and Church leaders are puzzled by the many problems presented by their young people during this unsettled period, and wonder why so many of them seem to lose interest in their Church and its work.

Most of the difficulties faced by the adolescent in these days are man-made, and result from disturbing and conflicting domestic and cultural influences; from lack of understanding of the adolescent by those on whom he depends. The understanding and leadership of the adolescent is therefore an important part of the pastoral function, and the good pastor can offer some very constructive and far-reaching service in his own relationships with young people and in the education of parents to make the most of their great opportunities.

During this important period young people prepare themselves, with the help of parents, pastors and teachers, for all the responsibilities of their future citizenship, personal, domestic, vocational and social. They enter it as dependent children and leave it as young adults, ready and anxious to stand on their own feet and to make their own decisions in every part of their lives. As they emerge from the safe harbour of childhood into the open seas of maturity these young voyagers through life meet with some of their most difficult problems at a time when they are often insufficiently prepared to meet them.

When we look at the adolescent we find a gloriously unpredictable and ever-changing person, who simply refuses to be compressed into any brief description. But we can look for a few moments at some of the main features of his changing personality so that we can possibly understand and help him to negotiate this difficult period of his life.

'Life', as Herbert Spencer once observed, 'is the continuous adjustment of internal relations to external relations', and each of these is rapidly changing throughout the greater part of this second decade.

Between the ages of 12 and 18 there is very rapid bodily growth and development, and the actively developing sex glands flood the body with potent secretions which have profound effects on the child's attitudes and feelings. The capacity to feel deeply is perhaps one of the outstanding features of adolescence. The emotions are often intense and unstable, and may alternate in the most unpredictable manner between ecstasy and despair, which makes it difficult at times for the adolescent to understand himself. His feelings may be hidden behind a mask of 'toughness' or bravado, or of calm self-possession which gives no hint of the bewildered and questioning spirit behind it.

In very sensitive and introspective children these emotional stirrings may give rise to all kinds of definite or nameless fears, and some children may even come for a time to doubt their own sanity. The situation is made still more difficult when the environment is unsettled or insecure, when the child's energies are sapped by over-work, over-study, physical illness, or emotional shocks, or when his imagination is misdirected by unsuitable films, broadcast sessions, or stories, or by bad companions.

The imaginative faculty expands very greatly in the adolescent, and the phantasy life may even interfere with his reasoning or his initiative. He then becomes still more unstable and often inconsistent in his attitudes and judgements. Impetuous at one moment and self-conscious or day-dreaming at the next, he is at once the delight and despair of parent and teacher alike.

Some of this day-dreaming is wholesome and productive. Many early ambitions that lead to greatness are born in the quiet depths of the adolescent imagination. At other times it may become an escape from the challenges and responsibilities of life, and in a few of the more seriously withdrawn it may go on to schizophrenia.

The emotional instability of the earlier years of adolescence is often reflected in strange bodily postures and gestures, ungraceful movements, and slapdash behaviour. There may also be a degree of self-consciousness with strangers, and fear of ridicule and discouragement. In the later years, however, there is generally a rapid recovery of grace and rhythm, the clumsy boy becoming the graceful athlete, and the gawky 'teen-age' girl becoming almost overnight the graceful, poised and charming young woman.

With the rapid bodily growth and emotional awakening there is an equally rapid expansion of all the child's intellectual faculties, especially that of memory. These are days of searching and criticizing in which nothing is taken for granted. A whole world is waiting to be discovered, and through reading, listening, questioning, observing and experimenting, stimulated by an insatiable curiosity, all kinds of facts are crammed into the child's eagerly interested mind. The general tendency at this stage, however, is for an accumulation of facts without much real correlation, which leads to some hasty and one-sided judgements and even bitter arguments and conflicts. We can well say with the poet Tennyson: 'Knowledge comes, but wisdom lingers.'

Another outstanding development in the second half of this decade is the awakening of idealism, one of the most important, and often neglected, of all the characteristics of youth. There may be urgent and powerful desires to set the world right: after all it is to be their world; coupled at times with a youthful impatience and intolerance, which may lead to many painful frustrations and disillusionments.

The relationship of the adolescent to himself in the earlier years is therefore one of intense feeling without stability, growth without gracefulness, knowledge without wisdom, and idealism without tolerance. This is followed in later adolescence by a gradual settling down and a progressive adjustment to his rapidly changing self.

The external relationships of the adolescent expand in widening circles from home, school, neighbourhood and church into society, the whole pattern of all these relationships being governed by his unfolding relationship to life itself.

In the home there is a gradual but very important change in the parent-child relationship. During childhood the parents generally have the whip hand, the power to enforce their will by punishment if necessary. During this period the child awakens to the consciousness of his own individuality and power, and a natural urge toward independence and freedom. Normally this should be accompanied by a gradual change in the parent-child relationship from a kind of 'benevolent dictatorship' to a 'democracy'. This change does not always happen smoothly.

From the child's point of view there is always some conflict between his growing desire for freedom and the various restrictions imposed upon him, ostensibly for his own good, by his parents. Much of this conflict is natural and inevitable: it represents part of the universal conflict between desire and duty. But to the child many of the restrictions, especially those imposed by over-possessive parents, will appear unnecessary and even unjust. In this way some of the seeds of revolt may be planted.

Outside the home the closest personal interests of the young adolescent are generally directed to others of the same sex. A boy or girl may be influenced far more by the leader of the 'gang' or 'group' than by either parent. This is part of the natural reaction away from authority toward independence. If this temporary interlude is treated by the parents as ingratitude or loss of confidence the child may be thrown into an almost intolerable conflict of loyalties. This could well interfere with any later return to full confidence on the more mature level of free and willing co-operation.

The general attitude of boys to girls in early adolescence is one of indifference and even scorn, but in these days may girls of 12 and 13 develop a sentimental interest in boys, which sometimes leads to such emotional exaggerations as 'petting parties' or possibly boastful accounts of imaginary happenings. These may be encouraged to some extent by film, novel, or the desire to emulate others or to feel 'grown-up'.

The middle years of adolescence bring a rapid awakening of interest in the opposite sex, sometimes accompanied by a succession of short-lived but very 'serious' 'calf-loves', devastating to the emotions and to all the other interests of the participants while they last. These initial thrills are generally more sentimental than sexual, and falling out of love may prove to be a greater strain than falling in—to the rest of the household as well as the central figure.

In later adolescence the affections steady down a little, and tend to become more fixed on a particular individual, possibly with some painful and disturbing changes. At the same time the sexual urge generally becomes stronger, and there may be increasing tension between powerful desires and the limitations of social convention and morality. The strain is often made heavier by the fact that marriage is generally impossible for some years for financial and other reasons. It is also made heavier when there has been any deficiency in earlier sex education.

Many young people find that the strains of this period incite them to a bitter rebellion against the moral code, and they may indulge in various adventures in immorality, which bring all kinds of further problems and bewilderments in their train. It is hard for those who have had the advantage of good training and sex education to realize the severity of these strains upon people who have had no such advantages.

The attitude of the adolescent to life is of course extremely variable, and it depends greatly on environment, experience, and the influence of people who mean something to him. But understanding, acceptance, and patient goodwill by parents, teachers, and pastors will have incalculable results for good when they are directed to the creation of the right kind of leadership, to help young people to fit themselves for a full and effective life.

The adolescent will not be driven, but when his confidence is won he will readily accept leadership, even of the wrong kind, as the Hitler youth showed. The quality of the leadership of the adolescent is therefore one of the most important matters for any country to face, so that the very best can be made of this vital material.

It must obviously be good leadership, based on reality, on the truth about life. 'If the blind lead the blind, both shall fall into the ditch' (Matthew 15¹⁴). It must also be capable of inspiring discipline by winning confidence, for free people cannot be driven.

There is plenty of good but uninspiring leadership, and much also that is bad but inspiring. Good and inspiring leadership is not easy to find or to develop, particularly as it also demands patience and understanding, a high level of devoted comradeship, and sufficient tact to preserve the self-respect of the adolescent. Lord Baden-Powell showed it in the Boy Scout Movement, and we see it often in good schools, in amateur sport, and in a large company of youth leaders produced by various branches of the Christian Church and such organizations as the Y.M.C.A. and Y.W.C.A. The ultimate in good and inspiring leadership comes from Jesus Christ through those who follow Him in any of these opportunities for leadership.

The scope and range of leadership of this kind must surely be unlimited. Personal character and ability in many different spheres of life, positive creative initiative and leadership, in work, play, in social, industrial, political, and ecclesiastical relationships, and in the most intimate personal and sexual relationships are all enriched and made more effective by good inspiring leadership. The pastor is in a most important strategic position in the community, and is called to give and to organize some of the most responsible and far-reaching leadership imaginable. The general account offered in these initial chapters is intended to provide some background knowledge to assist in that vital responsibility and privilege.

The goal of all leadership of young people may be stated in one word—fitness—using the term in its very broadest sense. They must be helped to fit themselves for marriage, for a career, and for citizenship in general. These are indivisible, and in thinking of how the adolescent can be prepared for later marriage we shall necessarily think at the same time of his needs for his future career and his future citizenship.

HELPING YOUNG PEOPLE TO ACHIEVE FITNESS FOR MARRIAGE

What can be done by parents, teachers, pastors, and youth leaders to help young people to achieve the highest standard of fitness for later marriage? It is clear that they must be helped to develop 'all-round' personal fitness—physical, intellectual, cultural, occupational, moral, and spiritual fitness—and also the ability to enter into good personal relationship with people of both sexes, and particularly to be wise in friendship, courtship, and choice of their life partners.

Physical fitness is to be sought and maintained by proper nutrition, fresh air, and sufficient exercise and rest, and by attention to any symptoms of ill-health. An important but often neglected physical training of young girls is a set of special exercises designed to develop the pelvic muscles which are closely concerned with parturition. Most of the customary exercises and sports help to develop the muscles of the abdomen and thighs but leave the pelvic muscles relatively thin and flabby. This probably accounts for many 'repair' operations in women after their childbearing days are over. It is obvious that good physical health and fitness is a great asset in any husband or wife, and indeed in any citizen, and many of the foundations of health and physical fitness are laid down in adolescence.

Intellectual and Occupational fitness is very largely achieved during the second decade of life. It is important that boys and girls should be encouraged to gain as much relevant knowledge and to cultivate as many abilities and skills as possible during this period. This will help them to become more self-reliant and responsible citizens and will also improve their fitness for later marriage. Such 'domestic' skills as gardening, 'first aid', and parent-craft are useful for boys and girls alike. Boys can also learn to be good 'handymen', and girls will make better wives if they have taken the trouble to become proficient in cooking, sewing, and simple nursing.

Cultural fitness: the cultivation of a love for good literature, poetry, music, and art, will also prove to be a valuable asset for most young people for the development of their own personalities and for better fitness for marriage.

Moral and Social fitness are closely related with one another. The development of character, the best of all possessions, requires disciplined training. The practice of generosity, neighbourly service, and self-control, even in small things, will help to build up the habits of creative initiative which greatly enrich the personality. Boys and girls should be helped to learn to become good 'mixers'; to keep to their own standards and not to be 'priggish' or demanding to other people. They should learn the grace of good sportsmanship and practise its application far beyond the limits of sport. All this needs practice and working-out by rubbing shoulders with all kinds of people, as well as example and precept. The collection and reading of good biographies, already discussed, will often provide some valuable inspiration for this great project.

In the special field of sex it is important for boys and girls to be encouraged to lay down habitual attitudes of positive healthy relationships. It is generally agreed that self-mastery begins in the inner thinking of people. If they are disciplined in their thinking and daydreaming they have laid strong foundations for the development of moral and social fitness, which is of the greatest importance for marriage and citizenship alike. Many of the relationships between the sexes will be influenced and even determined by the prevailing social attitudes, and the current ideas about the roles of male and female. The Christian fellowship is a society within society, and its general tone is greatly influenced by the character and personal attitudes of the pastor, backed by all the Christian heritage and tradition, and inspired by the Holy Spirit, fresh and inspiring in every age.

Spiritual fitness is the supreme kind of fitness, which provides the power without which the necessary discipline for moral fitness is difficult or impossible to sustain. Its ultimate source is the personal guidance and inspiration of Jesus Christ, and the Holy Spirit living and working in Christian people in history and in the present day, people who embody and show His character in any degree. It is cultivated by Christian worship, fellowship, and service. The growth of Christian Love (*agape*) in people is at first fitful and occasional, it may be experienced and shown only in people's 'great' moments. But with patient cultivation, and with faith and hope encouraged by the consciousness of the reality of Christian forgiveness and the privilege of fresh beginnings, it will generally steal more and more into the personality.

Courtship and Choice of Marriage Partner. These activities will depend greatly on the personal character and the scale of values of boys and girls, and also on many 'unconscious' factors mostly connected with early experiences and relationships. It is probable that most if not all people have an unconscious 'ideal' picture in their minds of the desired characteristics of the opposite sex. This was discussed briefly in the section of Chapter 2 that dealt with Jung's psychology, and something of this kind may explain many cases of 'love at first sight'. In view of these deep and mysterious factors, is advice regarding the wise choice of marriage partner futile? Ultimately of course the choice will be made by the young people themselves and this is as it should be. But there are some sound principles that can be offered to them to help in the far-reaching decision, if they are willing to follow their heads as well as their hearts.

(1) *Meet as many young people as possible of both sexes* in easy natural comradeship. Meeting a number of people of the opposite sex will reduce the risk of 'falling in love with love' and give better perspective. Meeting the same sex will tend to preserve a reasonable ability to 'give and take' and to keep a sense of humour. An active Church congregation with its associated clubs and fellowships provides many good opportunities for such social intercourse.

(2) *Allow sufficient time before making the decision.* Marriage must be able to stand the test of time, and most people go through more than one 'love affair' before meeting their real marriage partner. A degree of self-discipline is necessary to overcome the strong temptation to impulsiveness. Many people have a very plausible superficial 'technique' in courtship, which may impress the other one for a short period, but will not stand the test of time.

(3) See the prospective partner as much as possible in ordinary everyday living in his or her home. In this way many domestic and social qualities can be more clearly assessed than when all meetings are on special occasions when people are 'all dressed up' and on their best behaviour. It also provides a necessary opportunity for seeing the prospective partner in relationship with members of the family, and for getting to know the family. The common saying that 'you do not marry the family' is generally false. Any evidence of family domination or possessiveness should be taken as a warning.

(4) *Consider health and heredity* if the previous investigations have

been encouraging. In choosing a marriage partner people are choosing the nature and quality of their future children as well. There are not many important hereditary considerations, and these, together with the necessary considerations of health can best be safeguarded by consultation with the family doctor in each case.

(5) *Questions* of finance, housing, attitude to having and bringing up children, whether the girl will go on working for a time after marriage, and above all the attitude of each to marriage itself, need full discussion and agreement between the prospective partners before final commitment. When a serious disagreement on any of these matters is discovered after marriage it may cause much unhappiness and even do irreparable damage. People should enter the marriage contract, like any other contract, with their eyes fully open.

'*The Case for Chastity.*' Many young people find themselves in great difficulty regarding the handling of strong urges to express their feelings for one another in sex intercourse before marriage. In some cases the prevailing social attitudes tend to make self-control in this relationship extremely difficult, and many girls have to contend with very strong and superficially plausible arguments from their 'boy friends' as well as their own emotional urges. Young people need much more than 'thou shalt not', and more also than the attempt to dissuade them by a recital of the risks and dangers.

This 'negative case' is the one most frequently put to young people, and it rests mainly on three considerations: first, that of tradition, that no society allows licence in this matter, and that sex intercourse must be furtive and secretive; second, that there are serious risks, venereal disease, pregnancy with its grim alternatives of criminal abortion, illegitimacy, and a 'forced marriage', and severe psychological consequences particularly in the girl; and third, that unchastity before marriage makes infidelity after marriage more likely.

But this negative case of itself is quite inadequate and generally ineffective. To fight these strong temptations young people must be armed with something stronger than fear. The spirit of adventure in any normal young people thrives on danger and is only too eager to take a chance with the sublime confidence that no harm will come this time.

Chastity is a positive virtue: the honour and reverence due to men and women as children of God, which is the basis of what we call the dignity of human personality. Self-control is quite different from the unhealthy repression with which it is often confused, it is a healthy discipline needed in every part of life, and much easier to achieve when the earlier training has been good.

The 'positive case' for chastity rests on the true nature, meaning, and significance of human, as opposed to animal, sexual relationships, and this in turn depends on the value that is placed on human personality. To the animal, sex intercourse is little more than gratification of a strong inner appetite or desire, and some human beings see little more significance in it than that—and indeed think of man himself as little if anything more than a clever animal.

But as we have seen in the discussion of pre-marital preparation, human sex intercourse is a sacred action which expresses through the most intimate of all contacts between two people the complete abandoned self-giving of each to the other as part of their self-giving to God. It is an expression and pledge of love, which includes body, mind, and spirit, and an acting out together of the 'one-flesh-ness' established at marriage and embodied in the living together 'in the life-long companionship of a home and the complete intertwining of two lives'.[1] Apart from this total life together and the bond of total love, sex intercourse in the fullest human sense is a hollow sham, unless the partners regard man as no more than a clever animal.

When young people can help each other to cultivate this positive virtue of chastity it will cost them considerable self-denial, but it will bring them much greater and deeper self-respect and inner peace, and a joy in later marriage unknown to the self-indulgent. Chastity on the larger scale will bring much greater social cohesion.

There is a great need to make the fullest use of every possible opportunity of explaining

to a perplexed and rather impatient generation that Christian moral standards are not a code arbitrarily imposed upon certain people who, being Christians, are bound to submit to it, but are precisely those essential disciplines, issuing from deep insights into the nature of human beings and the structure of human society, apart from which there is, in the end, no real fullness of life, no richness, reality, or blessedness for *anybody*.[2]

We began these last five chapters by considering the urgent community need or much greater attention to the education of people for marriage and parenthood, and then attempted to offer the main

[1] F. R. Barry, Claude Mullins, and Douglas White, *Right Marriage*.
[2] G. L. Russell, *Sex Problems in Wartime* (SCM Press, 1940).

elements of a plan according to which it can be done, beginning with the pre-marital preparation of two young people whom we called John and Mary. This account touched on the medical contribution and then discussed the direct and indirect pastoral contribution to an understanding of marriage, love, and the sexual and personal relationships in marriage.

Some aspects of the marriage service were then considered, and then the important work of education for most effective parenthood. This included some details of the handling and management of babies, then the important work of helping parents to give religious and sex education to their young children in the home, and later to give understanding and leadership to help them to achieve fitness for marriage, parenthood, vocation and citizenship through the second decade of their lives. This would naturally lead to the pre-marital preparation, so completing the ever-recurring cycle.

It seems clear that while much of the work of education for marriage and parenthood is most fittingly carried out by parents, teachers, doctors, and marriage counsellors, the pastor by the very nature of his calling should be at the very centre of the whole project. He is particularly equipped to do some of the work himself, and can become equipped for much more of it. He also has a unique opportunity to equip parents, teachers, and even doctors to make the most of their opportunities.

If this great work can be taken up as fully as the community needs demand it might well become the most important and socially creative 'combined operation' of the latter half of this twentieth century.

SECTION THREE

The Healing Ministry

CHAPTER ELEVEN

The Church's Part in Healing

IT IS generally agreed that the Church has played an important part in the great healing enterprise through the greater part of the Christian era, and that it is still giving valuable assistance to the cause of healing today, especially in its medical missions in various countries. But there are many who believe that the real ministry of healing has now been taken over almost completely by medical science—medicine, surgery, psychiatry, and all their associated services—and that the work is being carried out with increasingly conspicuous success.

Such people may accept with gratitude the provision and administration of certain hospitals and homes by the Church, the services of pastors as hospital chaplains and visitors, and the private ministry of the Church to the sick as well as the healthy. But they do not generally regard these services as playing any essential part in the actual work of healing. They would probably believe that any material, domestic, or social factors which may be contributing to people's illnesses or impeding their recovery are being sufficiently attended to in these days by almoners and social workers.

Those who take this secular or materialistic view would be tolerant of any efforts of the Church to save the souls of men and women, as long as Christian ministers keep off the scientific 'grass'.

At the other end of the scale is the extreme 'religious' view, which maintains that the Church has an important part in healing, but sees it as mainly or even exclusively a priestly one, which uses prayer and the traditional sacramental methods of laying-on of hands and sometimes anointing with oil. These religious observances are carried out either privately in particular individual cases, or in the presence of a congregation in 'healing services' or in the sacrament of Holy Communion.

In order that we may see more clearly what part the Church may and should have in the great healing enterprise we must first consider the over-all nature of the healing process, and then look at the various ways in which we human beings may come to make the most effective use of the available healing resources.

We shall think of healing in its wider perspective, and include the prevention of ill-health and the promotion of good health as well as the recovery of health. We shall think of health as something more than freedom from obvious disease, and as something concerned with the soul and spirit of man as well as his body and mind. Health has been described as the combination of a fit body, a quiet mind, and a sense of worth-while purpose in life. The word comes from an Old English word which means wholeness, from which also the word holiness is derived. The great old Christian words 'salvation' and 'atonement' are also closely related with this wider conception of health.

It is generally agreed that health and healing are inseparable from life, that they come through a power given and constantly replenished with life. The ancient Romans called it the '*Vis Medicatrix Naturae*', and Christian people would rather describe it as the '*Vis Medicatrix Dei*'. We see healing as a rational, law-abiding process, at least in the overwhelming majority of cases, and we are justified in believing that those healings which we call miraculous are the outward and visible signs of the working of laws beyond our present understanding.

These laws of health and healing are intimately related to all the laws of life and growth, as part of a rational and consistent design and method of working of God. They govern the whole of life: every living thing and the total environment, and can be investigated and correlated through progressively emergent levels of life.

Healthy life, growth, and reproduction depend upon human co-operation with these laws, but they appear to be too vast and complex for any one human mind to comprehend in their entirety. For adequate and rational co-operation it is therefore obligatory for all would-be healers to study, formulate, correlate, and apply as many of the laws as may lie within the range of their possible comprehension, to recognize their limitations, and to co-operate with all the other healing agencies which may deal with other aspects of the total pattern. In other words the need for expanding team-work and continuing research is written into the very nature of things.

It is a fundamental truth that no human 'healer' can ever heal anything, he can only seek to co-operate with this inner vital healing power which is given freely and spontaneously by God. In some accounts of healing works that came through Jesus we are told that someone 'was made whole', the passive verb is used.

The surgeon may perform a brilliant operation for the removal of a gangrenous appendix, or some other organ or tissue which may be interfering with a person's health, but the surgeon's knife has no healing power. The healing power of God in the patient has to heal the operation area and the surgeon's wound, and restore the patient to health.

The physician, by using penicillin or some other antibiotic, may upset the reproductive power of many virulent germs, and so bring about the recovery of many people from diseases which would otherwise have been fatal or highly dangerous. But penicillin has no power to heal any of the inflamed and poisoned tissues, nor can it clean up the mess left by the action of the germs. The healing power of God in the patient has to do that.

The necessary co-operation with God's laws of life and health can be carried out in three closely related ways, so that the fullest possible healing may be made available to men and women.

The first is the provision of the most suitable environment, with which people can preserve the proper relationship, the second is the provision of suitable nourishment in sufficient quantity and availability, and the third is the attempt to discover, and neutralize or remove, all possible hindrances to health and healing.

These three ways of co-operation need to be carried out in every aspect of human life—physical and chemical, mental, and social and spiritual—if people are to be made whole in the fullest sense of that term.

It is the main task of medical science to provide for the fullest co-operation with the healing and health-giving power on the physical and chemical and the mental planes, and to an increasing extent on the social and spiritual. In this task it is necessarily concerned with environment, nutrition, and the recognition and neutralization or removal of hindrances to health and healing.

The environment is kept within the proper range of temperature and humidity in the physical sphere, and sufficient oxygen and other atmospheric components are ensured in the chemical sphere. A mental environment of consistency and reason, and a spiritual 'atmosphere' of devoted care are also provided to help in the healing process.

Nutrition is carefully looked after, beyond the physical and chemical nourishment of a proper diet, through the mental 'nourishment' of adequate information and explanation, to the social and spiritual 'nourishment' of fellowship and inspiration in the healer-patient relationship.

The various hindrances to healing are thought of and dealt with in similar manner. They may be physical, such as the separation between the edges of a wound, or movement between the opposing edges of a fractured bone. They may be chemical such as bacterial or other poisons. They may be mental, such as pain, bewilderment, conflict, anxiety or confusion; or social and spiritual, such as hatred, greed, jealousy, frustration or futility.

It is important to realize that mental, social, and spiritual 'poisons' exert a profound influence on the physical and chemical processes of the body, and are often potent factors in the causation and persistence of 'physical' disease. All modern insights into 'psycho-somatic' and 'somato-psychic' medicine are confirming the conviction that it is impossible to separate the soul and spirit from the body and mind of man. There are many examples to be found of the healing influence of 'spiritual restoration' on 'physical disease'.

A young woman of 21 had been in bed with proved tuberculosis of the lungs for more than three months, under the best medical care in the pre-antibiotic days. She was still running a high swinging temperature and feeling and looking ill, for no apparent adequate reason. She was a professing Christian, and her minister had visited her regularly, and had sought for healing through prayer and the laying-on of hands, with no obvious effect on her physical condition.

When she was faced with the question, 'Is there something troubling your mind?', she eventually unburdened herself of a number of long-standing emotional and spiritual conflicts, some of which were associated with a man who was pestering her to marry him and threatening suicide if she turned him down. She had no love for him, but feared and hated him, and feared the possible scandal if he carried out his threat. She had been telling increasingly difficult lies to her family, and was feeling a deep sense of guilt and despair. When all of this was confessed and faced, her temperature became normal within a week, her health improved rapidly, and in a few months she returned to work. She has since married and has presented her husband with three fine children.

The same kind of co-operation with the healing and health-giving power of God is seen in every kind of treatment of every kind of illness and injury, and the growth of 'social case-work' in relation to the work of hospitals constitutes a practical recognition of the vital importance of the social and spiritual aspects of physical as well as psychic illness.

We are now in a better position to consider the nature and the possible scope of the Church's part in healing, including the prevention of ill-health and the promotion of 'wholeness'. 'Wholeness', in its full meaning, involves the body, the mind (conscious and unconscious), the soul (which may be thought of as the self-conscious part of the personality), and the spirit (the 'God-conscious' part). It also involves the integration of all these into an 'in-divid-ual' (an undivided person) and the 'wholesome' relationship of the individual with his fellow-men and with God.

If they are to be made whole people must be helped to increase, as Jesus did, 'in wisdom and stature, and in favour with God and man' (Luke 2^{52}). This is wholeness or health as Jesus saw it, achieved it, and offered it in His earthly ministry. This is what He still offers through His living Spirit to His followers today, and through them to all mankind. His original commission to His disciples, none of whom were doctors, 'to preach the kingdom of God, and to heal the sick' (Luke 9$^{1-2}$), is still valid today, however much it has been ignored throughout the Christian era.

In one sense the vocation of medicine, with all its related services, can be regarded as a part of the healing work of the Church, and the extent to which the Church has failed to regard it as such is an index of the narrowness and rigidity of human thought in the earlier centuries. But even if we think of medical science as something apart from the work of the Church, and acknowledge its rightful possession of the main field of scientific healing, there is still a very large area in which no form of science is applicable: the co-operation with the healing and health-giving forces through the three spiritual avenues of environment, nourishment, and overcoming of hindrances. This is the special calling, privilege, and responsibility of the Church in the fullest co-operation with all the other healing agencies, and it is a work for which the Church has at its disposal all the potential resources necessary if it will but mobilize, develop, and use them.

The Spiritual Environment needed for health in its fullest sense may be described as the fellowship of the Spirit: of Christian Love. This should surround the child from birth, through the kind of parent-child relationship already described in part of Chapter 9, and it can be promoted through the total personal and educational, healing, and evangelistic work of the Church. Beyond the home it is the special calling of the Christian congregation to provide this health-promoting spiritual environment in the community. It seems certain that there are opportunities for healing and preventive service of this kind by Christian congregations far greater than we have ever realized.

The Spiritual Nourishment needed for total health involves the constant renewing of the inner resources of faith, hope, and love through worship, prayer, and service of the appropriate kind. Through any of these acts of worship men and women can lay hold of the four great gifts of the Spirit described in Chapter 3: light, power, deliverance, and fellowship. In mediating these gifts to mankind the Church is performing a greater healing service than is generally recognized, and one which will increase to the extent that people are helped to understand the meaning and purpose of worship, and to open their souls in self-giving adoration to God.

The Overcoming of Spiritual Hindrances to Health, such as resentment against God or against people, greed, fear, jealousy, grief, and the sense of frustration, futility, or despair, needs more than medical or any other 'science'. Many doctors, face to face with a person tormented by any of these spiritual poisons, would say with the Doctor in *Macbeth*: 'More needs she the Divine than the physician.' This is the great privilege and calling of the Church through an enlightened and devoted pastoral ministry: to offer people everywhere in the personal relationship between pastor and person, and in verbal expression in simple and plain terms, the healing and reconciling power of the Holy Spirit. Unless they are given in the setting of this personal relationship, preaching and teaching are often ineffective in overcoming spiritual hindrances to health, because emotions are little influenced by reason in many cases.

It will be seen that the Church's contribution to healing is one that involves the whole Church: laymen as well as ministers have an important part, individually and in fellowship, in each of the three avenues of healing work already described. We may therefore give some consideration to ways in which the Church can take up the task more fully and effectively, thinking first of ministers and then of laymen.

It is certain that ministers will be given more and more training in every aspect of the Church's healing-work, and that some ministers with special gifts will be trained as specialists in one or other field of healing. The training will need to be carried out at the undergraduate and post-graduate levels, through set lectures and special study, discussions, 'clinical' work, and in some cases through correspondence courses for ministers in outlying areas.

This training will necessarily include detailed consideration of the nature and practice of priestly healing, the different avenues of pastoral healing, and the important work of educating suitable laymen to play their part.

Laymen will need to be trained to exercise a healing and reconciling influence as individuals, as members of special groups, and as members of the total Christian congregation.

As individuals they will need to be confronted with the well-known commission of Jesus to His disciples, none of whom were doctors, to preach and to heal, to be the light of the world and the salt of the earth (Luke 9^{1-2}, 10^{1-9}, Matthew 5^{13-16}.) It seems logical to assume that every Christian is called to be a healing and reconciling influence wherever he may be. For this he will need to be educated and trained to some extent in the simple interviewing relationships and techniques, and in some cases in the deeper relationships of counselling.

As member of special groups who meet together for study, prayer, fellowship and service it is probable that Christian laymen can fit themselves, under the leadership of the pastor, for a quality and range of healing-service beyond anything ever imagined. The main aspects of their contribution may be considered under the same three ways of co-operation with the healing power of God as has already been described: environment, nourishment, and overcoming of hindrances.

A 'Social Group', made up of Christian men and women who may feel called to study and practise the fullest and deepest implications of the 'fellowship of the Spirit', could provide the necessary spiritual environment for those who may need it in a manner not generally available in our society. This may be of priceless value to the lonely, shy, diffident and troubled, and to the many people who are trying to re-establish themselves into human society after a prolonged mental or physical illness. Such a group would fulfil one of the functions of the Church and constitute the home and family on the larger scale, offering to many people the kind of love which they may never have received in their own homes, and through which alone their personalities may develop and he healed.

A 'Prayer Group' of dedicated people who meet regularly to learn together the deeper meanings and the most effective spirit and method of prayer may be of the greatest help in the 'priestly healing' work of the Church. Such a group could study the special principles and methods of 'priestly healing' and particularly of prayer for the sick and troubled. This would inevitably lead to steady growth in the total prayer life of each member of the group, and its influence would spread far beyond the group, into and beyond the whole congregation. This prayer group would provide the essential spiritual nourishment for many who may need it greatly, and who may somehow have failed to find sufficient spiritual reality in their lives.

A 'Pastoral Group' might also be formed, made up of men and women of suitable temperament and emotional maturity, who may feel called to some kind of pastoral healing. Such people would meet regularly and study together the art of interviewing and counselling, so that they could learn to understand and accept people, and become the kind of people in whom anyone could feel safe in confiding. In this way they could provide healing through helping people to discover and be delivered from many of the spiritual hindrances to healing already discussed. That this is no fanciful dream is shown by the most effective counselling given by laymen through Marriage Guidance Councils in many countries.

It is certain that this kind of pastoral healing of troubled individuals as well as troubled homes will be carried out more and more by dedicated trained laymen in future years. The work of such a pastoral group, like that of the pastor himself and in full co-operation with him, will be personal and educational as well as therapeutic or healing, and it will be evangelistic through and through.

The members of these three groups will inevitably find themselves brought into close relationships with one another by the very nature of their work, but it is vital that they should also be brought together and into contact with the total membership of the Church, through the fellowship of the whole congregation. This will provide a constant inspiration to the congregation, and will awaken many other members to the call to some form of special service. There may be other groups for other forms of personal and social service, also linked up in fellowship with the whole congregation and with the neighbourhood.

As members of the total congregation, laymen may be given steady education and training in the healing aspects of the Christian calling, through preaching, teaching, visiting, counselling, and through prayer and worship, and the work of various Church organizations. Some of them will learn much through special service in their own jobs or as members of a Church organization.

In all this work, much of which is being done very fully and without ostentation, the Church is doing something of very great importance for the mental and spiritual health of multitudes of people, not least of doctors, nurses, and other members of healing 'teams' in the community.

The hospital chaplain has a particularly important opportunity in this part of the work, because all future doctors and nurses pass through the 'bottle-neck' of a public hospital, and are accessible there, more than at any other period of their career, to the demonstration of the healing and health-promoting potencies of the Christian Faith. Apart from doctors and nurses the chaplain has close contact with many non-churchgoers at a time when they are more than ever open to the Christian Gospel expressed in action, the word made flesh.

The Over-all View: The Healing Church. Medicine and Religion were joined together in the Person and Ministry of Jesus Christ: Teacher, Healer, Saviour and Friend, and in His commission to His followers who were to form His Church. They were intended to be joined together in those who bear His Name, and the Healing Church is the natural successor to the Healing Saviour. Through human ignorance, narrowness and pride, they have drifted apart to some extent. But what God has joined together no man can finally put asunder, and each of the 'partners' is coming to a new realization of their essential unity. Medicine is realizing that the sick person needs to be made whole, and that wholeness means what it says. The Church is also realizing the incompleteness of any service which takes a limited view of wholeness.

Without overlooking all the devoted social and personal service being carried on by the Church, it may be said that the special and unique calling of the Church in the great healing enterprise would seem to be along three avenues of service: the provision of a health-promoting spiritual environment through the Christian Fellowship, which is what the Church has always been called to be; the provision of spiritual nourishment through worship and through the special form of worship which has been described as 'priestly healing'; and the carrying on of the pastoral work of Jesus Christ by offering 'pastoral healing' to individuals, homes, and societies in His name.

If we think of Medicine as a channel of Divine Healing through Science, including Psychology as the science of the mind, and 'priestly healing' as a channel of Divine Healing through Religion, then 'pastoral healing' can be seen as a kind of bridge between the two, which makes use of Psychology and Religion. It is clear that as the individual cannot be split up into parts, both priestly and pastoral healing, and the work of Christian congregations will be incomplete and ineffective unless they are conceived and administered in the fullest co-operation with all the other healing agencies that may be appropriate.

On the other hand the most efficient and devoted medical care may leave a person reasonably healed in body and mind, but still sick in his soul, and therefore incompletely healed even in body and mind.

When the healing Church comes into its own again through a real awakening and courageous initiative, it may well become the main integrating agent which will bring into proper relationship all the many healing agencies. In this way it may provide a real safeguard against the growing danger of specialism, which, necessary as it is, tends to separate man into parts. The world needs some integrating agency to see man as a whole, in relationship with his natural, cultural, social and spiritual environment; and to provide a kind of society in which he can grow to wholeness, and experience his wholeness. Here surely is the great vision for the Church as it faces today's human situation, from the sick individual to the sick world in space, and from now to eternity in time.

With this general consideration of the Church's part in healing we are now in a position to give more detailed consideration to the main aspects of the Church's healing ministry. We shall consider the act of worship described as 'Priestly Healing', and then go on to deal with some aspects of 'Pastoral Healing'. Under this latter term we shall consider Pastoral Counselling as a healing service, the Christian approach to some emotional and spiritual difficulties, the Understanding and Helping of the Mentally Ill, Marriage Counselling, and Visiting the Sick. These are all vital activities in 'The Church's Part in Healing'.

CHAPTER TWELVE

Priestly Healing

THE TERM Priestly Healing is intended to denote the various kinds of healing that are experienced as a 'by-product' of Christian worship. Whether healing is sought through prayer, the laying-on of hands, or the anointing with oil, and whether privately or in the fellowship of other people, the first object of the act of worship, as of all acts of Christian worship, is the fullest communion with God through Jesus Christ. While the aching desire for healing is naturally present there is no attempt to dwell on the hope of any particular result, but simply on the love and power of God as seen in Jesus Christ, with the fullest acceptance of any or no apparent healing of body or mind.

Priestly healing then is an attempt to bring the soul of the sick person into direct communion with the creative, redemptive, and healing power and love of God: it is healing at and from the very centre of the personality. In this it is quite distinct from any other kind of healing efforts, medical, surgical, psychiatric, and even from many attempts at so-called 'faith healing'; although of course any or all of these may be associated with it in any particular case.

The essential background and the main justification for all the Church's attempts to mediate the healing power of God to His ailing children in this way is the biblical record of the healing works of Jesus, together with His committal of His disciples to the carrying on of those works, and the available accounts of their works of healing.

These records provide many difficulties of interpretation. They are mostly incomplete, and often vague and indefinite. They appear to have been committed to writing some time after the actual occurrence of the events described by men whose minds were largely ignorant of the nature of disease and sometimes imbued with 'magic' and credulity. Furthermore, the Eastern idiom of speech and pictorial manner of description raises some problems in the separation of literal fact from vivid allegory and symbol.

But two solid facts emerge from the records. The first is that Jesus was recognized, by His enemies as well as His friends, as an outstanding healer. The second is that He took great care not to allow the intense and widespread needs of suffering humanity, and the urgent demands of sick people to deviate Him from His primary mission: the revelation of God to mankind. Again and again He charged those that were healed to tell no man, again and again He found it necessary to withdraw with His disciples from the thronging demanding crowd. And when He 'briefed' His disciples we are told that 'He sent them to preach the kingdom of God, and to heal the sick' (Luke 9^2).

We think of Him, with the writer of the letter to the Hebrews, as 'Jesus Christ the same yesterday, and today, and for ever' (13^8), and we have many definite sayings and promises to justify our efforts in His name. (Matthew 18^{20}, 28$^{18-20}$, and John 14$^{10-13}$ are outstanding examples).

'*The Master's Methods*'. A brief survey of the technique of Jesus in His more fully recorded works of healing will provide much help in all our efforts to carry on His healing ministry in His name and through His power. For this purpose we may consider two outstanding examples, each of which is described by the writers of the first three gospels.

The first is the healing of a boy who suffered from fits (Matthew 17$^{14-21}$, Mark 9$^{14-29}$, Luke 9$^{37-42}$). It needs little imagination to read between the lines, particularly of St Mark's graphic record, and to visualize the dramatic situation. We can see the father of the boy, worried and agitated, disappointed at the absence of Jesus, whose help he had come to seek, and even more disappointed at the failure of the disciples to help his son. We can also picture the crowd, probably full of advice and criticism, increasing the emotional tension and deepening the father's despair; the disciples, anxious to cure the boy and trying hard to do so, but without result; and the boy, the central figure in this first act of the drama, writhing in the throes of what was probably an epileptic fit. All these are familiar enough elements of many similar situations today.

Into this came Jesus, His face aglow with the memory of His recent experience on the Mount of Transfiguration, radiating confidence and power, so that all the people ran to meet Him, stirred with a new sense of expectation. Watch His perfect handling of the whole situation: the initial questioning, the rapid sizing up of the problem and of the lack of faith of the people; then the order for the boy to be brought to Him, the boy reacting with a more violent convulsion; the further questioning of the father, winning him from despair to faith; and finally the decisive attack at the exact 'psychological moment'.

Notice the superb timing of Jesus. His own preparations, the renewed expectation of the crowd, and the renewed faith of the father of the boy had all reached their peak, when the power was let loose, and the enemy overwhelmed. No wonder the disciples, disappointed at their own failure, but lost in admiration of their master, took the first chance of asking Him privately the inescapable question; to which came the well-known answer: 'This kind can come forth by nothing, but by prayer and fasting' (9²⁹).

Although some authorities omit the word 'fasting' it may be suggested that the word prayer may be interpreted as the fullest co-operation with God's power and love, and fasting as complete self-discipline which of course is really included in the term prayer. Through these great disciplines the healer can become a vital channel between God, the source of all healing, and the sick person; as Jesus the Great Healer, was the perfect channel for the creative and re-creative work of God. The sheer magnetism of His personality would have gripped the personality of the boy directly, even while he was in the throes of the fit; and also indirectly through His influence on the boy's father and on the crowd. In this way all the conflicting elements in the boy's personality were pulled together, and he was made whole.

There are many little conflicting 'selves' in all of us, which are never pulled together because we are not gripped strongly enough in our inner souls to be lifted right above our own little concerns. Medical science has still much to learn about the deeper reaches of the human personality, and about the healing potencies of the spirit.

The second example to be considered is the healing of the young man who was paralysed (Matthew 9²⁻⁸, Mark 2¹⁻¹², Luke 5¹⁷⁻²⁶). We do not know what caused his paralysis, but if we remember that in those days all disease was regarded as a punishment from God for wrongdoing, we may imagine the heavy load of bitterness, despair, and self-reproach that must have burdened the young man's soul, as the paralysis weighed down his body.

He may have heard rumours of amazing cures by Jesus, and wondered whether he would ever have the chance of seeing Him. And now comes the news that Jesus is here in Capernaum, addressing a meeting at a nearby house. It is now or never! Jesus might be moving on at any time. How could he reach Him? We are told that four good friends came to his rescue, and promptly carried him to the house. But there his hopes were dashed, he found the house crowded to the doors and there seemed to be no possible chance for him to be admitted. But his friends quickly proved their resourcefulness and determination. They collected some ropes, which were plentiful enough among the fishermen's haunts, lifted him up on to the roof, and then opened up the roof and let him down on his bed into the room, right in front of Jesus.

The young man must have been vividly aware of the buzz of surprise and curiosity in the gathering, and a growing murmur of indignation at the sheer audacity of the intrusion. And then he must have felt the penetrating gaze of Jesus. How would Jesus take it? But Jesus always managed to see a little farther and deeper than other people, to discover and appreciate the good in men, even when it was not immediately obvious. He realized at once the strong faith of the four men, and their devotion to their friend; and He saw through the paralysis of the young man's body to the deep unrest in his soul.

With a quiet bearing that radiated authority and power graciously blended with understanding, sympathy and love, Jesus looked down at the young man and said to him: 'Son, be of good cheer; thy sins be forgiven thee' (Matthew 9²). Although nobody seems to have spoken, we are left in no doubt of the seething astonishment and indignation stirred up by those penetrating words. We may recall that some very important people were there—scribes and Pharisees, and doctors of the law from many surrounding districts, and to them it was arrogant presumption for anyone but a priest to pronounce the Divine forgiveness.

To the young man, however, the surprise must have been accompanied by a sudden quickening of interest and expectancy. Notice again the perfect poise of Jesus in handling the crowd, and the sureness and superb timing of His attack.

And immediately when Jesus perceived in his spirit that they so reasoned within themselves, he said unto them, Why reason ye these things in your hearts? Whether is it easier to say to the sick of the palsy, Thy sins be forgiven thee; or to say, Arise, and take up thy bed, and walk? But that ye may know the Son of man hath power on earth to forgive sins (he saith to the sick of the palsy), I say unto thee, Arise, and take up thy bed, and go thy way into thine house. And immediately he arose, took up the bed, and went forth before them

all; insomuch that they were all amazed, and glorified God, saying,
We never saw it on this fashion (Mark 2$^{8-12}$).

We can well imagine the crescendo of expectation in the mind of
the young man, and the tremendous spiritual power let loose at
exactly the right moment by the positive command of Jesus, at which
every conflicting part of his disturbed personality was pulled together
in a self-forgetting ecstasy of the spirit.

From these records and those of His other healing works we can
draw some helpful conclusions about the 'technique' of Jesus in healing. We find that He often made careful inquiry regarding the nature
of the illness, as the modern doctor takes a 'history', and He used
different methods according to each particular type of trouble. He
frequently made use of physical agents and methods, hands, clay,
spittle, washing and bathing, as vehicles for the apprehension and
transmission of spiritual power.

Above and behind all these of course was His own physical personality, poised, confident, powerful, and radiant, and His perfect timing
and control. Throughout the record of His healing works we also find
evidence of His dependence on having or winning the faith of the sick
person and of those around him. Many times He said to the person
who was healed: 'Thy faith hath made thee whole.' He said it so
often, and in 'explanation' of so many works of healing, that we must
accept it as His considered conviction. We are told that when He
came into His own country 'he did not many mighty works there
because of their unbelief' (Matthew 13^{58}), or as St Mark records it:
'He could there do no mighty work, save that he laid his hands upon
a few sick folk, and healed them. And he marvelled because of their
unbelief' (6$^{5-6}$).

How are we in this twentieth century to regard the healing works of
Jesus? Are we to be sceptical about those which we cannot 'explain'
in our present state of 'scientific' knowledge? Or are we to admit
frankly, what the whole history of scientific progress has clearly
demonstrated, that 'there are more things in heaven and earth . . .
than are dreamt of in (our) philosophy'. Perhaps we can best answer
these vital questions by quoting some penetrating observations of the
Rev. Dr Leslie D. Weatherhead.[1]

Because of what He was, and because of His relation to, and trust in,
God, Christ was able to introduce into the lives of men living on the

---

[1] *Psychology, Religion, and Healing,* pp. 488, 489.

M

human plane, energies which belong to the divine or supernatural plane. The effect was what we call miracle. It was as startling to men as the effect of man's intervention would be to thoughtful and reasoning dogs—if we can imagine such—whose wounds and injuries were suddenly healed by calling in resources such as penicillin, familiar and law-abiding to man, but outside the range of canine understanding.

Miracles are not to be excluded. On a higher plane of being they are normal, law-abiding happenings. When they impinge on our plane, we call them miraculous and supernatural—which, indeed, they are; but they are only 'above' the nature we know. They are not to be regarded as, in any sense, a rupture of law. They are supernatural but not contranatural.

It seems equally absurd to suppose that there is a fixed and closed order, knowable by man, outside which nothing can possibly happen. So a dog might be imagined, solemnly deciding that nothing outside his understanding world could possibly happen. Man is not limited to what such a dog would recognize as the limits of the possible, and God is certainly not restricted to the limited operation of the realm of law which man has found out through 'science'.

Some healing work was apparently carried out by the disciples during the period of the earthly ministry of Jesus (Mark 6[7-13]). And after Pentecost many healings were apparently brought about through the ministry of Peter, Philip, and Paul, as recorded throughout The Acts of the Apostles. We also have the famous statement of St James, 'to the twelve tribes which are scattered abroad':

Is any sick among you? let him call for the elders of the church; and let them pray over him, anointing him with oil in the name of the Lord: And the prayer of faith shall save the sick, and the Lord shall raise him up; and if he have committed sins, they shall be forgiven him. Confess your faults one to another, and pray for one another, that ye may be healed. The effectual fervent prayer of a righteous man availeth much (1[1], 5[14-17]).

This healing power seems to have been lost fairly quickly by the early Church, and the history of priestly healing to the present day provides relatively few examples of healing through prayer, the laying-on of hands, and anointing with oil. 'Greater works' indeed have been done, and still greater works are being done year by year in the healing and prevention of disease by the power of God working through scientific medicine, surgery, psychiatry, and their associated healing agencies, and some important but unspectacular healing and preventive work has been done through the knowledge, faith, and devotion of Christian pastors. But many people are becoming convinced that the Church is called to a much greater healing work than anything carried out through priestly and pastoral ministrations so far, and attention is being increasingly given to the whole question of priestly and pastoral healing.

It is becoming more clearly realized that priestly healing through worship, prayer, the laying-on of hands, and anointing with oil, or through any one or more of these agencies, is something quite distinct from healing by suggestion. Suggestion may provide one element in the healing process, but priestly healing makes primary use of faith, which is something quite different from suggestibility or even from credulity. Suggestibility appears to be a natural characteristic of certain types of personality, and credulity is either associated with it or may be a sign of immaturity or simple-mindedness. Faith, on the other hand, is the response of the whole personality to something, or someone which has proved worthy of it: it is the recognition, acceptance, and self-obliterating committal to the highest we know, an openness to the spirit without demand.

If a person's faith is self-centred, if its chief or only motive is the desire to get well, or to receive any other benefit, it will probably be ineffective, because such shallow faith is all too easily overcome by fear. Such faith cannot make men whole because they are still beset by the fear of what may happen.

The fully effective faith is a God-centred faith; a faith in God because God is what He is; a faith which can honestly affirm with Job in the ancient epic: 'Though he slay me, yet will I trust in him' (13^{15}). Only a faith which is willing to accept any or no healing can free the body and mind from emotional conflict with its constant dissipation of energy, and so liberate in its fullness the healing power of the spirit of God. That surely is what faith meant to Jesus, and it must mean that to those who are made whole.

How can people receive, or find such faith? Most people want passionately to believe, but find their many different fears, desires, regrets and perplexities so strong and in such conflict that they feel no sense of reality in their relationship with God. Many of their strongest urges and feelings seem to be elusive, and out of range of their understanding or their control. The Jesus of history seems so far away in time and place that they cannot seem to feel the power of

His dynamic personality, which apparently was so great a factor in His original works of healing.

Jesus set out to win people's faith by giving Himself to them in loving serving friendship, as a visible, tangible Person. He commissioned His Church to be His continuing 'body', to offer His creative dynamic spirit afresh to every age as a visible, tangible reality, as the true fellowship of the Spirit. This is something which cannot be counterfeited, but if it exists it will be felt by people, and awaken an increasing faith in their personalities. All that Christian people say and do may have a part in transmitting this unique faith-winning Spirit of Jesus, but these things are incomplete and relatively ineffective until people can actually experience the creative power of Christian Love. As we saw in Chapter 3, only the complete personality (which involves fellowship with others) can speak adequately to the whole of man, and lead him to abundant life.

Faith of the right kind is therefore awakened and increased in people, not by arduous human striving, but by simple openness to the Spirit of God which is ever ready to flow into them through worship, fellowship, and through self-giving service. It is for the Christian minister and Christian layman to make these Divine resources real to people, and to be open channels for the vital healing transfusion of the Holy Spirit into their bewildered hungry souls. In this way the sick and troubled will become filled with such confidence of the unquenchable love and power of God that they will be lifted above the human over-concern with the 'bodily' result, and even be able to face the possibility of death as a form of healing of the personality.

Practical Considerations regarding Priestly Healing. All that has been discussed so far should make it clear that priestly healing should not be regarded lightly or carelessly, something that is worth 'giving a trial' or carrying out as a kind of 'sacerdotal routine'. Nor should it be regarded as an isolated event, something apart from all other methods of treatment. Above all it should not be thought of always as a 'last resort', when all other methods appear to have been ineffective.

Priestly healing should be taken seriously and 'rightly and duly' administered as befitting its sanctity. It needs and merits the fullest possible preparation of all concerned, and the most carefully considered planning, design, and technique. It should be regarded as an act of worship of the whole Christian fellowship, and the minister as the spearhead of the 'fellowship of the Spirit', backed up in his worship by the faith, love, and prayer of the whole fellowship. The whole act of worship is greatly enriched when it is possible for all the 'healers' who have anything to do with the sick person to take part, at least in spirit and in prayer, in full understanding co-operation.

It may well be that when priestly healing can be carried out in this way, in full relationship with all appropriate 'medical' treatment and 'pastoral' help, we shall find our healing activities raised to a new level of efficiency, and a new relationship with the total life of mankind. Priestly healing will then become more widely accepted as an integral and essential part of the great healing enterprise: one which indeed sets the standard and revitalizes the inspiration for all the others.

In general it would seem that this act of worship is most fittingly carried out in a relatively small compact fellowship rather than in open public services. The vital 'atmosphere' of faith, love, and creative prayer is likely to be interfered with if the service is allowed to attract people whose 'faith' is self-centred, and whose main motive is curiosity rather than worship. It is possible that large 'missions of healing' may be appropriate to some particular situations, and some people with particular 'gifts of healing', but such projects are of a different order from the priestly healing already described, and probably more dependent on suggestion. If there is a 'prayer group', as described in Chapter 11, it would naturally form the active nucleus of the small 'congregation', and provide a vital source of inspiration and power.

In all cases it is important to guard against any tendency to regard the actual healing service as the final act of healing, even when the sick person makes a very good recovery. There should be a real effort to follow up and to keep in touch with the recipients of all these priestly ministrations, to welcome into the Christian fellowship, and to give them the opportunity and encouragement to express their loving gratitude to God in further acts of worship and fellowship, and in loving service to His other 'children'.

This may be summed up most fittingly by another quotation from the Rev. Dr Leslie D. Weatherhead:

The intercession of people united in love for Christ and living disciplined lives, and the laying-on of hands undertaken after prayer and self-discipline by a priest or minister, or other person who is the contact-point, so to speak, of a beloved, believing, and united community, standing behind him and supporting his ministration to a patient who has been taught to understand the true nature of Christian faith. . . . This is the true ministry of the Church as such, and, in a sense, has nothing to do with psychology at all. This is the ministry which must be recovered, and which only the Church can do. For this ministry the words 'spiritual healing' should be reserved.[1]

These penetrating words offer the main clues to the kind of preparation which ought to be sought for the minister, the relatives and friends of the sick person, the congregation, and the sick person himself whenever possible. With this background, consideration may be given to some of the details of the preparation.

The general preparation of the minister may be considered in terms of the three great functions of the mind: intellect, emotion, and will. Intellectually he must constantly seek and cultivate a sound clear understanding of what he is trying to do, and of how he can best co-operate with the ways of God as he understands them. This will involve constant study, constant reviewing of his insights and methods, and regular discussion with other ministers, and with doctors, nurses, and with sick people and their relatives and friends. It will also involve careful collecting and reviewing of 'clinical' records, which will be discussed in a later section of this account.

The emotional preparation of the minister will include the constant cultivation of awareness and grateful acceptance of the infinite love of God, by regular disciplined meditation, prayer, and bible study. To become a fully effective channel for the healing power of the Spirit he will need to be genuinely willing to face and surrender all his personal desires and ambitions, fears and resentments, if necessary through confession of them to God in the presence of a dedicated colleague. He will also need to face everything that is not right in his life and in his relationships with other people, to make restitution of any wrongs where possible, and to accept the forgiveness of God through his honest repentance.

The volitional preparation of the minister is largely a matter of regular dedication and re-dedication to disciplined, self-sacrificing service, a committal that is implicit in the total work of all good Christian ministers. With regular disciplined practice, constantly inspired from without by his awareness of human need, and from within by his regular devotional life in the secret places of his own

---

[1] *Psychology, Religion, and Healing.*

soul and in the fellowship of his fellow-Christians, this dedication becomes so built into his character that it is spontaneous and 'unselfconscious'.

This general preparation of intellect, emotion, and will is intensified by a fitting immediate preparation, which may take any form that seems effective for the particular minister. For many it will be a period of quiet unhurried meditation and prayer, in which there is a fresh committal to God in self-surrender, and a 'handing over' to God of the whole situation with all its human anguish and concern, and all the associated hopes and fears.

The general preparation of the congregation, of the relatives and friends of the sick person, and of the doctors, nurses, and any other people who may be looking after him in any way, is, or should be, part of the normal ministry of the Church. It is carried out through preaching and teaching, and through the pastoral ministry of routine visiting, general conversation, and through deeper counselling where it seems relevant. It is made up of specific training in the Christian practice of worship, prayer, and the acceptance of Divine guidance, already discussed in Chapter 5, and of equally specific training in the main principles of Spiritual Healing, so that they can give the fullest co-operation to the great act of worship. Such preparation can be a thrilling progressive adventure in Christian service, and it will inevitably bring a deepening of spiritual experience, a vitalizing of faith, and an enriching of personal fellowship in communal worship.

The more immediate preparation of the congregation may be thought of in terms of intellect, emotion, and will, as for the minister. Intellectually they should have a clear understanding of what they are about to do and to attempt: to 'bring the sick person to Jesus' as the men of Gennesaret did of old, 'that they might only touch the hem of his garment' (Matthew 14[34-6]). They may be helped to see themselves as standing behind and supporting the minister who is their representative before God, and God's representative and minister to the sick person. In some such manner as this they can, with the minister, create a warm vital expectant 'atmosphere' of faith, hope, and the greatest of all, love, in which the sick person will be uplifted in spirit above all his little conflicting selves to feel the presence and the power of Him who makes men whole.

The emotional preparation of the members of the congregation is mainly an attempt to help them to overcome all negative feelings: doubt of God's love and power, criticism and resentment, and anxiety.

As we have seen in Chapter 5, any negative feeling or thoughts will certainly radiate with the positive ones, and tend to neutralize their beneficial power. It is, as St James pointed out, 'the prayer of faith' that 'shall save the sick', and those who take part in any such praying may well watch and pray in the spirit—and the words—of this most appropriate prayer:

Almighty God, unto whom all hearts be open, all desires known, and from whom no secrets are hid; cleanse the thoughts of our hearts by the inspiration of thy Holy Spirit, that we may perfectly love thee, and worthily magnify thy holy Name; through Christ our Lord, Amen.[1]

What an inspiration of genius it was to describe the vital inner feelings as 'the thoughts of our hearts'! The awakening of people to the sheer 'bigness' of the love of God, which can overcome all human pride and self-centredness, is greatly helped by regular and properly conducted prayer, fellowship, and communal outgoing service.

The volitional preparation of people is assisted by all acts of outgoing sacrificial devotion in the Name and in the Spirit of Jesus Christ. In many cases it will have been increased by acts of neighbourly devotion and sympathetic service to the sick person for whom the particular act of worship is being planned.

The preparation of the patient may be thought of under the two headings: medical and religious. The medical preparation should include the fullest possible scientific investigation: a thorough inquiry and recording of the history of the illness, the past history and family history of the patient, and the various symptoms; and a full clinical examination with all the required special investigations and tests. All this is, of course, a matter for the patient's doctor, and anyone else on whom he may call for help. The required treatment, medical, surgical and any other measures, will also have been at least set in motion.

Man is an 'in-divid-ual' and any effort to separate him into parts will naturally interfere with efforts to help him to be made whole. Either 'spiritual' or 'medical' healing without the other will generally be incomplete. But spiritual healing need not wait until the medical diagnosis and treatment are complete, or have done all they can. As long as the medical aspects of the situation are being attended to the

---

[1] *Book of Common Prayer.*

spiritual ministrations ought to begin as soon as possible, and go on right through the illness as part of the total therapy.

There was a time in the medical treatment of pneumonia when oxygen was only administered when everything else seemed to be failing and the patient appeared at the point of death. When it began to be used more generally some knowing patients became panic-stricken at the appearance of an oxygen cylinder at their bed-sides, thinking that this must mean that their chances of recovery were slender. The same kind of panic has come to sick people at the appearance of the minister, because in their minds such ministrations were only associated with 'last ditch' situations. It is vital that Spiritual help should come to be regarded (as oxygen now is in pneumonia) as an essential and valuable part of the total attack of the illness.

The 'religious' preparation of the patient may not always be possible, for example when the minister is called to a very sick or even unconscious patient, adult or child. This, of course, should not prevent the minister and friends from seeking the direct power of God through prayer, the laying-on of hands, and anointing with oil, or any one or two of them. But where it is possible without too much strain on the patient—and this should be a matter for consultation with the doctor or the nurse in any case of the slightest doubt—the patient should be specifically prepared for what is going to be done and sought on his behalf, so that he can give the best co-operation with the act of worship.

One part of the religious preparation is carried out through the pastoral ministry of the minister. Through personal counselling, as described elsewhere in this book, the patient may be helped to gain fuller insight into his deeper attitudes and prejudices, his uncritical assumptions and unconscious desires. In this way some of the spiritual hindrances to healing may be uncovered, faced, and allowed to be overcome by the healing power of the Spirit of God. Through more specifically priestly work he may be helped to face and confess anything that may burden his soul with a sense of guilt, and receive absolution. Through evangelistic work the pastor may help him to a clearer awareness of the love of God, the will of God for the fullest health of all His children, and the meaning of faith, worship, and prayer for himself. He is then in a better position to make full and effective use of his immediate devotional preparation for the act of worship by his own private meditation, prayer, and self-surrender.

To quote the Rev. Dr Leslie D. Weatherhead yet again:

Perhaps the ideal mental condition for the patient who is to receive the rite of the laying-on of hands is that of entire surrender to the will of God in the circumstances. If that can be health, he will praise God. If, for various human reasons, health cannot be restored, he must try to see that while God's intention is health, that intention may be temporarily defeated by human ignorance, folly or sin at some point or another, not necessarily in the patient's own life, but in that of the whole human race of which he is a member. But the patient must try to understand that there is always a secondary or interim will of God, and that God is never finally defeated, but, as in the case of St Paul, can weave even continued suffering into His plan, so that ultimately the patient is brought to the same point as that to which he would have been brought if health had been restored.[1]

This deep inner conviction is an expression of true faith in God, and this spirit is the true spirit of worship, difficult enough to describe, but even more difficult for people, sick or well, to achieve. Those who have it will find themselves thinking of illness, and all other possible calamities in terms of the penetrating admonition of Jesus; 'Fear not them which kill the body, but are not able to kill the soul: but rather fear him which is able to destroy both soul and body in hell' (Matthew 10[28]).

The actual form which the healing service will take must depend on the particular circumstances of the individual case, the particular attitudes and practices of the minister, and the attitudes and feelings of the patient and those around him. In general the whole atmosphere and arrangement of the service should be in tune with and expressive of the particular feelings of the patient and his friends. In particular the main prayers should express the spiritual needs as recognized by the patient and take up into themselves his thoughts about the situation. Above all they should be short and simple. The comments of Russell Dicks about prayer in the sick-room are relevant for all prayers for the sick:

The contents of prayer in the sick-room should be like the contents of the patient's food tray. Steak smothered in onions and french-fried potatoes are not given a patient in his early convalescence, however much he may desire them. He is given broth, tea,

---

[1] op. cit.

soft-boiled eggs, toast, or a similar meal. So with prayer in the sick-room.[1]

Many excellent prayers for the sick are given in that book.

Prayer for the sick should not be used as an oblique way of bringing home to the patient some worthy moral principle, nor should it be an instrument of coercion. It should show full acceptance of the patient's feelings, so that his attention is not diverted by a sense of shame or guilt for having them, but is allowed to be fully open to the light, power, deliverance, and fellowship of the Spirit of God, and to His quietness, confidence, and peace. The proper use of silence in the service may deepen and intensify this feeling.

At the actual point of laying-on of hands, the climax to which all the preparations and all the service so far should lead, the kind of prayer may be along the lines suggested by the Rev. Dr Percy Dearmer, in a suggested form of service, with a note of authority in it:

(*Then the Minister, standing by the sick person, shall lay both his hands upon the head of the same, saying these words*)
In the Name of God Most High, mayest thou be given release from pain, and may thy soul be restored into harmony with His immortal laws. In the Name of Jesus Christ, the Prince of Life, may new life come into thy human body. In the Name of the Holy Spirit, mayest thou have inward health and the peace which passeth under-standing.

And the God of all peace Himself sanctify you wholly; and may your spirit and soul and body be preserved entire, without blame at the presence of our Lord Jesus Christ. Amen.[2]

It would seem fitting and natural that when the patient has re-covered to any extent he should be encouraged to help others to the kind of spiritual experience that he has been given, in any way that may be open to him. The experience of Alcoholics Anonymous is that such grateful service to others is vital and even essential to the maintenance of 'wholeness', and the words of Jesus are extremely relevant: 'Freely ye have received, freely give' (Matthew 10[8]). The Christian fellowship is greatly strengthened by the inclusion in it of many people who are gratefully aware of the healing power of God in their souls, even if their bodies are still beset by some 'thorn in the

---

[1] Richard C. Cabot, M.D., and Russell L. Dicks, B.D., *The Art of Ministering to the Sick* (Macmillan, New York, 1936), p. 215.
[2] *Body and Soul* (E. P. Dutton & Co., New York, 1909). Quoted by Leslie D. Weatherhead, op. cit., p. 521.

flesh'. The pastor will find the fullest effectiveness in his healing ministry when he can mobilize many of the recipients of it to back up and inspire the continuing work.

Many other aspects of this ministry to the sick will be considered in a later chapter which deals with the work of visiting the sick. This is closely related with all that has been dealt with in this chapter, but if included here might possibly confuse the situation to some extent. It is perhaps better regarded as part of pastoral healing, which in itself is inseparably intertwined with priestly healing.

The keeping of records and assessment of results. It is very difficult for a minister to make or keep adequate records of the results of 'priestly healing' for many reasons. In the first place he has no way of making sure about the diagnosis except what he is told by the sick person and possibly by his doctor. A full diagnosis would need to include more than an account of the nature of the bodily and even the mental abnormality. It would also need to assess the inner feelings and the personal relationships, which are very difficult to assess in definite terms. Another difficulty is that the priestly ministrations will generally be associated with those of many other people: doctors, nurses, physiotherapists, almoners, and possibly pastoral ministrations as well. It is very difficult to disentangle the various influences, and quite undesirable to attempt such a task. A third difficulty is that the results can only be adequately described in terms of healing of the body and of the more definite mental disorders. The healing of the spirit, or the total personality can be felt and seen much better than it can be described. And lastly the minister is incompetent to assess any 'medical' results, which may even be impossible for a doctor to assess adequately without very large numbers of cases and carefully arranged controls.

The cause of spiritual healing has not been helped by the many sketchy and uncorroborated reports that have been issued from time to time by over-enthusiastic devotees. The care taken by the administrators of the Medical Bureau at Lourdes provides a splendid example of what is required for accurate and objective reporting.

It is probable that the best records in the future will come from hospitals or homes of healing where the fullest medical investigations of sick people can be undertaken before and after the full medical, pastoral, and priestly 'treatment' is carried out, and from which those who have been cared for in this way can be 'followed up' for some time to assess the permanence or otherwise of the results. If these records, containing full details of all the different forms of treatment, are then assessed by a representative panel of qualified people it will be possible to gain much more reliable knowledge of results, and some clear impression of the part which priestly healing has played in them. In this way we may gain more insight into the most effective methods of co-operating with God in this very important act of worship.

Until now priestly healing has been largely 'individual', carried out by certain people who have realized and demonstrated the 'gift' of healing. It is probable that there are many more people who have it than ever realize the fact. It seems likely that future developments of this work will be carried out by ministers in the perspective of the total ministry of the whole Church: minister and congregation. After all, the healing Church in this sense is the logical and fitting continuation of the healing Saviour.

In conclusion it may be said that there are many indications of a very healthy awakening in the Church to the need for recovering the healing power that has been in abeyance for so long. This awakening, coupled with a new level of insight into the whole nature of healing, may lead to a great advance in human welfare, to something which may well bring, nearer than ever before, the brotherhood of man throughout the world.

CHAPTER THIRTEEN

Pastoral Healing through Personal Counselling

WE HAVE seen that the Church's part in healing may be conceived and carried out through three related avenues of service: the provision of a health-promoting spiritual environment through the Christian fellowship of congregations, possibly offered in more tangible fashion through 'social groups'; priestly healing, which may also be enriched by 'prayer groups'; and pastoral healing through pastors and any 'pastoral groups' of laymen. It is essential that all this healing work should be done under the informed and inspiring leadership of Christian ministers, and that it should always be carried out in the fullest co-operation with the relevant 'scientific' healing services, medical, surgical, psychiatric, and social. This total view of healing rests on the well-founded conviction that all these methods, scientific as well as religious, are divinely ordained channels through which men, women and children may be made whole.

We have seen too that pastoral healing finds itself concerned with science (mainly psychology and sociology) as well as religion, and that it fits into the total pattern as a kind of bridge between priestly and scientific healing. With a proper sense of vocation, temperamental suitability, and an adequate training for the work, the pastor, minister or trained layman, has a unique and exclusive opportunity to see the needy person as a whole: as a person among persons in relation to God and His world. At its best his contribution can fill in a serious gap in the great co-operative healing enterprise, and counteract many of the deficiencies associated with specialism. This is an ideal which will inevitably become realized more and more in the future, especially when laymen become awakened and trained to take their part.

The essential foundation of all pastoral healing is the personal relationship and creative interaction achieved in pastoral counselling, a healing service which is at once very old and very new. It is old because it has come down to us from the earliest days of primitive medicine men, priests, and tribal chiefs. Plato, Socrates, Moses, and many other wise men used it freely and effectively, and Jesus gave it a prominent place in His ministry. The Christian Church has always made use of it in its educational, therapeutic, and evangelistic service to the community.

It is new because it has now taken into itself many fresh insights and methods from the experience of a variety of other professional activities and disciplines, from psychology, anthropology, sociology, and from the practice of psychiatry, child guidance, and many other similar activities. Above all it is still learning by constant careful critical review of its own work.

The work of counselling is based on some fundamental facts of life. The first of these (discussed in the first section of this book) is that man is not a 'rational' being—he is strongly influenced by a multitude of emotions, habits, customs, conventions, and prejudices, many of which are 'out of range' of his ordinary awareness. He is even more 'blind' to his inner attitudes and urges when he is in the grip of disordered, conflicting, or intense emotions. His insights are blocked by strong 'defence mechanisms', many of which are unconscious through the automatic mental device of repression.

The second fundamental fact on which counselling is based is that no man is self-sufficient. Men and women are born into a community, and cannot exist, let alone grow, without mutual support, help, encouragement and challenge. The physical resources necessary for life, growth, and healing come directly or indirectly from the raw materials of the earth through various forms of primary production and cultivation. But most of them need to be brought to men and women in assimilable form by other human beings: miners, refiners, farmers and distributors. Similarly the intellectual and cultural heritage, progressively discovered, refined, and correlated by our ancestors, is also brought to men and women in assimilable form through human beings: researchers, refiners, philosophers, writers, printers, and teachers. Similarly again we need the counsellor to bring the progressively revealed, discovered, refined, and correlated spiritual heritage to troubled and needy people in assimilable form, and at the same time to mobilize and assist the creative spiritual forces within them.

Christian counselling is based on the conviction that human society is not self-sufficient: that man is insufficiently helped in the more complex difficulties of life by other men through their own wisdom and capacity because they are blind and fallible, and ultimately in the same 'boat' as he is. As Jesus himself said: 'Can the blind lead the blind? shall they not both fall into the ditch?' (Luke 6³⁹). While practical human wisdom is of immense and essential value in its own field of reference, the ultimate meaning and purpose of life and the worthwhileness of human striving can only be found in the larger perspective of more than human wisdom: the progressive revelation of the nature and purpose of God, the author, creator, preserver and director of life. The Christian gospel is offered to man as the Good News about God, Man, and Society, embodied clearly in the Person of Jesus Christ, not in philosophies or principles, and 'made flesh' anew in every age by His continuing 'body' the Christian Church. It is applicable to every aspect of human life, as the ultimate frame of reference in which all human wisdom and all human strivings are judged.

Many people are diffident for various reasons about seeking personal help in their inner bewilderments, tensions, and conflicts. Some of them try to protect their sensitive, troubled and hurt personalities by withdrawing into their shells and fighting a lonely, single-handed battle with their aching desires and frustrations, often appearing calm and even cheerful on the surface. This inner battle may go on for so long that they cease to be aware of many of the 'bottled up' tensions within them, and when the situation becomes unbearable it may be difficult for any helper to make adequate contact with the real causes of the trouble.

Some of these troubled people would have looked for help much sooner if they had known who to go to. Talking with relatives and friends may involve questions of loyalty, and although people are mostly generous with advice it is often conflicting, and generally fails to meet the needs of the situation. They may be diffident about going to a minister, either because they do not attend his church regularly, or because they think he would not understand their problem sufficiently. The doctor, they may feel, might think their trouble outside his domain, or might regard it as trivial. In some cases they have taken their courage in both hands and sought help from someone, but have sensed a lack of understanding, or received a stone when they came for bread.

One striking result of the impact of Psychology on mankind is that many people have begun to feel that they should be able to solve their own problems without having to bare their shamefaced souls to any other person. To satisfy the popular demand we are being offered a swelling flood of books and magazine articles on 'popular psychology', telling people how to overcome all their 'complexes', real and imaginary, 'how to win friends and influence people', and generally to live a full and satisfying life. The novelist has not been insensitive to the general interest, and the cinema has grasped the golden opportunity to spread an over-simplified psychological 'gospel' all over the world. And for those who want help in particular problems there are special newspaper and magazine columns, and even radio sessions, glad to give advice freely and plentifully.

In these and similar ways people are finding some help in their individual difficulties. They are also gaining some understanding of some of the deeper motives underlying human attitude and behaviour, and the comforting realization that they are not alone in their troubles. But most of this help is superficial and temporary, and it is all too common for the troubled person to discover that in spite of all the good advice he sinks deeper and deeper into the depths of psychic despair.

The Christian religion has always offered healing to those 'in trouble, sorrow, need, sickness, or any other adversity', and it sets out to do so through pastoral healing by trying to deal with the deeper causes of the trouble, rather than with the superficial manifestations. It is well known that when we can bring peace to the inner personality—the mind, soul and spirit of man—many so-called physical disorders are prevented, relieved, or even healed.

We have seen that the essential foundation of pastoral healing is the personal relationship and creative interaction achieved in pastoral counselling. The dynamics of this relationship, and the way the interaction is handled will necessarily depend on the nature and the personal maturity of the participants. Assuming a reasonable degree of personal and social maturity in the counsellor the structure of the relationship will depend on the maturity of the 'client', the person who comes for help.

This can be understood more clearly if we think of the different kinds of counselling which are found appropriate to different age levels. Very young children need much 'directive' counselling, of a negative restrictive kind, represented by 'Thou shalt not ——'. Older children are helped by 'directive' counselling of a more positive, expansive kind, represented by 'Thou shalt ——', or 'Do this'. And with increasing maturity the counselling should become less and less 'directive', and more concerned with enabling the person to help himself through the achievement of better insight into his own and

N

other people's attitudes, and into the way life works. What is called 'non-directive counselling' sets out in this way to help people to find their own solutions, and to grow to greater maturity and social responsibility through the experience.

The nature of the counselling relationship and technique will similarly depend on the kind of culture and the degree of maturity of the particular society in which the person lives. In a fully authoritative society the client will probably have little capacity—and possibly little opportunity—for independent judgement or social responsibility, compared with his opposite number in a free democratic society. The counsellor also will be working with underlying assumptions more fitting for an authoritative relationship than the democratic.

This variability may help in the understanding of apparent anomalies and differences in the general nature of the counselling relationship as it can be traced through history, and as it may be seen in relation to different types of personality and to different countries today. The Ten Commandments were given to a people in the immature stage of social maturity, just emerging from a long period of slavery, and their main 'counsel' was in terms of 'Thou shalt not ——'. At a more advanced stage of personal and social development the descendants of the same people were given much more positive, but still directive, 'counsel' by Jesus, such as 'Thou shalt ——', and 'Do this ——'. But He pointed to the still more advanced stage of human development and promised the further gift of the Holy Spirit to lead men into all truth (John 16$^{7-15}$).

These three stages, each built on and given in fulfilment of all that had gone before, are eloquently described by the writer of the letter to the Hebrews: 'God, who at sundry times and in divers manners spake in time past unto the fathers by the prophets, hath in these last days spoken unto us by his Son, whom he hath appointed heir of all things' (1$^{1-2}$), and 'The Holy Ghost also is a witness to us: for after that he had said before, This is the covenant that I will make with them after those days, saith the Lord, I will put my laws into their hearts, and in their minds will I write them' (10$^{15-16}$).

During the last thirty years there has been a very great development in the understanding of the proper aims and methods of all kinds of personal counselling, as the inner workings of the human mind have become better known. The Counsellor-at-Law has earned an increasingly honoured place in the community. Personnel managers and vocational guidance experts are doing important work in Industry. Schoolmasters are seeing more in their calling than the teaching of 'the three R's' to the young. Psychiatrists and physicians are doing more and more counselling as part of their daily work, and the growing experience of social workers and almoners, and child guidance experts, has brought a great advance in our understanding of the many aspects, and the aims and objects of personal counselling. Pastoral counselling in its modern form has profited very greatly from the experience of practically all of these other counsellors, and is also offering its own contribution to these other related fields of counselling work. It is also developing more than has ever been possible in all its history from constant critical reviews of its own methods and results. With the technical help of the tape recorder and similar instruments, it is now possible to preserve accurate records of whole interviews and series of interviews, from the study of which the valid principles and methods of good counselling can be established, and training of new counsellors carried out. Typical records are now being transcribed and published, with safeguards against recognition, for study in any part of the world.

In many countries the Church is only beginning to become aware of and to make any adequate use of the rapidly expanding knowledge and experience available for this important work. Many Christian ministers and laymen are quietly doing some good pastoral counselling in spite of all kinds of difficulties, but Christian ministers in general are still given all too little official education in these countries in matters concerning the understanding of people, and particularly in modern counselling techniques. They are launched into the community among troubled and even mentally ill people, and compelled to learn for themselves how to deal with them. It is one of the aims of this book to offer some help in this delicate and far-reaching work.

It is the experience of all skilled counsellors that the problem presented by the client is generally not the real one, but the 'outward and visible sign' of an inner and more fundamental personality problem. If the presenting problem is dealt with—by 'good advice', or 'moral support', or by 'having a word' with a supposedly offending party, any apparent relief is generally short-lived. The deeper personality problem or deficiency will show itself in further personal or social upsets, and the client (and his relatives) will move another step down the road to despair.

As we have seen in the first section of this book, we do not know our own minds very well, we are far less 'rational' and consistent than we like to think, and strongly influenced by emotions, habits, customs, conventions, and prejudices, of which we are mostly unaware. When these dynamic forces get out of balance or in conflict in a person he will often feel and act in ways that are difficult for him, or anyone else, to understand. When, in spite of well-meant, but superficial advice he finds himself more bewildered and in still greater conflict with his fellow-men, it is inevitable that he should become disillusioned and even cynical. But with modern counselling methods it is possible to help such personal and social misfits to gain real insight into their inner feelings and attitudes, and then to redirect their destructive and conflicting urges to positive creative ends.

The aim of modern Pastoral Counselling, as of most other kinds of personal counselling, and of social case-work, is not to give advice, nor is it to provide ready-made solutions to various personal problems. That kind of 'help' would deprive the client of what may well be his best or only chance of gaining insight into his inner attitudes and prejudices and his real needs. It would also tend to make him dependent on the counsellor when further difficulties make their appearance.

The whole aim of Pastoral Counselling is to create a personal relationship of such quality that the client will feel able progressively to unburden his pent-up emotions, and let go his deeply buried psychic defences. In this way alone will most people gain the necessary insight, and sufficient awareness and release of their creative energies. Then they are in a position to look at their problems, and themselves, more objectively, and in further discussion with the counsellor to work out their future attitudes and actions. The experience of such help will generally enable people to grow to greater maturity and social responsibility.

This 'client-centred interview' has proved itself beyond doubt to be the most effective counselling method and principle in the hands of psychiatrists, social workers, vocational guidance experts, and most other counsellors, as well as pastors. It preserves for the client with any actual or potential capacity for doing it, the right and privilege of deciding his own personal attitudes, and taking responsibility for his own choices.

At this point something should be mentioned about the relationship of Pastoral Counselling as undertaken for Christian healing to such other healing and helping activities as the confessional, spiritual direction, social case-work, and the work of the psychiatrist.

In the confessional the Church offers to the penitent sinner the absolution and remission of his confessed sins in the name of God, the Father, the Son, and the Holy Spirit; and the opportunity to begin again a new life. The confessional as generally offered does not seek to build up a personal relationship, nor does it generally involve deep or prolonged discussion, or set out to deal with problems other than the sense of guilt.

Spiritual direction seems to be mainly appropriate for the edification and guidance of the converted, or of people with good insight into their own inner attitudes. In this sense it is an educational rather than a healing activity. In many ways, however, it may approach fairly closely to the later stages of the counselling technique.

Social case-work involves much counselling, and from its nature, and the general quality of the worker-client relationship it is a channel of Christian healing that touches on the work of the pastor in many of its aspects. The social worker deals with people whose presenting problem is mainly economic, domestic, or social, often intensified by illness. But the real problems behind the various presenting ones are very often in the deeper realm of personal character and personal relationships, where the Pastor has an important part to play.

It is inevitable that the pastor will find himself involved in 'social case-work' at times, just as the social worker will find herself in the pastoral field. It is probable that with the further development of both pastoral and social case-work their respective fields will become better differentiated in practice as they now are in theory, the pastor's function being seen as that of ministering to people's deepest personal needs, and the social worker's in the more practical field of administration of the material, technical, and personal resources for social welfare. But however clear the differentiation of their respective functions may be it seems certain that pastor and social worker are destined to work in close collaboration and even to overlap greatly in what they may do in any particular piece of work.

The psychiatrist sets out to bring healing to the mentally ill in various ways, one of which includes a 'client centred' activity closely related in principles and practice with counselling. This section of psychotherapy seeks to help the mentally ill to gain insight into their disturbing and conflicting mental processes. But here again there is bound to be much overlapping in the work of the psychiatrist and the pastor, because there is a vast 'no-man's-land' between frank mental illness and the simpler emotional disturbances that come within the pastor's field of work.

In addition to the difficulty of delineating the frontier between mental health and mental illness, which is great enough, many people will feel the need of pastoral help while they are under the care of psychiatrists for definite mental illness, as they do while under medical care for physical illness. The pastor must therefore be prepared to work in close co-operation with psychiatrists as well as with social workers, and possibly to be a co-ordinating influence between all the professional helpers who may be dealing with the particular person.

But there is one point at which the pastor goes farther than these other helpers. The psychiatrist as such is not specifically concerned with what the person does with his health when he gets it, what life-goal he is aiming at, what purposes he lives for. This is also true of all the other professional helpers. The pastor has the responsibility of going this important step farther, and seeking to help the person to abundant living in his personal life and in his wider relationships —with his fellow-men and with his Creator—to become, in those famous words of Dorothy Sayers, 'a man, among men, in a world that makes sense'.[1]

The actual differentiation between the fields of work of the pastor and the psychiatrist will always be vague and flexible. It will depend partly on the training of the particular pastor, and his ability and suitability for counselling work, partly on the spiritual outlook of particular psychiatrists, and partly on the attitudes and desires of those who need help. It is important, however, that pastors should not in any way try to encroach on the medical field, or set out to enter the ranks of psychotherapists 'by the back door'. They should be trained to recognize the symptoms of mental illness, even in its early stages, and do all they can to see that medical help is obtained. And the more understanding they show in this respect and the more competence in their own field, the more frequently will psychiatrists come to give their co-operation and to encourage their patients to accept pastoral ministrations alongside their psychotherapeutic efforts.

[1] In Preface to *What is Christian Education?* by Reeves and Drewett.

It will be seen that pastoral counselling is an activity which cannot be circumscribed by any definite horizon. It is for every counsellor to keep constantly in mind the need to recognize his own limitations, and the advisability of suggesting other kinds of professional help. It is also most vital that the counsellor should be aware of the other therapeutic and helping resources in the community, and to establish the fullest personal relationships with them, so that good team-work will always be possible. This will be of great educational value to him and of incalculable benefit to those whom he serves.

Some pre-counselling opportunities and requirements. Before counselling in its true sense is possible the client must realize his need for help. People who are brought against their will, or who only come to oblige someone else, are not suitable for counselling unless and until they can come to realize and admit some need. In the same way when the pastor realizes that a particular person needs his help in such an urgent situation that he feels bound to take the intiative by calling or seeking an interview with him, no counselling is possible until that person accepts the offer of help in the spirit of felt need.

There are some important pre-counselling requirements in such cases as these, which have been clearly stated by Seward Hiltner [1] and illustrated by the example of the initiative taken by a pastor when unfavourable rumours were found to be circulating regarding the conduct of one of his prominent church members. The general requirements of a pre-counselling interview may be summarized (following Hiltner) as follows:

Help should be offered in such a way that it can be refused easily and without embarrassment, and asked for later if desired without 'loss of face'.

It should be clear to the client that any attitude he adopts will be understood and accepted, and any possible incorrect expectations on the part of the client should be clearly denied.

The counsellor should then be willing to wait for the client to make the counselling approach spontaneously, even though he may know the client's need and desire for help, and even though he is being urged by the client's relatives to 'do something'.

Beyond the recognition of the need for help the client will also need to realize that the problem concerns himself, at least to some extent, before counselling is possible, and also that the aim of the

[1] *Pastoral Counselling* (Abingdon Cokesbury Press ,1949), pp. 125-31.

counselling is that he shall be assisted to help himself. If he thinks of the counsellor as someone who is going to do something for him, or to offer a ready-made solution to his problem or difficulty, the true aims of the counselling process may have to be made clear to him at some stage in the interview, or else counsellor and client will find themselves working at cross purposes.

Every part of the total work of the minister may be thought of and used as a pre-counselling opportunity, as a way to win the confidence of people in his understanding, acceptance, and ability to help. The average person in trouble will not readily unburden his soul to another person until he feels that he will be understood and accepted without criticism, and above all that everything he says will be kept in sacred confidence. The pastor will seek to win such confidence through his preaching, teaching, and writing, and through personal conversation in visits, interviews, and chance meetings. His conduct of the formal worship and sacraments of the church, and of the various church organizations may also help to win people's confidence in his understanding and discretion. The best of all pre-counselling opportunities, however, is in the good counselling work itself: we are known by our fruits, and many people who come to the pastor for this kind of help do so because they know of others who have been greatly helped through his counselling.

Finally, we may refer to the general methods of making pastoral contact with people and winning confidence, discussed in Chapter 1 of this book, which apply most particularly to the counselling relationship.

The client and his troubles. What kinds of trouble in people are suitable for pastoral counselling, and what types of situation should put the counsellor on his guard? Those questions must be discussed from the point of view of what we may term the presenting problem, which, as we have seen, is often the 'outward and visible sign' of an inner and more fundamental personality problem.

Most of the people who come for counselling help will do so because of some acute crisis or long-standing burden, related to some external or internal situation. Many of them will have tried to deal with the apparent problem without the help of anyone else, or will have tried to take the advice of some relative or friend. In such cases they will generally have used their energies uneconomically and wrongly, and found themselves even more confused and bewildered, often anxious, resentful, and filled with the sense of guilt or failure.

They may have rationalized their own attitudes and become bitter about the attitudes of other people, or 'the Church'. The harder they try to deal with the situation the further they drift toward a paralysing despair. They are lacking in insight mainly because they are emotionally 'pent up', and blocked from release of their tensions by automatic unconscious 'defence mechanisms'. Hence the great value of making pastoral contact with them in the early stages of the trouble.

For purposes of discussion the actual presenting problems may be divided into four main groups. Some of them will fit into more than one of the groups, perhaps all four; and some will also be closely related to the field of work of other professional helpers and call for good co-operative team-work.

The first group will include people who feel a definite need. This may be physical (better housing, clothing, food or finance); or social (companionship or fellowship); educational (marriage or child guidance); or occupational (an actual job, vocational guidance, or something to do to fill in time). The main need of some people will be simply for emotional support or for reassurance.

The second group will include people who seek help in adjusting themselves to a new situation, actual or possible. It may be a broken engagement, the loss of a loved one, a major operation, a long or serious illness in the person or in some near relative or friend; or it may be the approach of blindness or deafness, or the loss of an eye or a limb.

The third group will bring together people who are finding some difficulty in their social relationships. It may be that the client is concerned about the disturbing attitude or behaviour of another person or persons: a wife, husband, child, 'in-laws', neighbours, colleagues, or people with whom he works. On the other hand the client may be conscious of his own shyness, awkwardness, loneliness, or the difficulty of getting on reasonably with other people. There may be difficulty in finding a satisfactory mutual basis for some co-operative work, such as bringing up the children, or budgeting for the housekeeping. The social disharmony may be so great that the client has come up against the law for truancy, delinquency, vandalism, or crime.

In the fourth group we may include people whose main difficulties are felt to be within themselves, although of course they will generally have some disturbing effect on their social relationships.

Some of these people will be distressed by inner tensions. They may feel nervy, jittery, restless, over-sensitive, easily hurt or insulted, anxious, and apprehensive about relatively minor matters, or 'all bottled up', filled with hatred, jealousy, or self-pity. Many of them will find themselves giving way to outbursts of temper, and saying things which they don't really mean, and are sorry for afterwards.

Others will confess to a deep feeling of depression, either from a definite sense of failure or guilt, constant frustration, misfortune, or the sense of futility, or for no apparent reason. The depression may be felt as physical weakness, in which the slightest effort seems to bring utter fatigue, and they are ashamed because they are unable to pull their weight in the home or at work.

Others again will be indecisive, unable to make any decisions, lacking in confidence, or consumed by gnawing doubts. Some of the bewilderment may be of a specifically religious or philosophical nature, or they may be troubled about more practical matters of morality, or of general attitude or behaviour.

Lastly, among those with inner disturbances there will be some who suffer from persistent obsessions or compulsions. Some of them will seem queer or eccentric, and many of these will feel no need for counselling but will try rather to convert the counsellor to their way of thought. Others will be pestered by some persistent or repeated unwelcome thought or insatiable inner urge to gambling, alcohol, or drug addiction, sexual practices of some normal or abnormal kind, incessant activity, or even the desire to harm someone they love. Others again will have the urge to be over-scrupulous in some way, often in religious or moral attitude or behaviour—they 'strain at a gnat and swallow a camel'.

These four groups of troubled people, those who feel a definite need, those who seek help in adjustment to a new situation, those who find difficulty in their social relationships, and those who feel disturbed within themselves, will cover most of the field of therapeutic pastoral counselling. Some of these people will be seen to be more suitable for psychiatric help, and the pastor will be very wise to refer them without delay to their family doctor or to some other appropriate source of treatment. The most obvious indications of the various types of mental illness should be well known to all who do pastoral work, and they will be discussed in a later chapter of this book.

It will be clear that many of these difficulties we have described are faced and overcome by numbers of people without any personal help at all. People get into difficulties often because they have not learned to deal adequately with the inevitable stresses of life, because their point of view is too narrow, rigid, or short-sighted. But it is generally the best they know, and they are convinced that their attitudes are those which any sensible person would take. In this they lack the necessary objective insight for proper adaptation to life.

There are some kinds of people with whom the pastor should be very cautious about counselling. The most important of these are of course the mentally ill, in which group we may include people who are found to have shown sudden changes in character or personality, people with bizarre religious attitudes, and also people who have had previous counselling or psychotherapy without obvious result. Some pastoral help may be offered to such people, but no attempt should be made to give counselling except in full co-operation with a psychiatrist. The aged and ageing, and those who are having 'involutional troubles', are also unsuitable in most cases for counselling, except in full co-operation with their physician. The same applies to people who are physically ill. They may be offered simple pastoral help, but no attempt should be made to give counselling except with the fullest co-operation with their medical practitioner.

In some cases the pastor will find it very difficult to decide whether the trouble is within his field or whether it is an expression of mental illness more suitable for the psychiatrist. Many people suffering from various forms of neurosis or psychosis can be very plausible indeed, and the inexperienced pastor may find himself more deeply involved in their tangled situation than he had anticipated. In particular the pastor should be very cautious in his responses to people who make serious accusations against one or more other people. Many of these may turn out to be of a delusional character. Paranoid psychoses are more common than is generally realized, and many of them are not serious or troublesome enough to warrant committal to an institution. The more intense delusional states are generally fairly easy to recognize by the wide range and bizarre character of the accusations, but the milder forms may be much more difficult.

In cases of real doubt which do not seem to warrant an immediate recommendation for medical advice it may be helpful to allow a few counselling interviews with great care to keep to the methods which will be suggested in a later part of this chapter, and then to review the situation and decide whether or not to allow it to continue. In particular it is important for the counsellor to refrain from agreeing or disagreeing with the accusations, and from any expression of condemnation of those who may be accused. It is also most important that he resist the temptation to give any specific advice in the situation. When one particular person is named as the 'villain' it may help to ask whether that person would like to come for a talk with the pastor. In such cases it should be made clear that the purpose of such a discussion is simply to find out how the other person feels about the situation, not to regard him as an accused person who is expected to defend himself. The counsellor must always keep clear of any attempt to make him into a judge, and still more of any involvement in the client's personal attitudes or actions.

To give one example, we may take the case of a woman who came to a counsellor for help in dealing with what she described as a sadistically cruel husband. She poured out a very convincing story of long-standing domestic tension, and of her own patient, devoted, and even sacrificial efforts to restore the relationship. She accused her husband of repeated acts of infidelity, and asserted that his acts of cruelty were simply designed to make her leave him. She had been to more than one lawyer, but accused each one of them of taking her husband's part. The husband was quite willing to come and it was soon quite obvious that his wife was suffering from a paranoid psychosis, for which she had had repeated psychiatric treatment.

The counsellor and his attitudes. Even the simplest kind of interview, for such a straightforward purpose as the sale or puchase of something, or the obtaining of purely technical information, is affected to some extent for good or ill by the feelings and attitudes of the participants. But when the interview is undertaken for the purpose of helping someone in a deeply personal problem the feelings and attitudes of the participants become the dominant factor in the whole enterprise. As the client in most cases of pastoral counselling is in a state of some emotional conflict and tension, and extremely vulnerable to the feelings and attitudes of other people, it is clear that the attitudes of the counsellor will always have the most profound effect on the whole outcome of the counselling.

When we remind ourselves that all human beings have their inner emotional conflicts, tensions, and vulnerabilities, and that the counsellor, being human, has his share of them, it is clear that he has a very great responsibility to do all that is possible to minimize the influence of his own attitudes throughout the counselling project. This is made even more difficult when we remember that many people have the urge to help in the solution of other people's problems as an unconscious compensation for their own sense of inferiority, failure, or frustration. When they are unaware of this, or unable or unwilling to accept it, they are all the more likely, without realizing it, to project their negative attitudes into the counselling situation, and thus to do more harm than good to many troubled people.

Beyond the special knowledge and wisdom, and the understanding of human nature needed by most technical consultants, the good counsellor will therefore need a deep and objective understanding of himself. He will need to be thoroughly aware of his own limitations, his uncritical assumptions and desires, and in general his emotional needs. Only then can he give the steady consistent leadership which will release the healing forces in the client.

This inner awareness is an elusive and very difficult quality to achieve. Doctors do not generally embark upon the career of psycho-analyst until they have submitted themselves to a prolonged analysis, and the same principle holds for the would-be counsellor. It is very greatly to his advantage, and to the advantage of his future clients, that he should open his soul fully and deeply to an experienced counsellor for the purpose of being helped to the most complete self-awareness.

It will also help greatly if, while watching the client's reactions in counselling interviews he constantly watches his own, and asks himself the right questions about them. 'Why', he may ask, 'did that remark, or that mannerism, stir up feelings of hostility in me?' Or 'Am I being over-protective to this person—and why?' The continual honest facing of such questions as these will help him to learn all the time from his work and from his clients, and it will help still more if he can find opportunities for facing them with his colleagues from time to time.

Many of his attitudes may appear to the counsellor as good Christian qualities, such as compassion, righteousness, or the burning desire to help people. The desire to be of use is a deep and divinely altruistic quality in man, and the development of honest self-respect and self-regard through the creative service of others seems to be an essential part of God's own design for human society. Compassion and righteousness are good Christian qualities as long as they are kept in the perspective of the long-term welfare of the persons who come for help.

Here is an example of the faulty use of compassion. In the course of her narrative a woman confesses to a haunting fear that she may be in the early stages of insanity, a very common anxiety among troubled people. The keen and sympathetic counsellor rushes in with appropriate reassurances, backed by good logical reasoning. But he is disappointed to find that the client's anxiety seems even greater, and he is then faced with an acute dilemma. Is he to go on repeating the reassurance at every demand for it, or should he stifle the discussion by refusing to do so? The counselling process has become sidetracked into a personal conflict and the client's recovery greatly delayed.

This woman will have had some deep and, to her, convincing reasons for her anxiety, many of which she has not yet found courage enough to talk about, some of which she may not yet be aware of. Every effort at reassurance is countered by the inner conviction that if the counsellor could know why she feels as she does he would not be able to reassure her, and yet she feels an inner compulsion to demand words of reassurance.

The counsellor's reassurance was a response of sentimentality rather than wisdom; he was not then in a position to understand the woman's feelings, and his function was to find and deal with causes rather than symptoms. He might have encouraged her to go on unburdening by a simple comment showing understanding and acceptance of her feelings, such as 'You feel sometimes that things are getting beyond you', or possibly, 'Perhaps you could tell me more about this feeling, and the things which have made you feel that way'. The fact that her feelings are accepted without any horrified surprise will give all the reassurance that she can take at this stage, and pave the way for any later interpretation which may be required.

This example shows how delicate the work of counselling can be, and how the counsellor's best efforts can be spoilt by some of his apparently noble qualities. His compassion needs to be tempered with the disciplined patience of the searcher for better understanding and long-term welfare, or it may easily degenerate into sentimentality which sacrifices the ultimate welfare for a specious reassurance.

Perfectionism or over-conscientiousness is another common quality in the Christian pastor, minister or layman, which may all too easily project itself into the counselling relationship and do considerable harm. Many religious people have had a fairly strict, even repressive upbringing, and their 'super-ego' may well become over-dominant as a result. Of course it is perfectly normal to have high ideals and worthy ambitions and conscientiously to try to live up to them. But it is all too easy for such ideals to creep stealthily above their 'station' and to become insatiable demands.

The counsellor will generally be unaware of this subtle change, but he will feel the results of it in a constant state of emotional tension. His work will appear important to him, as it should, but he will go beyond that view of it to the false view that it is indispensable. He will then lose the ability to relax and play, which is bad for his health, harmful to his wife and growing children, and to the people with whom he undertakes counselling. They will see in him no 'treasure hidden in a field', no 'pearl of great price', and the Holy Spirit will not flow through him as it should. Life, as they sense it in him, will appear almost unlivable to them, and his counselling will be greatly hindered, even though he may not consciously try to impose his rigid standards on them.

But the constant sense of inferiority and failure which goes with this perfectionism will make it virtually impossible for this kind of counsellor to avoid judging or envying other people, in spite of his frequent self-criticism and his acceptance of the Christian admonition about removing the plank from one's own eye before looking for splinters in a neighbour's eye. 'From envy, hatred, malice, and all uncharitableness' he needs the good Lord's deliverance. Only then will he become human enough to love and accept other people and to leave their inner attitudes and feelings to their own consciences, enlightened by the Holy Spirit as radiated through him. Without the radiation of love, joy and peace, and the other 'fruits of the Spirit' any client may well be sceptical of the spiritual endowment of the counsellor.

Another possible result of a rigid repressed upbringing is that the counsellor may have failed to reach a satisfactory sexual adjustment in his own life. Unless he can bring the highest spiritual resources to this situation he will be compelled to ignore or suppress many powerful urges within him, which will bring some deep emotional needs. If he is an introspective, over-conscientious person these difficulties will be intensified by an elusive but profound sense of guilt. Tensions and conflicts of this kind, and any others, need to be talked out fully and frankly with an able and experienced counsellor for the pastor's own sake and for the sake of the whole of his ministry.

If the counsellor finds undue pleasure in the relationship with a client of the opposite sex he should regard it as a real danger signal and be very constantly on his guard. One of the difficulties in all counselling of troubled people is to prevent the client from becoming too attached to the counsellor and too dependent on him, and this will be greatly increased when there is any emotional attraction on the counsellor's side, however much it may be rationalized. It will also interfere greatly with the counselling by making the counsellor too protective.

When the counsellor has a healthy awareness of his limitations he will not attempt to take the sole responsibility for dealing with people who may need a psychiatrist or physician, a lawyer or a social worker, or perhaps a more experienced counsellor. There may be an important part for the counsellor to play in co-operation with any such other helper and this will be to the counsellor's lasting benefit as well as that of the client.

The counselling technique. As with interviewing, discussed in Chapter 4, there can be no set rules which will apply to all types of counselling, but there are some principles which have been found to be valid, and some methods which have been proved to be helpful as long as they do not interfere with spontaneity, flexibility, and friendliness. For purposes of description the counselling technique is divided into successive stages, but in actual practice there will always be considerable overlapping between the different parts, and sometimes there will be a return to an earlier stage when the need for it arises.

The client's first impression should be of a calm, restful, unhurried atmosphere, and a warm but simple welcome. He should be offered a comfortable chair, and given time to settle down and collect his thoughts. If unknown to the counsellor he should be asked to give his name and address, and a few simple particulars about himself and his reasons for seeking help. This will lead naturally to the invitation to give an account of what is troubling him.

While the counsellor is taking in the details of the story he will also be doing something much more important—and difficult. His main purpose at this stage is to 'feel into' the client's emotions, and everything else is subservient to that task. He will be watching the facial expressions of the client, the movements of his hands and of any other parts of his body. He will be listening to catch every shade of feeling from what the client says, the inflexions of his voice and the way he tells the story. He will think of the various items in the narrative in terms of what they mean to the client. He will do nothing to impede the flow of emotional unburdening, even if at this stage it is little more than a torrent of hostile abuse. An occasional question expressing interest and acceptance will often help any initial hesitations in the client.

The one great purpose of this part of the counselling interview is that the counsellor should come to understand, not so much what has happened to the client, but how the client feels about everything. He will keep the actual facts at the back of his mind for future use if necessary, but the whole counselling technique is based on the conviction that the necessary insight cannot generally be achieved by the client until he has been given the opportunity to unburden all his pent-up feelings, conscious and then unconscious ones, which will often find their way into consciousness as the unburdening proceeds in the permissive accepting relationship.

At any pause in the narrative the counsellor will take the opportunity to show the client that all his feelings are understood and accepted without criticism by the kind of brief comment which summarizes what feelings the client has communicated, which may be quite different from what he has said. For example the client may have said in heartfelt tones: 'Why should this happen to me?' What he is communicating is not the desire for a philosophical explanation, but the feeling of anguish; and the appropriate comment from the counsellor would not be an attempted answer to the question but an acceptance of the feeling, such as 'You feel pretty sore about it'. The counsellor must make his comment in such a manner that he communicates the understanding and acceptance, and this communication is also more important than the actual words used. In this way the client is encouraged to go on unburdening, a process which is known as catharsis.

In this 'creative listening', a relationship of what is called empathy is expressed and built up by the counsellor. It has been described as a progressive 'feeling into' the client's feelings, not with any idea of agreeing or disagreeing, supporting or rejecting, praising or blaming, but simply discerning, understanding, and accepting.

This part of the counselling process requires considerable time, patience, and self-control, particularly when the client strays off the main point into all kinds of apparently irrelevant detail. He will often look for emotional support from the counsellor through some such question as 'What else could I have done?', or 'Don't you think that was pretty mean?' But the counsellor should keep clear of judgements. In any case there has been no chance of

o

hearing the other sides of the story, and he is a healer and not a judge.

The best kind of response to such questions is generally to make a simple comment which shows acceptance of the feeling. In these two cases the comments might be, 'You did everything possible about it', and 'It wasn't what you would have expected from him (or her)'. Such comments generally encourage further unburdening. If the counsellor tries to stop such appeals for support by such a comment as 'Look here old chap, you mustn't ask me to pass judgement', it may well appear to the client as lack of acceptance, and hinder the essential flow of feeling. After all the client is entitled to ask for support if he wishes to do so.

If the counsellor has some touchy and vulnerable points in his own personality he may easily find himself on the defensive in the face of any hostile attitudes, and he may unwittingly project his own moralistic demands and his emotional needs into the counselling relationship. If so he will generally switch the whole process off the track into a personal argument and put an emotional barrier between himself and the client. This will hold up, and may even defeat, the whole purpose of this part of the interview, which is to allow the most deeply pent-up feelings to discharge themselves, and thus to make way for insight.

Another danger at this stage is that, in his desire to help, the counsellor may be over-protective. Few of us have entirely outgrown the romantic ideals of our childhood, and the vision of the 'knight in shining armour' coming to the rescue of the 'beautiful damsel in distress'. When a nice girl begins to unburden some painful material with the partially protective introduction, 'You'll think I've been very foolish', it may be very tempting for the modern 'knight-errant' to rush in with utterly premature reassurances and 'understandings'. This may block a difficult and painful unburdening, but one without which a deep sense of guilt or hostility may go on festering in the client's personality. Here again a simple comment, such as 'You don't feel particularly happy about it', is nearer to the truth, and will generally be far more helpful in the long run than any impulsive premature reassurances.

It is inevitable that many clients will project some of their pent-up hostility, and some of their frustrated love on to the counsellor; perhaps each of them alternately. This is called transference, negative and positive respectively, and if handled without 'counter-transference' it may be used to help in the client's insight and growth. If it stirs up hostility or affection in the counsellor it will do great harm.

This attitude of empathy—feeling into the client's emotions with understanding and acceptance—is the first essential of all good counselling, and this kind of creative listening will provide a unique experience for the client. It is a sad commentary on our human relationships that all his previous efforts to tell somebody how he feels will have produced some advice, often with actual or implied criticism, or an attempt to cheer him up by minimizing the feeling or telling him that other people have the same or worse trouble. Such well-meant efforts generally convey lack of acceptance and often lack of understanding, and add to the burden instead of helping him to meet it. But the dawning realization that the counsellor understands and accepts his feelings, many of which he feels a little ashamed of having, will generally open the flood gates to the progressive release of his pent-up feelings.

As the emotional outpouring goes on, the client will generally begin to let down some of his well-guarded psychic defences, and come to see, possibly for the first time, some of his own faulty attitudes. These may have been obvious to the counsellor much earlier, but any attempt to point them out to the client would have driven him back behind his unconscious defences and made insight much more difficult. It is vital to the counselling technique to realize that insight is something achieved from within through the correct personal relationship, not something imposed from without.

A simple example of this method of handling the early stages of counselling is in the case of a man who came saying that he was in despair about his domestic situation. He and his wife had taken his mother-in-law to live with them and had given her a comfortable home. But now she never stops interfering with their private affairs, and his wife has become a nervous wreck as a result. Mother-in-law has nowhere else to go, and he has tried to reason with her without any success. Now he often loses his temper with her, and then he has two weeping women and two scared children on his hands. Then there is a pause in the story. What kind of comment would be most appropriate?

Some people would offer some advice at this point, such as: 'Couldn't you ignore the interference for the sake of peace?' Others might try to pour oil on the troubled waters by generalizing: 'I know quite a lot of husbands in the same boat.' Others again might offer the moralizing comment: 'You shouldn't lose your temper, that never does any good!'

None of these would help the client at all, he has thought of every one of them already in any case. The most helpful type of comment at this stage would probably be, 'You feel rather bitter about it at times', which simply reflects his feeling and encourages him to go on unburdening. He will probably say something like this, 'Yes, and I don't think she shows much gratitude for what we are doing for her', and the unburdening will go on.

An important stage in the unburdening appears when the client expresses some hint of ambivalence or emotional conflict. The counsellor again reflects back the conflicting feelings by an appropriate comment which shows acceptance, but no judgement. For example when the husband already mentioned came to this point the appropriate comment was: 'You feel these surges of hatred of your mother-in-law, and yet you still have quite a soft spot for her.'

The acceptance and clarification of such contradictory feelings without praise or blame, and without giving advice about them will be of great help to the client. He will probably have had the idea that their presence is an indication of stupidity or weak-mindedness, or even some kind of mental abnormality, and this kind of calm recognition and acceptance will help him to realize their normality better than any attempt to assure him that they are.

This expression of ambivalence will also indicate the dawning of better insight on the part of the client, and, rightly handled, will pave the way for the awareness and expression of further positive feeling, such as: 'But I suppose I have brought some of it on myself.' It is important to be on the look-out for this and to show simple recognition and acceptance without commendation.

The dawning of positive insight will enable the interview to move on from the initial stage of catharsis to the second stage of clarification and interpretation, in which the client may be helped to see himself and his attitudes in better perspective and reality. This may well take the form of suitable creative questions, which will keep him thinking, and participating actively in the discussion. It will also keep the emphasis on the main purpose of the counselling which is to help him to help himself, and it may help to overcome further resistances.

One aspect of the clarification may be achieved by trying to relate the main difficulties and problems to certain patterns of attitude and behaviour laid down earlier in the person's life, and by looking with him past the external factors, which he probably regards as the dominating ones, to the internal strains which have made him so vulnerable to ordinary happenings. In doing these things the counsellor must feel his way cautiously. If the client accepts his question or suggested explanation he can go on, but if it seems to stir up any defensive attitudes it is probably better to go back and encourage a little more catharsis. If the interpretation is ignored it suggests that the particular matter is not exerting any great influence on the client's attitudes.

As an example of this kind of approach to clarification we can take the case of a man who came because of an increasingly difficult domestic situation, which he felt was having a bad effect on the two children as well as on himself and his wife. He unburdened a lot of hostility concerning his wife which he attributed to the feeling that she had been neglecting him for the children ever since their arrival. He had come to the expression of some ambivalence, admitting to considerable love for her and dependence on her as well as the annoyance and hostility, and then he volunteered the positive conviction that he had behaved like a jealous child at times.

The question, 'Did you ever feel that way toward your mother?' opened the way to his growing insight into the real situation, that he had been a little over-dependent on his mother, and therefore drawn to a wife slightly older than himself who 'mothered' him, and was glad to do so because of something in her personality. Their partnership on these terms was mutually satisfactory until the children came. But then his wife found herself with one and then two strongly demanding objects for her mothering, much more naturally demanding on her maternal instinct, and her husband's exclusive dependency came to an end. The rest of the story arose from his hostile reactions to the 'deprivation'.

When this man began thinking along the positive line of seeing his original dependence as a large factor in the production of the vulnerability in his marital relationships his inner creative resources for growth were set free, and the children soon found him a stable father instead of one who competed with them for their mother's affection and attention.

If all this had been pointed out to the client at the beginning he might have recognized some of the factors in the situation, but his unconscious defence mechanisms would more likely have caused him to justify his attitudes, and then he would have failed to do anything positive about this dangerous family situation.

This psychological approach to clarification and interpretation is generally essential, but it will be incomplete unless it is deepened by an attempt to relate the whole situation, thus clarified, to the Christian conception of life—of God, Man, and Society, as it is expressed in the Christian Gospel and embodied in the Person of Jesus Christ. The essential setting for this further clarification and interpretation will have been established already through the counselling relationship of empathy, progressively experienced by the client from the beginning.

People often think of the Christian faith as a set of propositions which must be believed, or a set of rules which must be obeyed. Theology and morality have an important place in the Christian religion, but the essence of the Christian faith is that it is first of all a Gospel: good news of what God has done, is doing, and will continue to do for man, expressed in a Life, in the Person and Attitudes of Jesus, in whom 'the Word was made flesh' and dwelt among men, so that they 'beheld His glory, the glory of the only begotten of the Father, full of grace and truth' (John 1^{14}).

The first essential of Christian counselling is that, sincerely if incompletely, the Word is again and again 'made flesh', and the Spirit of Christian Love 'transfused' into the client through the counselling relationship. Without this any specifically Christian interpretations will be deprived of much of their vivid reality and living power. In this setting of Christian empathy the light, power, deliverance and fellowship of Jesus Christ can be gradually brought to the bewildered and troubled personality of the client, so that they can exert their healing, reconciling, and redeeming influence, and help him to abundant life as described in Chapter 3 of this book.

Specifically Christian interpretation may be offered in various ways. For clients with any knowledge of the life and teaching of Jesus an effective method is through the use of questions, perhaps the favourite method of Jesus Himself. We may point people to facts which are well known or verifiable in their own experience, as Jesus frequently did, and then ask them the appropriate question about these facts of life. This method is illustrated very well in parts of the Sermon on the Mount (Matthew 6^{24-30}, 7^{9-11}).

Another valuable type of question which can be addressed to those who may know something of the life and teaching of Jesus is about

His own attitudes to people. For example a vital question to a person who finds it difficult to feel the reality of Christian forgiveness is: 'Did Jesus ever withhold forgiveness from anyone who sincerely asked for it?'

As far as possible therefore the religious clarifying questions should be about matters of fact—historical facts, and facts about nature and human nature. In this way the client's reasoning will have at least a solid foundation. In the same way information should be given wherever possible in terms of fact rather than belief, of news rather than views.

There are specific Christian interpretations which apply to each of the particular emotional difficulties commonly faced by troubled people, and these will form the subject of the next chapter. But before leaving the question of clarification and interpretation it must be emphasized that pastoral counselling is not based upon any idea that 'Religion' should 'solve' problems. Problems are solved by people, and religion sets out to offer the spiritual resources which they need for the task of 'overcoming evil with good'. Many people have a childish 'dependent' attitude to religion, and imagine that they can use it as a kind of magic formula for escaping the difficulties and hardships of life.

Pastoral counselling is ultimately based on the understanding relationship which should be sought, not only between counsellor and client, but also between them and reality, not in terms of human desire, but rather in terms of the nature and action and will of God as seen in Jesus Christ. In this it is, like priestly healing, an act of worship. This may not be at all clear to the client at the beginning, but with good interpretation it will gradually dawn on him as the counselling proceeds.

As new insights develop and clarify, the client will begin to see their application in more positive attitudes, and still further in creative action. This will then be based on balanced insight and Christian love and dedication, rather than on self-deception and fear. It may be that 'the still, small voice' is heard better and more initiative developed in a period of creative silence, or perhaps in a short, simple and natural prayer. In these final stages of the counselling process the client will grow in wisdom and confidence, and the ability to take fuller responsibility for his own decisions. He will no longer expect more from life than it will give, but will set out eagerly to develop and use his real abilities in the service of his day and generation.

How long should counselling go on? Most counsellors find that up to six sessions of about an hour each are sufficient for the reasonably difficult personal problem. When there is no sign of positive insight after some four to six interviews in which the correct methods have been followed the counsellor should ask himself whether the particular problem may not be more appropriately dealt with by a psychiatrist.

Many people cannot or will not achieve insight through any known counselling technique, but no client should be regarded as hopeless without being offered the best possible chance of finding insight. Of course every counsellor should be aware of the main characteristics of mental illness, and recommend psychiatric or other medical help at once in every suspected case. The subject of mental illness will be considered in Chapter 16.

CHAPTER FOURTEEN

The Christian Approach to some Emotional Disorders

IT MUST be made clear at the beginning of this chapter that in every case the troubled person must be given the fullest opportunity to unburden himself of his pent-up feeling before any attempt to apply 'sweet reason', logic, or any Christian or other interpretations is likely to be effective. All the material in this chapter is intended to be part of the 'clarification and interpretation' stage of counselling, in which the counsellor should always be ready to allow further 'catharsis' when there are any signs of emotional tension in the client. Emotion always tends to distort people's thinking and to make them, at least for a time, inaccessible to even the clearest logical reasoning.

It may also be stated that the counsellor does not set out to help people with such disorders as resentment, guilt, anxiety and frustration in general, but with their particular experience of any or all of these troubles. The general ideas discussed in this chapter are intended to offer some specific help which may be applied by the counsellor as he may find it appropriate when the client is ready to give calm consideration to his difficulties with a real desire for clarification.

As discussed in the last chapter this kind of help is offered in the form of questions, illustrations from life or from human nature, and also in the form of direct information where it seems appropriate. As far as humanly possible the counsellor should avoid direct advice, for reasons which have been considered in the last chapter.

I. RESENTMENT AGAINST LIFE, OR AGAINST GOD

This deep emotional poison is probably an important factor, which is often unrecognized, in the causation and persistence of many physical illnesses, as well as neurotic and psychotic disorders. If we remember that our first and most influential idea of the character of the heavenly Father generally comes from what we see and experience in our human parents, it is easy to see that deprivation of love, security, and reverence for personality in early childhood may well bring about this deep disharmony. In other people it may be the outward and visible sign of a deep sense of guilt, the rationalization of some serious moral lapse, which may not easily be unburdened in the early stages of the counselling.

In many cases, however, this resentment shows itself directly as an intense bitterness, disillusionment (often concerning 'the Church', or one or more 'Christian people'), or self-pity. It may be asserted that God must be either callous or powerless.

'You feel competent to judge God, or life', the client may be asked. 'Can the finite human mind, so "recently" arrived in the age-long pageant of life, pass judgement on the profound mysteries of life and death?' 'Can we find in the life or the teaching of Jesus any suggestion that God is our servant: that life sets out to offer us what we would regard as a "fair deal"?' These are further possible questions on the same theme.

A possible illustration is that in a long and difficult military campaign it always falls to the lot of some of the bravest and most valuable soldiers to bear an entirely disproportionate share of the total hardship and suffering, even though the Commander is neither callous nor powerless. We are like front-line troops in a small section of 'the battle of life', and cannot ever see the whole campaign. Like the good troops in the military campaign we can only trust the Commander, who, in Jesus Christ, has shown Himself worthy of trust in the battle of life.

A possible philosophical contribution is that if goodness meant a kind of indemnity against suffering, then we should tend to be good for what we could get out of it. And then there would be no such thing as 'goodness', because unless goodness is practised for the sake of goodness it ceases to be goodness. As somebody wisely remarked: 'Suffering disinfects our goodness of egotism.'

These of course are only very small nibbles at a profound and many-sided mystery, which has baffled the wisest of men. But they may help to start the client along some fresh avenues of positive thinking if they are offered when the opening appears and not imposed on him in the form of an eloquent sermon. This applies to all the ideas expressed in this chapter.

A second type of question may be found appropriate in some cases: 'Even if we were competent to judge God, are we judging Him fairly?' It may be suggested to the client that he draw up a kind of Balance Sheet of life. On one side he might include all the bad things he suffered from life which he did not deserve, and on the other side all the undeserved good things. The debit side is generally easy to fill, but he may need some help in remembering all the undeserved good things. What about fire, electricity, agriculture, art, music, literature, law, medicine, and all the other benefits freely handed down to us from men and women who worked, suffered, and even died to create and preserve them?

In the face of the very long list of undeserved benefits, which have come to us through our contemporaries, as well as our ancestors, because of our membership of the human family, is it just, or even rational, to dwell predominantly on the bad things which constitute our share in the liabilities of the family? Does it lead us to overlook the fact that many of the bad things can be improved if we will gird our loins and tackle them?

The positive act of remembering God in this way and adequately counting our blessings is a vital act of worship, which will naturally issue in thanksgiving and in its expression in self-giving service. This is the one essential 'cure' of the insinuating disease of self-pity, and an important way to better total health. Some of the emotional energy which had been used in the 'rebellion' will then be redirected to positive creative ends.

II. RESENTMENT AGAINST OTHER PEOPLE

It is important to recognize the resentment of a paranoid mental illness, because it is waste of time and even harmful to try to 'clarify' the paranoid mental processes. They can generally be suspected by the character of the accusations, but these are sometimes very plausible and difficult to detect. The main indication to the counsellor in the doubtful case may be the persistence of the 'unburdening' unrelieved by any evidence of positive insight. This alone should lead him to consider the advisability of psychiatric help.

Personal resentment assumes for him who bears it the ability and the right to judge other people, and we may therefore consider the questions: 'Are we competent to judge other people?' 'Can we penetrate deeply enough into any human personality to be able to assess at their true value all the different influences which have combined to produce the attitude and conduct to which we object?'

Such questions may help the resentful person to see the possibility that the offender might have done what he did for a set of reasons which appeared to him adequate, even if he were mistaken or misguided. The critic may also come to see that he is not so faultless himself as to be fit to cast a stone. The trouble with all human relationships is that we all have a convenient blind spot regarding our own inconsistencies and very clear vision of those of other people. It is all too easy to condemn, but condemnation only stirs up more defensive rationalizations in the other person, which widens the breach still farther.

The resentful person may also be helped to see that he is 'cutting off his nose to spite his face', that the nursing of ill will poisons the personality to an extent far beyond the realization of most people, and may even help to bring about physical and mental illness.

But in spite of the fullest opportunities of unburdening and all the clarification that can be given, people still go on hating. As Nicolai Berdyaev has grimly maintained: 'The world is poisoned by hatred'. This is one form of what is called in the Bible, 'possession by an evil spirit'. As Jesus said to Nicodemus: 'Spirit gives birth to spirit' (John 3⁶), and this surely applies to evil as well as good spirits.

Anything more than a temporary and superficial hatred is an evil and tenacious thing, and the overcoming of evil with good is always a costly business. To overcome such hatred it takes nothing less than an active unquenchable persistent sacrificial goodwill. That is of course what the Christian understands by love, and it is found in its supreme beauty and power in the Person of Jesus Christ. It is reflected in men and women in every age, through whom His spirit has enlightened, inspired, and redeemed mankind.

Beyond all His idealism He is the supreme realist of all time, and here as elsewhere the best findings of modern psychological research are but echoes of the deep insights expressed two thousand years ago in the life and teaching of this amazing Carpenter.

Jesus had the most profound insight into the whole question of personal relationships, and where anyone imagines that he knows better it can be suggested that he will find on further reflection that he has failed to allow for some of the less obvious but inescapable facts of life. His teaching about hatred may be recommended to the resentful client to ponder over (Matthew 7¹⁻⁵, John 8⁷, Matthew 5²⁰⁻⁶, ⁴³⁻⁸, Matthew 6¹²⁻¹⁵).

But Jesus did more than teach the value and power of unquenchable Christian love. He practised what He preached, hating injustice and wrong but loving the wrongdoer. He bore no ill will even through the extreme provocations of injury, humiliation, desertion, betrayal, and crucifixion. In the very shadow of Calvary, His attitude found eloquent expression in the famous prayer: 'Father, forgive them, for they know not what they do' (Luke 23^{34}).

In that living and vivid picture of God, who forgives men and women to an extent far beyond anything they can do to be worthy of it, is there something which can tug strongly at the soul of resentful man? Can it lift him above the common human attitude of 'I'll get even', and win him to the deep conviction that 'I, who have been so forgiven cannot be content until I can forgive my neighbour in the same way'. This is the great ideal pointed to in the parable of the unforgiving debtor (in Matthew 18$^{21-35}$).

If, as sometimes happens, the client finds it difficult to believe that men and women have been forgiven beyond their deserving, a simple bodily illustration may be offered. Here is a man who 'sins grievously' against his stomach by eating and drinking far more than he should of completely unsuitable materials, so that he gives himself an acute attack of gastritis. But within a day or two the effects of the 'sin' are completely removed, and he is 'forgiven' without any deserving on his part.

Another possible illustration is that a good human being will forgive a wrong even though the wrongdoer neither does nor can do anything to deserve it. If we, being evil, can do that, how much more will God do so?

These are but a few of the relevant aspects of a vast subject which demands and deserves all the thought and study that can be given to it. But in conclusion it may be stated with conviction that if there is any better or more practical ultimate 'remedy' for hatred than the Christian Religion, sacrificially expressed and clearly expounded, the world has not yet heard of it. And who can measure the world's need for this 'remedy'?

III. THE SENSE OF GUILT OR FAILURE

As with resentment we must exclude from this account any people who may suffer from what is called neurotic guilt, and the sense of guilt or failure associated with the affective psychosis known as melancholia. Here again they can be recognized partly by the rather exaggerated or bizarre nature of their feelings, and partly by the fact that they do not show evidence of any positive insight after several counselling sessions.

Many people find it difficult to unburden themselves of their deepest feelings of guilt because they are so ashamed of them, and in some cases because they have previously unburdened themselves at some cost to their pride, and found little or no understanding or acceptance. Some people seem to have grown up with a very distorted idea of God, which endows Him with an almost sadistic revengeful spirit, which would be unbecoming even to an average human being.

Many people everywhere find great relief from the burden of guilt through the ministry of the Church. The love and forgiveness of God have been made real to man through worship and sacrament over the last two thousand years at least, and confession and absolution have brought healing to the human soul from very early times, long before the emergence of psychiatry, and to an extent far beyond its power. But sometimes people fail to experience the reality of forgiveness through the religious approach by itself: they need pastoral as well as priestly healing.

Some of these people will come to discover in good counselling that they are prevented from feeling the full reality of forgiveness by the haunting realization that they can never wholly undo the wrong. At this point the simple reminder that they are in very good company, that of the whole human race, that nobody can ever wholly undo any wrong, may bring a new light on the situation, and a change from despair to a new hope.

The Christian religion, based on reality in its view of man and his life, does not ask for impossible conditions in its offering of forgiveness of sins. The essential condition is not life-long remorse, but repentance: change of attitude to the whole of life. It involves facing the sin honestly and humbly, being willing to 'take our medicine', to do all that we can to make amends, and to express our changed attitude still further by forgiving all who may have injured us in any way. Then, in faith and gratitude, we may accept the forgiveness of God and make a fresh start in life, freed from the burden, and all the better in character and understanding for the experience.

The parable of the prodigal son, which might be more appropriately called the parable of the forgiving father, provides a perfect illustration of this realistic Christian attitude to the sins and stupidities of men and women. The father was always ready to restore the relationship which had been broken by the son's attitudes, but this could not happen until the son 'came to himself', until he faced the real truth honestly and humbly, that he had thrown away his right to sonship. His request to be made as one of his father's hired servants was no easy matter for one of the 'aristocracy'; and it showed his changed attitude, and opened the door for the father's gracious restoration, beyond any possible 'deserving'.

Here is a simple human example in the form of a modern 'parable'. A little boy went to the glass-fronted cabinet in the drawing-room and picked up a piece of Dresden china, a priceless family heirloom, not realizing that it had any particular value, although he had been told not to touch anything in the cabinet. His father happened to come into the room, and the boy, startled by his appearance, dropped the piece, and broke it beyond repair, and seeing his father's expression, came sobbing to him.

The good father may have something to say about meddling, but he does not demand the impossible from the child, the replacement of the heirloom, or compensation for its loss. He takes the burden of the 'sin' on his own shoulders, forgives the child far beyond the child's power to be 'worthy of forgiveness', and restores the relationship. If the child then goes about day after day weighed down by what the father has been glad to forgive, it will only increase the burden on the father's heart.

If a fallible human parent can be so loving and merciful as to accept the burden of his child's wrongdoing and to forgive so freely, how much more will the heavenly Father forgive us His children, not because we can ever deserve it, but through His 'manifold and great mercy'? And can we see that any unwillingness on our part to accept the forgiveness in the spirit in which it is offered is only adding to the total burden of life in the heart of the Creator?

We may carry the human illustration a little farther and remind ourselves that the sensible human parent does not expect complete success from his child's every effort. He is very proud of the child who will come to him and say: 'I didn't get it right, but I'm going to try again.' We may surely believe that God expects from us, His children, not constant success, but constant trying: doing our best in spite of failures, and not expecting the impossible from other people.

Finally, we may remind ourselves that it is impossible for anyone to have the inner tranquillity which comes from harmony with life while he is allowing himself to nurse ill will against anyone else. This has been abundantly confirmed by the psychiatrists, but it was seen and expressed with unmistakable clarity by Jesus some two thousand years ago, and this great fact has been affirmed by men and women ever since then in the Lord's Prayer, not always with full realization of its implications (Matthew 6¹²).

IV. ANXIETY AND APPREHENSIVENESS

Anxiety is a universal human attribute, a negative product of the faculty of imagination. It may be described as the 'black sheep of the family' of fear: the degradation of the essential and valuable protective mechanism of fear to the useless destructive futility of worry. Fear generally has a definite object, which, as Paul Tillich points out, 'can be faced, analysed, attacked, endured'.[1] 'One can act upon it,' he continues, 'and in acting upon it participate in it—even if in the form of struggle. In this way one can take it into one's self-affirmation.'

Anxiety, on the other hand, has no definite object to grapple with. It is generally not even concerned with a present danger, but rather with an elusive, indefinite, ghostly threat of some future danger. And yet, to a varying degree, it produces much the same effects on the body as fear, charging it up for immediate action which in this case is premature and unnecessary. It thus produces a harmful state of tension which may have serious effects if frequently repeated.

Paul Tillich[2] draws a distinction between existential anxiety, which is referable to human existence itself, and pathological anxiety, which is referable to the various experiences, conflicts and tensions associated with the individual and social living of human beings. He rightly points out that pathological anxiety, which includes neurotic and psychotic anxiety, is the concern of medicine and psychiatry, and not the concern of the minister as minister, although he must be fully aware of it, and although he may radiate healing power for mind and body and help to remove it.

Existential anxiety on the other hand, bound up as it is with the principles of pure being, cannot be removed, but may be an object of priestly help (it seems clear that he includes pastoral help in this), so that it can be taken up into what he calls 'the courage to be'. Tillich divides this existential anxiety into three forms: the anxiety of fate and death, the anxiety of emptiness and meaninglessness, and

---

[1] *The Courage to Be* (Nisbet, 1952).   [2] ibid.

the anxiety of guilt and condemnation. It is clear that the necessary help in excessive anxiety of this kind must be dependent on philosophical and religious considerations beyond the reach of science as such.

The necessary help in pathological anxiety, on the other hand, is generally dependent on psycho-dynamic considerations mostly subconscious and beyond the direct reach of philosophical and religious considerations. Many apparent failures of religion to help anxious people are certainly due to the overlooking of this distinction. When any degree of pathological anxiety has been analysed and dealt with by the psychiatrists there may still remain some excessive existential anxiety which will then be more open to priestly and pastoral help. The two forms of anxiety will inevitably tend to overlap.

What then is the Christian counsellor to offer his client when the time comes for clarification and interpretation in the counselling process? Not an eloquent statement of complex philosophy, nor a profound interpretation of religious dogma, but rather a simple picture of Jesus Christ the greatest power in heaven and earth for the overcoming of anxiety. This picture is offered first in the quality of the counselling relationship, and this is further delineated by the well-considered questions and statements of the counsellor.

Jesus Himself lived a life of complete control of anxiety, 'the courage to be', and also went up and down the Palestinian countryside helping other people to do the same. With unerring insight He gave to mankind in a few brief sentences, an account of the basic nature and the essential control of anxiety which has never been bettered.

He went to the inner cause of 'existential anxiety' in the saying 'Ye cannot serve God and mammon, therefore I say unto you, Be not anxious for your life' (Matthew 6$^{24-5}$). To the extent to which we try to serve mammon rather than God, to put ourselves, our loved ones, our possessions or our reputations at the centre of life where God ought to be, threats to our existence or security (or theirs) will inevitably generate anxiety.

In His portrayal of the Kingdom of God—the one kind of society which combines freedom and order, and preserves the infinite value of the individual and the welfare of society in dynamic equilibrium—He pointed to the reconciliation of individualism and collectivism which will remove many of the causative factors in anxiety.

And recognizing how premature is the emotional and physical

P

tension of worry, He said: 'Be not . . . anxious for the morrow. . . . Sufficient unto the day is the evil thereof' (Matthew 6³⁴).

The 'prescription' of Jesus for the control of anxiety follows naturally: 'Deny [or disown] yourself, take up your cross, and follow me' (Matthew 16²⁴), 'Seek ye first the Kingdom of God' (Matthew 6³⁶). Put God at the centre where He belongs, and life will make sense.

Beyond all His offering of knowledge about the meaning and purpose of life, of God, Man, and Society, Jesus also won the faith of people so that they committed their lives to His leadership. Above all, by His complete devotion to them, He ignited in their hearts the all-consuming fire of love.

These three great qualities—knowledge, faith, and love—are the three great weapons available to us through Jesus Christ in achieving, and helping others to achieve, the control of anxiety. To illustrate their practical application we may remind ourselves of the manner in which the British people faced the overwhelming 'existential anxiety' of the German 'blitzkrieg' of 1941. Here is an example of the way in which millions of ordinary people faced and overcame the most intense and prolonged threat to their very existence.

They were given knowledge. They knew where they stood, and they were promised 'blood, toil, tears, and sweat', appropriately reminiscent of what Jesus promised His disciples.

They found faith—faith in themselves and in each other, faith in Winston Churchill and his Government, faith in God. For many of them faith in God may have been vague and uncertain, but there was in all of them the divine instinct of human freedom and dignity, the deep if unspoken conviction that even death itself was preferable to life under the Nazi regime.

They also found love: an amazing comradeship which broke through the traditional British reserve beyond all expectations. We have seen that anxiety charges up the body for immediate action. The British people discharged that tension in the most positive and creative manner, by giving their active devoted service to their fellows in whatever way they could, as air-raid wardens, members of bomb-disposal squads, and in ambulances, canteens, and a variety of other essential services.

We could summarize it by suggesting that knowledge illuminates anxiety (and thus reduces 'fear of the unknown'), faith neutralizes it, and love casts it out (1 John 4¹⁸).

To apply these great assets most effectively we need first of all to make a definite committal of a self-disowning kind, then to undertake a programme of disciplined training in the fellowship of other committed people under the best kind of leadership, and then to find ways of expressing our committal in appropriate action. It is significant that this is the kind of programme which has been found necessary for the generation of morale in the armed services, where it is of life-and-death importance. The Church can offer a programme of the same kind.

It may be stated in conclusion that courage is by no means an exclusively Christian virtue, but when high courage is joined with Christian faith and love it will do more than bring control of anxiety, it will inspire others to stronger faith and love and it may turn apparent defeat into far-reaching victory, as it did at Calvary.

V. FRUSTRATION AND FUTILITY

In the counselling of troubled people these two emotional disorders, the sense of frustration with or without that of futility, will be very frequently unburdened. In some cases the actual unburdening will be sufficient to enable the client to see the way through to positive attitudes and actions without any particular interpretation or other help from the counsellor. But when further help is needed for the overcoming of these devitalizing difficulties it may be useful to look with the client at the way in which great men have tackled them.

To take the sense of frustration first, St Paul provides a most helpful example. His efforts were opposed at every turn, not only by his enemies, but even on many occasions by the leaders of the early Christian Church. Much of his life was beset by difficulties, hardships and frustrations (2 Corinthians 11[24-9]). Imagine his feelings in a Roman prison, chained to a Roman jailer. Most of us, with St Paul's passion for doing a job well, would have regarded such a calamity as a complete frustration. But St Paul was not the man to cry over spilt milk. He accepted the situation and then considered what good use he could make of it. He used the 'gift' of time in prison to write some remarkable letters which are still read all over the world and increasingly treasured. His contact with the jailer brought about a radical change in that man's life.

In spite of all the apparent frustrations St Paul succeeded in becoming one of the greatest evangelists of all time, because of the way he looked at and dealt with his frustrations. He knew what he was saying when he wrote to the Romans: 'Who shall separate us from the love of God? Shall tribulation, or distress, or persecution, or famine, or nakedness, or peril, or sword? . . . Nay, in all these things we are more than conquerors through Him that loved us' (Romans 8$^{35-7}$).

The early Christians were persecuted and dispersed, but again they saw their difficulties as opportunities for greater spread of their faith, and became 'more than conquerors' in spite of frustrations.

The biographies of great men and women illustrate the fact that such people have not left their mark on the world because their ways were made easy. They succeeded in spite of all kinds of frustration and even apparent defeats. What made them great was their spirit, which refused to admit defeat, and inspired them to keep doing what they could in spite of all apparent frustrations.

When confronted by such examples people will often say: 'That's all very well, but I'm not a St Paul or one of the great!' That may be true, but the same secret of life and the same power to become 'more than conquerors' which these people used is available to all men.

Our duty then in every kind of circumstance is to use the time, talents, resources and opportunities available to us in the best way that we know: to tackle every situation as well as we can and to do what we can to fit ourselves to do better in the future. And that is all! So often we are unwilling to stop at that, we want to produce a certain result, or to prevent something from happening. When we become tangled up with results we are in effect 'trying to play God', to control something beyond our control, and the result is naturally a sense of frustration.

The supreme example of victory over frustration is found of course in Jesus Himself. He was never deflected from His purpose, even by such apparent frustrations as the failure of His disciples, the fickleness of the crowd, and the moral ineptitude of both Jewish and Roman authorities. He did what he could with the opportunities available, and left all the results, or lack of apparent result, in His Father's hands. In that spirit of perfect co-operation with God He faced the agony of the Cross, and transformed the most vivid symbol of defeat into an eternal symbol of victory.

The sense of futility, closely related with that of frustration, is a conception in our minds which is dependent on our attitude to life. It is therefore largely a religious question.

Looking again at the life of Jesus we can see that it was made up of humble and unostentatious acts of service. His patient efforts to teach His disciples about the idea of world brotherhood were apparently futile, because He went to His death without having succeeded in convincing any of them. The 'secular' historians of His time apparently thought His life not worthy of much attention. And yet He has been and is likely to continue to be the most decisive of all influences in human life. Because we do not see immediate or spectacular results, we have no warrant for regarding anything we have done as futile.

The teaching of Jesus, by word and deed, is that we are not isolated individuals facing a hopeless futile task alone, but living agents in the hands of the Creator. We can perceive enough of His great plan and purpose to be able to carry out an intelligent part. In God's great strategy, devoted service is of the highest importance. 'Whoever shall be great among you, shall be your minister, and whosoever shall be chiefest shall be the servant of all' (Mark 10[43-4]). Jesus illustrated this, and at the same time sanctified 'drudgery' for all time for Christian people, by His washing of His disciples' feet. 'If I, then, your Lord and Master, have washed your feet; ye also ought to wash one another's feet' (John 13[14]).

The teaching of Jesus that this life is but a small part in a much greater life, which we can only call eternal life, also strikes at the taproot of futility, in its assurance that the acts of service that we do, and the character we build, do not just peter out in futility at our death, but are part of an infinite purpose extending far beyond any of our horizons.

The Christian attitude to futility therefore is that man's true significance is as the child of God, unable to achieve anything worthwhile in his own power, but of infinite value and significance as a living instrument in God's purposes. We are not just workers, nor even just fellow-workers, but 'labourers together with God' (1 Corinthians 3[9]), and we are given the resources we need for that high purpose to the extent of our willingness to accept and cultivate them.

The conquest of futility, then, is in the true perspective of life offered to mankind by Jesus Christ; in our acceptance of His leadership in the very heart of our personalities. This does not mean trying to escape the things we may regard as futile, nor even merely enduring them. It means allowing them to be transformed, by a kind of divine alchemy, into opportunities for devoted and creative service.

In more specific practical terms, if the futility is felt in work which does not seem to give sufficient outlet for special gifts or capacities, it may be right to look for more suitable occupation, or possibly to review the present work with a view to finding more opportunities of friendship and personal service. On the other hand there may be other possibilities of spare time activity: new interests, hobbies, or avenues of service which may compensate in some way for any lack of scope in the work itself.

There may be some would-be reformers who see little or no result from all their devoted efforts. The futility they feel may come to be seen as mainly centred on their own plans. This wider perspective may help them to victory over the dead weight of futility, and a new energy and enthusiasm which will bring much better results.

VI. LONELINESS

'A great city, a great loneliness.' So runs an ancient proverb. With increasing concentration of people in the cities of the world and the changing conditions of modern life, the poignant paradox of loneliness in the crowded city—the utter negation of human comradeship—has grown into one of the great modern problems. It is probably a forgotten factor in many disorders of personality, and a powerful hindrance to recovery.

In attempting to deal with loneliness we must exclude on the one hand those in whom it is a symptom of psychotic illness, for whom the main help is in the treatment of the psychosis. On the other hand we must exclude those who may desire solitude in the conviction that it allows their best contribution to effective living. Neither of these groups of people will generally submit themselves for counselling.

As with other emotional disorders the first contribution of the counsellor is the showing of understanding and acceptance through allowing all pent-up feelings in the client to unburden themselves freely. This in itself will remove much of the despair of loneliness, and open the door to a fresh look with the counsellor at the whole of the client's situation. It may be necessary deliberately to think of unconventional avenues of personal service in the light of any particular talents or opportunities which the client may have. It may also help to look with him at the many opportunities for friendship and service in Church fellowships and in societies held together by some common interest.

In whatever field of human life it is undertaken, the giving out of devoted service, even of the simplest and most humble kind, will inevitably lead to some real relief from loneliness and to the creation of new and enduring friendships. The words of Jesus, 'He that loseth his life for my sake shall find it' (Matthew 10^{39}), are specifically applicable in the relief of loneliness, but lonely people may need patient help before they achieve insight into the many factors which have combined to disturb their spontaneity in social relationships.

As we have seen previously there is a great field of Christian service open to members of Christian congregations in the relief of loneliness. This may apply in some countries on the national level, particularly in those which are welcoming large numbers of immigrants and 'displaced persons'. Such Christian service may need very great patience and perseverance when offered to people who may have been deeply wounded in spirit through 'man's inhumanity to man'. But the more of these qualities it needs the more important it will be for the future of humanity.

In many places there would seem to be a need for new adventures in social service on the part of the Church, possibly in co-operation with other organizations. Community centres of various kinds are being created and built up in some areas, and it seems vital that the leadership of the Church, possibly at the inter-denominational level, should be offered and accepted in all such community projects. It may well be that Community centres will become one of the main enterprises of the Church in the future, if their development is undertaken wisely and with due regard to particular needs and resources.

VII. GRIEF

The ministry to grief-stricken people, from bereavement or any other calamity, is one of the most frequent privileges of the pastor, and, more than most other emotional difficulties, grief comes within his special field of work. That is not to say that his ministry will not be helped by insights which come from psychological research, and in fact our knowledge has been greatly enriched in recent years by the discoveries of research workers.

In dealing with people suffering from grief we must distinguish between the 'natural' grief reaction, which may be helped greatly by good pastoral care, and what has been called 'morbid grief', which is generally in need of competent psychiatric help before it will become amenable to pastoral help.

Each type of grief is accompanied by bodily as well as mental symptoms, and morbid grief can best be recognized by the fact that it generally appears quite a long time after the bereavement or other cause, and often in a rather distorted form. Dr Henry H. Brewster [1] reports the case of a woman of 40 who had what appeared to be an excessive grief reaction. She was totally incapacitated, and it was found during psychotherapy that her emotion was more concerned with a brother who had died twenty years previously.

The natural grief reaction begins immediately after the person's receipt of the news of the bereavement or other precipitating event, with a feeling of being stunned or overcome with mental anguish. This is followed by a dazed, unreal feeling, often accompanied by inability to believe that the event can have happened. There may also be a feeling of being lost, or a conviction that the bottom has dropped out of life.

Sleeplessness and listlessness are common, sometimes alternating with touchiness and even hostility to those good friends who are trying to offer consolation and sympathy. The grief-stricken person may want to be left alone, but again this may alternate with a passionate desire for the company of friends and relatives. He will often move restlessly about the house starting to do all kinds of things but not finishing any of them, and feeling useless and indecisive.

The grief-stricken person will very often have a deep sense of guilt, which he justifies by recounting all the ways in which he has failed to understand or to serve the loved one, and all the sins of commission which he feels he has committed in relation to him. This sense of guilt is sometimes held back because of the feeling of shame, but the person may be most grateful for the opportunity to unburden it to someone who understands and accepts it. There is also a very common tendency to idealize the departed person, especially when there have been strained relationships with him during his life. It is most important for the pastor to understand and to accept these feelings, however inconsistent they may appear, and to encourage the fullest unburdening of them, even when it is repeated on many occasions.

The bodily symptoms generally seem to come in waves, often

---

[1] 'The Grief Situation' in *Psychiatry and Religion*, edited by Joshua Loth Liebman (Beacon Press, Boston, 1948).

arising when he thinks or is reminded of the loved one. Tears well up into his eyes and a lump comes into his throat, and there may be long sighs or unrestrained sobbing, sometimes even difficulty in breathing or swallowing. There is often an empty hollow feeling in his stomach but food is uniformly tasteless and he has no desire for it. His limbs may feel heavy and weak, and everything seems to be an effort.

The acute symptoms generally remain fairly intense for about two weeks, and then gradually abate, with some recurring waves of greater intensity, over the next three or four weeks if the person is willing to face the situation reasonably. The conventional social and religious observances of the first few days after the bereavement are all designed to encourage the unburdening of feeling, even to the point of therapeutic anguish. The gathering of relatives and friends, the many expressions of sympathy and fellowship through personal contact and through telegrams and flowers, and the tributes paid at the funeral service all minister to that end.

The period immediately following these public observances will often be suitable for the more private and intimate personal therapy of pastoral counselling. This may be carried out to some extent by doctors and by understanding friends as well as by ministers, and there are some principles which have proved valid by practical experience.

In the first place the person should be allowed and even encouraged to unburden his feelings, to recall and talk about as many pleasant experiences with the loved one as desired. Tears should be accepted with understanding and reassurance, and the counsellor's understanding and acceptance should be shown in manner: a steady hand on the person's shoulder or a firm hand grip, as well as in simple words. At this stage there is no need for attempted explanations, only understanding and acceptance of the person's feelings, as in the 'catharsis' stage of counselling. This is particularly needed during the days following the funeral, when a period of deep depression and bewilderment is often experienced by the bereaved person.

As the emotional intensity diminishes there may be an opportunity for some clarification or explanation, and particularly the application of the Christian Gospel to the situation. This must be approached with sensitiveness to the person's feelings, and when there is any further indication of guilt, resentment against God, or other negative feeling, it may be wise to encourage more catharsis. At some point in this part of the pastoral help the counsellor may be able to affirm his confidence in the person's faith and courage, and his ability to face the situation and come through it.

A temporary break from work and people may be of great help, but the person's active life should be resumed as soon as possible. Later it may be of advantage for him to consider whether the gap in his life can be filled by any new work or social relationships. Parents who have lost their only child, for example, might come to consider the advisability of having or adopting another, or of giving some particular personal service to needy children.

In some cases the person seems to cling to an idealized image of the loved one, and this may greatly hinder his social re-establishment in the months or even years following the bereavement. Such people need pastoral help greatly, and in some of them there is a gradual drift into morbid grief. When a reasonable period of pastoral help does not seem to remove this unreal attachment to the image of the loved one psychiatric help may be necessary.

The morbid grief reaction generally begins with an inappropriate response to the grief-producing situation. The person will often be 'frozen', unable to talk about the loved one, and unable to cry. He will often move about the house in a vague, apparently dazed fashion, and will seem withdrawn and unresponsive. On the other hand there may be exaggerated hostility, directed against anyone who may have had any part in the care of the deceased. In other cases the bereaved person may become restless and over-active, unable to sit still. He may even do stupid things on impulse which he would not have thought of doing otherwise. These symptoms are quite comparable with those of the affective psychoses, melancholia and mania, and bereavement may in some cases actually precipitate such psychotic reactions.

Another possible expression of morbid grief may be through bodily illnesses: what are called 'psychosomatic disorders.' Rheumatoid arthritis and spastic or ulcerative colitis are possibly the commonest of these. In many such cases the emotion of grief is combined with many other disordered feelings, such as resentment, guilt and fear, as it is in most cases of morbid grief. In such cases the grief may have been so deeply repressed that it is not discovered except by prolonged psychotherapy.

Before leaving this important subject of grief it may be of some value to offer some ideas about the meaning of death. Many people are quite bewildered about the whole subject, and if the pastor can help to clarify it in his ordinary educational work as well as in his therapeutic work with the bereaved, he will be doing something of far-reaching importance.

We may begin by reminding ourselves that death is a process rather than an event. Everywhere in nature we find the two opposing but intermingled processes of life and death continually going on. Nature, in fact, presents an endlessly recurring cycle of life, growth, development, and reproduction on the one hand; and death, decay, atrophy, and retrogression on the other; with life always coming out on top, taking hold of matter and making it burst forth through death into new cycles of life. 'If Winter comes,' observed the poet Shelley, 'can Spring be far behind?'

But what of human personality: the most recent arrival in the vast unfolding pageant of life? What happens to the invisible intangible human personality at the death of the physical body? With all its brilliant achievements in the realm of knowledge, science is still unable to answer the great questions about the nature of life or death or immortality, which still remain in the realm of intuition and conviction based on faith.

Faith is not credulity, or, as the schoolboy suggested, 'believing what you know is not true'. On the other hand, faith is not sight. It is somewhere between the two, because it has what may be termed an experimental basis. We try out the object of our faith in ways in which we can try it out, and then, having found it dependable, we venture with it into the unknown, believing. Faith in immortality then, is not belief without proof, but belief beyond proof: it is based ultimately upon firm foundations of experiment, experience, and logical reasoning.

The actual event of death has some interesting points of similarity with that of birth. Inside the mother's womb the developing child has two closely intermingled bodies; that which is needed for pre-natal life, which includes the placenta and the umbilical cord; and that which is being prepared for the next stage of life, which includes the lungs, intestines, and other organs quite unnecessary for intra-uterine life. At birth the first body, which has then fulfilled its purpose, dies and is cast off, and the second body enters into the life for which it has been steadily prepared in the pre-natal life.

During our life on earth we also possess two 'bodies' which are as closely intermingled as the two bodies in the pre-natal stage of life. The first of these is what we know as the physical body, which is needed for this stage of our lives, and the second is an invisible but definite personality: a kind of 'spiritual body' which we call character. This spiritual body seems to have some influence on the shape and form of the physical body, and to preserve its own unique identity in spite of the active, bustling changes which go on unceasingly throughout life in every living cell of the physical body. It may be compared with the calm restful melody in music, which soars serenely above the surging arpeggios of the accompaniment.

Can we think of the event of death, then, as the discarding of the now obsolete physical body, and the entry into its larger life of the spiritual body, the true personality, inaccessible to our material vision, but infinitely more real, for good or ill, than the ever-changing unstable flesh which served as its scaffolding?

If the child inside its mother's womb could know what it had to face in the process of birth, it could well be apprehensive or even quite despairing of any possibility of negotiating the severing of its one known life-line. Birth would then be a tremendous venture of faith, as death is to us.

This analogy may be carried still farther by imagining what would happen if there were twins inside their mother's womb who could explore their little world and communicate with each other as we do. When the first of them is born, the other one could only say, 'Poor chap, he's gone!', as we do when confronted with the apparently final event of death. He could never realize that the 'poor chap' had gone through birth into a new life more wonderful than he could ever imagine or be told about, and into the loving arms of people who had gone through the same gate of birth before him. Can we then believe that we pass through the gate of death into the loving 'arms' of those who have gone before us, and that although our only visible 'life-line' is severed there is a more suitable one ready to take over as we pass through?

This hypothesis is justified by the conviction, born of experience, that the universe is a uni-verse; it is 'all of one piece'. It does not do violence to any scientific principle, except the utterly discredited one that 'out of sight means out of existence'. It fits in with the Christian doctrine of the unbroken life and 'the Resurrection of the Body'. It envisages life as an unbroken sequence of growth and development of personality or soul, and the only real death as the spiritual death resulting from deliberate rebellious withdrawal from the Creator of all: the one and only source of life.

The scientists are convinced of the indestructibility of matter and of energy. Personality is far higher in the scale of creation than either matter or energy, and therefore presumably more worthy of preservation. And such preservation would involve continuance of the personal relationships of love, service and some form of recognition, which are inseparable from personality.

It seems quite irrational to accept the dogmatism which arises from unaided human reason, however confidently it may be presented, because it rests on the fallacy that human reason is at any time the last word. In fact the whole history of scientific progress shouts to the world of the utter foolishness of such an attitude. Every new generation produces men and women whose discoveries shatter the over-confident assertions of their scientific predecessors.

The proper scientific attitude to these profound mysteries would seem to be one of awe and reverence, with honest recognition of the limits of our knowledge at any time, and the frank admission that the whole structure of scientific reasoning itself is built on a great venture of faith: the belief in the essential consistency of the universe and the rationality of human reasoning.

Both humanist and Christian views about life and death depend on faith, the humanist on faith in human reason alone, and the Christian on faith in God as well. But unlike the humanist view the Christian faith about the meaning of life and death is based on a series of events in history: the life, death, and resurrection of Jesus Christ, the accounts of which have survived the most searching critical scrutiny of generations of brilliant scholars.

Belief in eternal life, of which our present life is an essential part, is at the centre of the Christian faith. It offers a rational meaning to the experience of bereavement, together with the fully justified expectation of reunion with loved ones as well as fellowship with them in 'the communion of saints'. Apart from bereavement the Christian belief in the Resurrection of the Spiritual Body offers added meaning to our everyday life. It sets it in a much wider perspective as part of a grand design, far beyond our puny little minds to grasp, but conceived and executed with infinite wisdom and infinite love.

The Christian, then, as he looks at death, is brought back more forcibly to face the meaning and value of life, with its quickly passing opportunities and its pressing tasks. And while the cynic is tempted by the despairing cry, 'Let's eat, drink, and be merry, for tomorrow we die', the Christian, looking farther, can say with deep conviction: 'Let's work, pray, and be friendly, for tomorrow we live!'

VIII. SOME SEXUAL DIFFICULTIES AND CONFLICTS

In general there are three main avenues of approach from the Christian standpoint in the prevention and overcoming of difficulties concerning the sexual aspect of human life. They have already been described in the first section of this book as the three great resources which can transform man's internal character structure: education, psychotherapy, and religion.

Sex education is obviously an important and essential part of any attempt to reduce the frequency and intensity of sexual difficulties and conflicts. But as we have emphasized in the second section of this book, any effective sex education must do far more than give people specific information about the anatomy and physiology and psychology of sex. Knowledge without character might only offer more opportunities for misuse of sex. One of the reasons why people get into difficulties is that most of their knowledge has come from very unreliable and unbalanced people, the dirty yarn at school or in the neighbourhood, the furtive inspection of crude sensuous literature and pictures, and many other unhealthy sources of information.

The place in which the proper early sex education can best be given in its essential setting of naturalness, intimacy and reverence is of course the good home. Here as we have seen it can be fitted into the everyday life and all the personal relationships in the home, and linked up completely with the early religious education. When this early sex education is well done the child will generally be immune to many of the possible adverse influences in school or neighbourhood, and far less interested in unhealthy literature, pictures, and conversation. When it is either evaded or given in distorted form by parents in the home, the child will generally be much more vulnerable to these noxious influences, and will be very likely to come up against some difficult and bewildering problems.

Psychotherapy in its broadest sense, from relatively superficial interviewing in the simpler cases, through pastoral or medical counselling in the more complex, to the most searching psychoanalysis by the well-trained psychiatrist, is the essential basis of the treatment of practically all sexual difficulties. It is necessary to be clear about this, because many people have the idea that 'gland treatment' will solve most of their sexual problems. In competent medical hands treatment by sex hormones of the appropriate kind may have an important part in some cases where there is definite evidence of their need, but the overwhelming majority of sexual difficulties, even those of mainly 'constitutional' origin, will only be relieved when they receive first-class psychotherapy.

In all but the simplest cases which respond quickly to pastoral counselling the pastor will be very wise to refer people with any sexual difficulties to a competent doctor, either the person's own 'family doctor' for preference, or else to a medical specialist in that field.

In any counselling for sexual difficulties it is necessary to help the client to gain some insight into his feelings and attitudes and into his psychic background, through which those attitudes were mainly built up. His earlier relationships with his parents and his siblings, and their relationships with one another, the manner in which he received, or failed to receive the fully integrated sex and character education, and his relationships in school, clubs, and later in his work and his social interactions—all these and more will need to be considered by counsellor and client together, and brought into relationship with the rest of his life and his scale of values.

Religion is often wrongly thought of as something which will 'solve the problem', or which should solve it. Problems are solved by people, and religion is one, but not the only one of the resources which are available to help people in their efforts to better living. The views of Alexis Carrel on a wider field are applicable here: 'Separately, the priest, the teacher, and the doctor are incapable of ensuring the success of life; they can only do so by pooling their knowledge.' [1] Sex is not an isolated part of the human personality, but rather a vital energy infusing all parts of our personality and one of the ways in which we express our character and our attitude to life and to people—and to God.

As we have seen previously in this book the Christian Religion offers light, power, deliverance, and fellowship to men and women to help them toward abundant life. It is possibly the one adequate inspiration and motive power for the disciplined training which will establish positive habits of self-mastery, and the one adequate source of the patience needed to keep on working at it.

We cannot leave this part of the question without pointing out

[1] *Reflections on Life* (Hamish Hamilton, 1952), p. 181.

one very simple yet necessary element in the management of many sexual disorders. 'Occupational therapy' is a useful part in the treatment of many nervous disorders, and is almost essential in those connected with sex. As the verse of Isaac Watts expresses it:

> *In works of labour, or of skill,*
> *I would be busy too;*
> *For Satan finds some mischief still*
> *For idle hands to do.*

Many of these disorders feed on idleness, and they also tend to be more difficult to control when people are spending much of their time in such sedentary pursuits as studying for examinations. Many university students find that unless they can make opportunities for healthy sport, preferably in company with other people, their sexual impulses are more difficult to deal with. Any good manual work and any good sporting opportunities that can be organized will be of considerable help to people who may be trying to overcome their sexual difficulties, as long as the other aspects of the treatment are being well carried out.

From these general considerations we may now turn to give some consideration to the kind of approach and help which may be offered to people in various sexual difficulties who may come under the care of the pastor.

Masturbation or self-stimulation is one of the commonest of these. It is probable that all men and women go through a period of life in which they practise some form of self-stimulation, and the general view in these days is that this is a normal part of their sexual development. Many young people who are unable to marry because of insufficient money or housing, and who are committed to the ideal of chastity, find that the urge to self-stimulation is beyond their power completely to resist. When they are of an introverted type of temperament, or have come to think of the practice as sinful or in some way harmful, their lives may be rendered unhappy and even despairing by the fruitless struggle against it. Many of them will have become shy and reticent about it, and too sensitive to seek help at the beginning of the trouble.

The pastor may suspect the presence of this difficulty in the more serious young men and women when they find it hard to look him in the face, or when they seem to be weighed down by a sense of guilt beyond anything that they have been able to talk about. When the counselling relationship has become well established it may be possible for the counsellor to give such a person the opportunity to unburden his or her feelings by a suitable question, such as: 'Do you sometimes find your sexual feelings difficult to keep under control?' That may be sufficient, or it may open the way for a further question: 'Do you sometimes have to give yourself some relief of tension?'

When the client unburdens his feelings about self-stimulation it is generally best to give plenty of time for a full 'catharsis' with no attempt at interpretation or reassurance until the counsellor has been able to find out what the situation means to the client, and possibly what made him come to think of it in that way. Unless this is done his attempted reassurances may well appear as just another conflicting view of the matter, which only increases the client's bewilderment.

Self-stimulation has been well defined as 'the sexual experience of an isolated individual'. It may of course happen even in married people, particularly when the previous habit was strong, and when one partner has stronger and more frequent sexual desires than the other can meet. In many cases it is accompanied by sexual phantasies, which may also bring feelings of guilt in the introspective person.

The first stage of interpretation is generally a clear and simple statement of the biological facts, which are now so generally accepted by competent authorities as to be beyond dispute. The main facts are as follows:

It is something that everyone experiences as part of his growth to maturity.

The act in itself does no harm to the body or mind, the 'energy' lost through it is of no consequence, and it makes no difference to any future potency or suitability for marriage.

Over-introspection and persistent anxiety about it only tend to give it a more prominent place in the person's attitudes than it ever could deserve. These things will have the same effects on the person's life as introspection and anxiety about anything else would have.

The Christian approach is surely that it is not wrong to be tempted, that God offers the power for growth to mature and abundant living, and that He would expect of us, not constant success in overcoming, but constant trying; doing our best with all possible help, and leaving all the results, or lack of them, in His hand. The whole approach in thought and prayer should be positive. The client should be encouraged to accept himself as he is for a start, and then to see himself as progressively more mature and victorious by the grace

Q

of God, as he sets out in all-round training for physical fitness and in all kinds of social service. Praying to God 'to deliver him from this vile habit' will only impress the negative thoughts and introspections still more deeply in his mind.

It is necessary therefore to help such people to victory over guilt, anxiety, and self-consciousness, as well as the actual domination of the self-stimulation. To overcome any undesired habit takes time and patience, but when the person can come to accept himself—as the counsellor in the name of God has accepted him, he will then be able to hold his head up among people, and be less inhibited in his work and his social relationships.

The pastor should constantly remind himself that the deep sense of guilt and anxiety over masturbation may sometimes be a symptom of a mental illness. When such feelings seem to be exaggerated, or inaccessible to the clarification offered at the right time in the counselling, he should consider referring the person to a suitable doctor for help.

Homosexuality is another sexual problem which will bring quite a number of people to the pastor for help. As with masturbation it is probable that all people pass through a stage of development, generally during the first half of the second decade of life, in which their inclinations are more toward the company of people of the same sex than toward young people of the opposite sex. With normal development to personal maturity most of them find these homosexual inclinations gradually replaced by heterosexual feelings. This is usually complete before the age of twenty, but there are many people who find themselves stirred by homosexual impulses for very much longer, sometimes for the whole of their active lives.

As with heterosexual feelings homosexuality varies in intensity in different people, from a mild occasional stirring of desire to an insatiable and constant passion. In the milder cases there may also be some heterosexual desire. Many people with well-marked homosexual impulses have other inclinations and often bodily conformation more appropriate to the opposite sex.

A number of homosexuals suffer in silence, or carry on as best they can with their impulses. When they find themselves forced into prolonged close contact with people of the same sex, for example during periods of military or other service, or at schools or university colleges, their urges sometimes disturb them to the point of despair, or tend to break through their self-control.

The incidence of homosexuality in any community is quite impossible to assess with any accuracy, in spite of 'Kinsey Reports' and other investigations. Even those who regularly practise homosexual intercourse in various forms take good care to guard against discovery, and only the occasional excesses which burst out into public awareness are available as a factual background for our surmises.

It is generally believed by psychiatrists and biologists that there are two main factors in the causation of homosexuality: constitutional and psychic. It seems clear that males and females are never quite wholly male or female in their biochemical or their psychic constitution, and that some of them are constitutionally of one sex and anatomically of the opposite. Such people have been described as examples of an 'intersex', and this condition also occurs in other animals.

It also seems clear from the work of Freud and other psychiatric authorities that at least some homosexuals arise from purely, or at least mainly psycho-pathological causes: abnormal relationships with adults which interfere in any way with the normal growth to maturity are often found. The commonest of these is probably the over-persistent attachment of a boy to his mother. It is possible that such an attachment would hinder the normal development of heterosexual relationships, especially when the mother is over-possessive.

Many homosexuals appear to be emotionally and sometimes physically immature, even when, as often happens, they are intellectually and culturally advanced. These are possibly homosexual mainly from environmental rather than constitutional causes, and some of them may be able to develop heterosexual attitudes with adequate psychic and environmental help to greater maturity.

The mainly constitutional homosexual does not generally show evidence of immaturity, but will often show bodily characteristics and marked personal attitudes of the opposite sex. The 'masculine' woman and the effeminate man are well known in most if not all cultures, and there is no convincing evidence that any kind of treatment will alter their physical or psychic constitution in any significant manner.

There is still much to be elucidated about this whole problem, and about the effects of prevailing social and cultural factors on the whole question. It is probable that in many cases both constitutional and environmental factors are closely inter-related. Male homosexuals have been divided into 'active' and 'passive' types according to their predominant attitudes, and the passive male homosexual will generally be effeminate in build. In some cases the person will adopt alternate active and passive roles according to the particular circumstances. Similarly female homosexuals can be divided into 'active' or 'masculine' types, often with masculine build and temperament, and 'passive' or 'feminine' types, more female in build and temperament.

What contribution can the pastor make to help people who may unburden such difficulties as these to him in counselling?

The first and most important is probably acceptance and a willingness to understand. This involves neither condoning nor condemning of the person. Most homosexuals feel a sense of isolation from the general community, which may drive them into closer relationships with their fellow-homosexuals. The more sensitive among them will be greatly helped by a spontaneous empathy on the part of the pastor, as long as he guards against any attitude which could possibly arouse the sexual feelings of the male homosexual. This may be difficult when, as often happens, the male homosexual attempts to become attached to the pastor in some subtle way, but with quiet compassion steadied by the kind of dispassion which transmits the love of God, the relationship can be kept under control.

Next the pastor can ask the right kind of questions about the client's feelings regarding self-control, and try to bring them into relationship with the light, power, deliverance, and fellowship offered by Jesus Christ. Self-control in these urges can be related to the necessary self-control in every other aspect of life, and to the self-control in the field of sex which the heterosexual people need to cultivate for personal and social maturity.

Thirdly, the pastor may be able to offer the help of the Christian fellowship in the cultivation of normal healthy friendships, and in the disciplined training in physical fitness, emotional maturity, and in creative social service.

All these contributions are best offered in most cases in the fullest co-operation with any medical or psychiatric help which the client may be having, or may be willing to seek. It is generally a good safeguard for the pastor to recommend such medical help in all homosexual cases, because the problem is generally too complex to be adequately dealt with through pastoral counselling alone.

Finally, it may be said that in any but the mildest cases the pastor must be prepared for many disappointments. Despite all their assurances many homosexuals have lapses, often in response to particular situations for which they are not sufficiently prepared. Such lapses should be accepted without condemnation, and used to discover more about the client's vulnerabilities and to help him to better insight into them. A sustained belief in the client, in spite of all his lapses will again be of material help to him in his lonely battle. The pastor's understanding friendship will also be of help to him in his efforts to live with the deep homosexual urges, and to sublimate them in creative service, even of a sacrificial kind.

Sexual frustration is very common in most communities, and may be far more common among members of Church congregations than is generally realized. It is mostly found among those men and women who do not marry for one reason or another, but is by no means uncommon among married people. Many people involved in this trouble are very reticent about it, and suffer in silence, unless a good counsellor can build up the kind of relationship in which they can unburden their feelings.

Sexual frustration often shows itself in various kinds of emotional tensions, particularly in women, for whom there are fewer social outlets for the frustrated feelings than are available to men. Women too are more emotionally sensitive, and probably more in need of emotional satisfaction than men, whose sexual attitudes are generally more physically orientated.

Sexually frustrated women often become shrewish, a little bitter and cynical, cold, and sometimes deeply jealous. Some of them do valuable service in Church organizations, for example as Sunday-school teachers. When they are 'nervy' and 'touchy' they may not provide the most suitable emotional environment for young people. In many cases they feel great need for help but find it difficult to take the initiative and ask for it. Often they do not know who they should seek it from. Many of them are looking for fellowship in the Church, but find that their fellow members are not able to understand their touchiness, and barriers arise which increase their sense of despair.

Here again the first necessity on the part of the pastor is a good understanding and acceptance, which is not altered in any way by the client's bitter criticism of the Church, or of other church members, or of herself. This understanding may be shown in preaching and in all relationships with people, and this will bring many who suffer from frustration for personal counselling, in which still further understanding and acceptance can be shown.

In the actual counselling the client should first be encouraged to unburden all her pent-up feelings, and when there are signs of positive insight the situation can be faced in relation to the light, power, deliverance, and fellowship offered by Jesus Christ. Many other emotions, such as the sense of guilt and anxiety, and often loneliness, will generally be associated with the frustration, and will need to be dealt with in the counselling if the person is to be helped to recover the grace of a balanced personality, and to be made whole. Other socially acceptable channels of expression of the frustrated instincts may be found in co-operative adventures in service. The maternal instinct which is denied its most natural expression may sometimes be seen as a positive asset for the love and care of young children in schools, crêches, kindergartens, and homes. The results will be best when the service is undertaken as an offering to God, rather than primarily as a self-centred desire for relief of tension.

The same principles apply to women who may suffer from the sense of frustration in middle age. It may be that they have depended on their sexual attraction of their husbands more than on their deeper qualities, and are now beginning to feel that they may lose their hold. In other cases they have been depending on the feeling of being needed by the children, and now the children are growing up and leaving home, and their mother does not feel needed any longer.

Here again a frank facing up to the new situation with understanding and acceptance, and then assessing the client's resources of time, ability and experience, possessions, and opportunities with a view to their best use in Christian stewardship, will often bring new insights, and positive action will then help to a richly rewarding new chapter of life. Of course the best help in such situations is to be awake to their inevitability, and to build up new ways of 'being needed' before the situation arises.

Sexual perversions may occasionally come under the notice or the field of counselling of the pastor. In practically every case he should do everything possible to induce the person to obtain medical help. Some of the people who come under the control of the law for actions which demonstrate any form of sexual perversion will be suffering from a psychopathic or even psychotic disorder, and will need expert help and possibly institutional treatment. Any pastoral help should be given only in full co-operation with the psychiatric and legal management of the situation.

The pastor may sometimes be brought into contact with a man of previously unexceptional behaviour, who, for no apparent reason, has committed some abnormal action, such as exhibitionism, or voyeurism. Here again it is most important to make sure that the person comes under psychiatric care. Such unexpected and perplexing actions are often the first symptoms of a mental illness, sometimes even of some physical illness.

In co-operation with any such help the pastor may offer the spiritual grace of understanding and acceptance, and the opportunity for full unburdening of his feelings in that atmosphere of Christian love. This may prove the one solid foundation for hope in the mind of the client, who will feel bewildered and guilty, and rejected by his fellows. This kind of situation provides one of the great opportunities for pastoral healing.

CHAPTER FIFTEEN

Understanding and Helping the Alcoholic

THE VARIOUS disorders associated with the immoderate consumption of alcohol constitute an increasingly vast and complex problem in most countries, personal, domestic, social, and national. Alcoholism has, in fact, become one of the greatest unsolved problems of our civilization, undermining and even ruining countless valuable lives, breaking up numbers of previously happy homes, contributing greatly to the increasing toll of road accidents, and seriously reducing national productivity and prosperity.

For the pastor, apart from his wider interest in social and national welfare, it provides a frequently recurring challenge to his personal understanding and skill, and above all to his Christian patience and tolerance. An attempt will be made, therefore, to summarize the most common forms of Alcoholism, and to give some account of the causative factors and of the pastoral contribution to the care and treatment of those who suffer directly and indirectly as a result.

(1) *Acute Alcoholism*, the commonest of all alcoholic manifestations, which may occur in any grade of severity from the 'merry' or 'near drunk' to the 'paralytic' or 'dead drunk'. It is generally agreed by the pharmacologists that alcohol is a narcotic poison rather than a stimulant, and that any appreciable percentage of alcohol in the circulating blood brings about a definite prolongation of 'reaction time', and interference with judgement, even when there are no obvious signs of actual 'drunkenness'. This is probably an important factor in many road accidents.

In many cases this condition is the result of irresponsible or unwise 'social' drinking, sometimes in celebration of some happy or exciting event, sometimes as an attempt to 'drown' some sorrow or to bring some momentary 'colour' into a dull drab existence. Apart from the fact that mental fuzziness causes accidents, which unfortunately may involve other people, the main danger of this kind of situation is that it may be an early stage in the development of an addiction. This is particularly important when young people feel that plenty of alcohol is necessary to make a party 'bright'.

The best treatment of the 'drunk' is generally to get him home to bed as quickly as possible. A drink of hot milk, tea, or coffee may be of some help if he is able and willing to swallow it easily, but no drinks should be forced on an unwilling or semi-comatose person, because of the risk that some of the fluid may find its way into the lungs. 'Corpse revivers' are sometimes useful, but are best left to the doctor to give when necessary.

It is a very good routine step in the management of any but the mildest intoxication to look for such other possible troubles as a head injury, a stroke in those past middle age, or a high fever. Any of these may be associated with the intoxication, or may produce a condition which may be mistaken for it when the person has been given alcohol in small quantity before the trouble or in an attempt to 'revive' him.

Apart from these measures, and possibly a good laxative at the appropriate time, it is only necessary to allow the person to 'sleep it off'. He may need some pastoral friendship and help later.

(2) *Alcohol addiction* is a serious condition in which a person has become a slave to alcohol, and is unable to give up drinking to excess, even though it has ceased to give him the relief or pleasure it once did, even though it brings the loss of a good job, of all his friends, and of his wife and home. Women are also very liable to this condition, with similar consequences. A somewhat related condition, known as dipsomania, is one of recurrent depression with the strong urge to alcohol, but the person appears to have good control between attacks.

The alcohol addict seems to lose all concern for the sufferings of others, and he will make all kinds of promises, but seems unable to carry them out. One serious example of this is when a young man in this condition manages to persuade a girl that she is his one salvation, that marriage with her will enable him to give up the habit and to make a fresh start. If she accepts his promises, the results are nearly always disastrous, and the extreme plausibility and persuasiveness of the alcoholic may make it very difficult for her to refuse, particularly if she is altruistic and conscientious.

The causative factors of this complaint are not altogether clear. Frequent drinking is obviously an important factor, but only a relatively small proportion of frequent drinkers become addicts, although the total number in most countries is very large, as can be realized from the membership of the organization known as 'Alcoholics Anonymous'. There may be some emotional immaturity or lack of balance in the personality which predisposes to addiction. Some of the addicts give a history of coming from a broken or disturbed early home environment, with considerable insecurity and lack of adequate parental care.

No treatment is likely to succeed in delivering an addict from his complaint unless he has come to a strong, sustained, and genuine desire to be cured, and a readiness to endure the 'blood, toil, tears, and sweat' involved. In many cases a fairly long period of institutional care seems to be a necessary beginning, and the institutional routine, communal discipline, understanding leadership, together with various kinds of occupational therapy, often help to give him a new confidence and a new feeling of health and vigour.

Membership of 'Alcoholics Anonymous', with consistently faithful carrying out of their well-known 'twelve steps', has proved to be the most effective way to permanent victory over the addiction. For details of this the reader is referred to the readily available literature of the organization. From the pastoral point of view, it is interesting to see that the twelve steps, which have evolved from practical experience, are very closely comparable with the sequence of steps through which the prodigal son accepted his opportunity to make a fresh start.

In all his attitudes to the addict, it is important that the pastor should regard the condition as a serious illness, which is in urgent and extreme need of Christian understanding and acceptance, and which would be greatly intensified by moralizing and 'preaching'. There is also great scope for good pastoral care of those who suffer as the result of living with the addict—wives, husbands, parents, or children. This care is much more effective when it is fully backed up by the understanding and goodwill of the whole Christian fellowship.

'Antabuse' and other remedies are for medical judgement, and are only serviceable in suitable institutions.

(3) *Chronic alcoholism.* This includes a number of abnormal mental and physical states which may follow the continued excessive consumption of alcohol, whether or not there is addiction as already described. Most of the manifestations are not directly due to the alcohol, but seem to arise from the nutritional and other consequences of the continued drinking. In many cases they appear to be intensifications of previously existing abnormalities. For example, some mild epileptics seem to be made worse by continued alcoholic excess, and the epileptic mentality may also encourage excessive

drinking. There are also many people who suffer from a mild psychosis, often a schizoid personality (withdrawn and suspicious), which encourages and is made worse by continued drinking. It is important for the pastor to have some understanding of these possibilities.

Some account will be given of the most important of these states: Alcoholic Hallucinosis, 'Delirium Tremens', 'Mania a Potu', and 'Korsakoff's Syndrome'.

Alcoholic Hallucinosis generally begins suddenly with intense fear, together with auditory hallucinations (the hearing of 'voices' or other sounds), or the misinterpretation of existing sounds. The person may have 'ideas of reference' (the belief that others are talking about him or are threatening him). He will generally know who and where he is, and will realize that he is suffering from hallucinations, but may be so upset that he even attempts suicide. It is probable that this condition is one of the effects of continued drinking on a person with a pre-existing schizoid personality. It generally occurs in younger people, between 30 and 40.

'Delirium Tremens' is probably the best known of the acute break-downs of chronic alcoholism. It is usually found in people over 40 who have been drinking heavily and consistently for five to ten years, either socially or in connexion with their work. They are usually of the extravert type of personality and of what is called 'Cyclothyme' temperament—prone to extreme swings of mood.

There may be some prodromal symptoms, such as insomnia, restlessness, panics and nightmares, which may recur several times before there is an attack of delirium. It is of interest that the symptoms of delirium tremens are noticed almost entirely at night.

The main symptom is of course delirium, which, if it is not fatal, is generally limited to about four days. There are generally vivid visual hallucinations of what is described as a 'cinematic character', switching rapidly from one to another, and they are mostly of fast-moving small animals such as rats. There is extreme terror associated with these hallucinations, with sweating and great restlessness. Occasionally they are accepted with some amusement. The person generally knows who he is, but is vague or ignorant about time and place. He will often realize the nature of his trouble. There may be some vomiting and disturbance of equilibrium. In severe cases there is often collapse, which may be fatal.

It is now generally held that the sudden stopping of alcohol in a chronic drinker cannot be blamed for precipitating an attack. Where it may appear to have done so, further investigation will show that the attack had already commenced when the alcohol was stopped. It may be precipitated by an injury or infection.

The treatment of 'D.T.s' is of course medical and generally institutional, and the sooner medical aid can be obtained the better the outlook will be. Here again it is most important that a search should be made for possible head injury or fever. Once again, the sufferer may need first-class pastoral friendship and help when he has recovered from the acute breakdown.

'*Mania a Potu.*' In this puzzling condition the person is suddenly caught up in intense rage, which may lead to extreme violence. It happens even after partaking of an amount of alcohol which might not be expected to produce any ill effects. The person later describes it as a 'blackout' and maintains that he has no memory at all of what happened. In most cases, it first comes under notice after some criminal act has been committed. There has been some previous consumption of alcohol, but when examined, the person shows none of the characteristics of drunkenness. It seems as if the alcohol must have precipitated him into blind impulsive uncontrolled rage or destructiveness, which has lasted for a relatively short time. During this time he may have performed diabolically skilful actions, but afterwards he has no memory of anything that has happened.

These people are usually unstable personalities, impulsive and generally irresponsible, prone to sudden temper or violence. The alcohol seems to remove the restraining factors, such as they are, and to pave the way for the sudden violence. Such people are difficult to assess, like all 'psychopathic personalities', and even more difficult to deal with.

'*Korsakoff's Syndrome*' is a combination of progressive dementia with severe peripheral neuritis and other physical manifestations of chronic alcoholism. It generally occurs in people more than 50 years of age who have been drinking constantly for many years. The main mental features of the complaint are extreme loss of memory for recent, even immediately recent events, and extreme disorientation in both time and place. Those who suffer from it often try to evade the failure of memory by making up fantastic stories. This is a true psychosis and needs expert medical and often institutional care.

There are some other similar states associated with chronic

alcoholism, but they are of medical rather than pastoral interest. It is important for the pastor to have some awareness of the different manifestations of alcoholism so that he can give some understanding as well as offer empathy and goodwill to those with whom he may come into contact.

CHAPTER SIXTEEN

Understanding and Helping the Mentally Ill

I. WHAT DO WE MEAN BY 'MENTAL ILLNESS'?

MENTAL ILLNESS may be defined as 'any recognizable disturbance of the functioning of any part of the mind: emotion, intellect, and/or will, with or without disturbance of bodily function; sufficiently pronounced to be regarded as abnormal in the particular person'.

This is a very general and rather vague definition, and it is necessarily so because there is no clear-cut dividing line between health and illness of the mind, any more than there is between health and illness of the body. This is true in a particular individual, and is even more obvious when we think of different people. What may be regarded as mentally healthy in a coal lumper may seem abnormal in a minister.

There is no real distinction, either between mind and body, or between different parts of the mind, except for convenience in description. Illness is a reaction of the whole personality to internal and/or external stresses, or a breakdown of the person's capacity for adaptation to life. It may be mild or severe, brief or prolonged, and there may be single or recurrent disturbances.

Mental illness may be classified broadly into three overlapping groups:

(a) *Disorders mainly of emotion or feeling*, represented by what are called 'psychoneurotic' and 'psychosomatic' disorders.
(b) *Disorders mainly of intellect or thinking*, represented by what are called 'psychotic disorders' (including mental defect).
(c) *Disorders mainly of will or conduct*, represented by what are called 'psychopathic disorders'.

There cannot be any actual dividing line between these three groups, because each part of the personality influences all the others. For example the so-called affective psychoses, mania and melancholia, would appear at first sight to come under the first group, but the primary disorder in such cases seems to be in the thinking function.

When we consider the various manifestations of the different kinds of mental illness it is clear that there are many people who experience symptoms comparable with some of them, but who never come under the care of either psychiatrist or pastor. Some of them are labelled 'peculiar' or 'eccentric', but their peculiarities are not sufficiently disturbing to themselves or to their relatives or fellow-citizens to bring them into conflict with the law. It is part of the price we pay for human freedom that such eccentric, and even mentally ill people may cause great inconvenience, and even harm, to others, but cannot be compelled to come under medical care unless they appear to be potentially dangerous to themselves or to others.

The pastor is often in the position to discover the presence of indications of mental illness before the person or his relatives would suspect it or face it. It is important therefore that he should know something of the early and later manifestations of the different kinds of mental illness, and in any suspected case that he should do everything possible to persuade the person to seek competent medical help at once. He should also have some understanding of the nature and development of these illnesses, and of the attitudes and feelings of those who suffer from them. This is particularly important because mental illness is seldom understood by people, and the understanding of their feelings by the pastor or Christian counsellor will do much more than is generally realized to help in the recovery of many of the mentally ill.

Some attention will therefore be given to the various kinds of mental illness which come under the three headings already mentioned: psychoneurotic and psychosomatic, psychotic, and psychopathic, remembering that they are not so much 'diseases' as types of reaction of the whole person to a complex pattern of stresses.

II. THE PSYCHONEUROTIC AND PSYCHOSOMATIC
REACTION TYPES

These are expressions of emotional tensions and conflicts in some kind of illness, in which the relationship of the disordered emotions to the symptoms is not clearly understood by the patient. They lack insight into their own inner attitudes, but have insight into reality. They are mentally maladjusted to the strains and stresses of life, and the particular symptoms in any person point to the kind of maladjustment. They can be divided for convenience into five main groups.

(*a*) *The Worriers.* These are generally dependent, clinging, compliant people, even if these characteristics are sometimes hidden under an apparently aggressive demanding exterior. Their anxiety may be generalized and appear as apprehensiveness, nerviness, and indecision without any adequate justification; or it may be experienced as specific, but inappropriate fears, or 'phobias'. This type of reaction is often called 'anxiety neurosis'.

(*b*) *The Depressed and Despairing.* These are generally withdrawn people, who suffer from either a sense of guilt, failure, remorse or unworthiness, over-scrupulosity or other religious bewilderment; or they may constantly complain of feeling exhausted in mind and body, with inability to concentrate or to show any initiative. This kind of reaction is often called 'neurasthenia'.

(*c*) *The Aggressive, Hostile, Touchy People,* who often feel a sense of frustration, or even victimization. Their general attitude is one of suspicion and condemnation. They are 'against' everybody, but demand that everybody should comply with their wishes, and fulfil their expectations.

(*d*) *The Obsessed People.* These are people whose lives are beset by constantly recurring unwelcome, often horrible thoughts (Obsessive-ruminative Neurosis), or more commonly by unwelcome dictatorial urges to do things which would seem stupid or unreasonable to any normal person (Obsessive-compulsive Neurosis). Examples of obsessive urges are the washing of hands every time anything is touched, the urge to go over and over again to the kitchen to make sure the gas has been turned off, or that the back door has been locked, and the urge to step on every square of the pavement, and to go back and step on any one that has been missed. Almost any kind of obsessive urge may intrude itself into the mind of a person with this disorder.

(*e*) *People with Bodily Symptoms or Bodily Disease of Emotional Origin.* When they are unaware of the emotional disorder it is generally called 'Conversion Hysteria'. When they are aware of the emotional disorder, but not necessarily of its relationship to the bodily symptoms, the trouble is usually described as a Psychosomatic Disorder.

It will be obvious that most people suffering from a psychoneurotic illness will come under more than one of these groups, and that there will be all kinds of variations in the manifestations of the illness. There may also be abnormalities of conduct which suggest a degree of psychopathic disorder, and sometimes there will be psychotic episodes in the course of an apparently psycho-neurotic illness. But the classification of these disorders is still very useful for purposes of description and recognition.

How does a Psychoneurotic Illness come into being? In assessing the many causative factors in this kind of illness we must consider the individual himself, his inadequacy to adapt to life, his vulnerability to all kinds of stresses, and also the nature and intensity and duration of the stresses. Another important factor in the development of a neurotic illness is the kind of reaction he makes to stresses and other experiences. Some attempts have been made to divide these disorders into Character Neuroses, in which the most prominent causative factors appear to be in the person himself, and Situation Neuroses, in which the environmental factors seem to be more influential in bringing about the illness. But in most cases it is impossible to separate these closely intertwined sets of causative factors.

It seems reasonably certain that some people are born with a kind of constitutional inadequacy for the difficulties of life, that people differ in their psychic as well as their physical constitution. But it is difficult to separate inborn characteristics and tendencies from those which arise during the early years of life, especially when the parents who provide the genes also provide the early physical and social environment.

In our consideration of environmental factors we must give some attention to the earliest environment of the growing child: the mother's womb. It is possible that deficiencies of intra-uterine nutrition and oxygen supply may have profound effects on the developing child, and the effect of maternal Rubella gives an indication of the effect of poisons which can pass through the placenta on the development of the child. The actual trauma of birth may also produce far-reaching changes on the personality of the child, particularly when there is actual injury to the brain or later pressure on it from haemorrhage.

These, however, do not appear to be of great importance in the causation of most cases of neurotic illness. It seems probable that, allowing always for the possibility of constitutional sensitivity to the strains of life, most cases are generated by environmental factors. Every child, except the mentally deficient, is endowed with the necessary resources for growth and maturing of personality as well as of body, if given favourable conditions.

R

We have seen that one of the most important of the child's early needs is for a full and constant relationship with a mother or a permanent mother substitute, and for the maternal qualities of love, dependability, and reverence for the child's personality. We are reminded that these spiritual qualities are as necessary for the growth of any child's personality as are protein, carbohydrate and fat for the development of his body. We have referred to the work of John Bowlby on the effects of maternal deprivation, psychic (through failure to give love of the right kind) as well as physical.[1] Maternal deprivation, or rejection of the child in any way by the mother, is particularly injurious to the child during the first four years of life.

During the next three years there is normally an expansion of the child's social relationships to the father, to others in the house, and beyond it to kindergarten, school, and neighbourhood. The child is still dependent on the mother, and now to an increasing extent on the mother-father relationship. He is learning to control the expression of his feelings through healthy friction with the desires and the rights of others, and needs the outgoing accepting love and trust of his parents, and the encouragement of his efforts.

These are some of the favourable conditions for the growth of a healthy personality. When the early environment is lacking in such necessities the child's growth to mature, self-reliant, social responsibility is interfered with. This may occur because of parental ignorance, or incapacity or unwillingness to offer the right kind of love, security, and the sense of being wanted and valued to the child. It is often a result of parents' own emotional tensions, conflicts, frustrations and neurotic needs, through which they become over-exacting, inconsistent, or over-protective to their children. This may happen in many 'religious' homes, and may also be seen in teachers in schools or Sunday-schools.

It is the whole psychic and Spiritual 'atmosphere' which counts rather than any particular single attitude, or traumatic experience. When the child feels consistently sure of his parents' love, dependability, and their reverence for his personality, he can take and adapt himself to severe strains and stresses and conflicts.

When the child is deprived of these essential resources for mental health he will fail to develop the necessary foundation of inner security, and will lose his natural spontaneity in what Karen Horney

[1] *Maternal Care and Mental Health* and *Child Care and the Growth of Love.*

has called 'Basic Anxiety', 'the feeling of being isolated and helpless in a world conceived as potentially hostile'.[1] Life then seems to him fundamentally unlivable, his whole relationship to life and to God is then on faulty, insecure, vulnerable foundations.

This 'basic anxiety' will be deeply imbedded in, and will tend to dominate, the child's whole outlook. It will prevent or hinder the establishment of effective personal relationships with others, except possibly those who can show consistent Christian Love over a sufficient period to win the child's confidence and overcome the basic anxiety. When the child fails to develop adequate personal relationships because of basic anxiety the anxiety tends to increase.

The child must react in some way to this basic anxiety, and his reactions will necessarily be immature, and will bring counter reactions from the failing parents, which will add still more to his basic anxiety, and tend to bring increasing bewilderment and despair.

There are three possible ways of reacting, described by Karen Horney as 'clinging, rebellion, or withdrawal: moving toward, against, or away from others'.[2] He is driven by his psychic discomfort to try one or all of these, and according to his inner nature and to the reactions of his parents he will come to work out a habitual reaction pattern in which one of these three ways has altogether excluded the other two.

This rigid psychic pattern is in marked contrast to the flexible pattern of the healthy person, who reacts to different stresses through whichever one seems appropriate. We all experience the need to be a little dependent at times, to be aggressive at other times, and to withdraw and be alone in other situations. But the neurotic child has to use whichever method has become his habitual pattern, whether it is appropriate or not, as an attempt at a 'solution' of the particular problem, or the achievement of some kind of 'equilibrium' with his life.

The first 'solution', then, according to Karen Horney, is in the establishment of one of these rigid habitual patterns of reaction to other people, and to the stresses of life. And this is seen in the three main neurotic patterns of childhood.

The Clinging pattern is seen in the timid, nervous, worrying child, who often suffers from night terrors, stammering, cyclic vomiting, or from asthma.

---

[1] *The Neurotic Personality of our Time* and *Neurosis and Human Growth.*
[2] *Neurosis and Human Growth.*

The Rebellious pattern is seen in the hostile aggressive child, who often indulges in temper tantrums, or possibly in lying, stealing, or truancy, or in the more oblique unconscious rebellion of nocturnal enuresis.

The Withdrawal pattern is seen in the shy solitary child, who tends to live in an imaginative world of phantasy to an extent which interferes with normal work and social relationships. There may be more than average thumb-sucking, and an exaggerated sense of guilt and unworthiness.

None of these patterns of reaction will 'solve' anything, or help the child to develop self-confidence or spontaneity, and he is thus forced as he grows up to further efforts to achieve self-realization or adjustment to life.

The second 'solution' then, in Karen Horney's view,[1] is of necessity in the child's imagery, in rationalizing the previously created habitual reaction, in making a virtue out of a necessity. We see this too in many young people, particularly in those who are seeking help in the fellowship of the Church. Clinging and compliance are thought of as goodness and even saintliness, rebelliousness and aggressiveness as courage and strength, and withdrawal and aloofness as independence and self-sufficiency. In this way the person tends to abandon his real self for an idealized, unreal 'self', as a compulsive attempt at self-realization.

But the demands of this idealized self are perfectionistic and insatiable; ideals, which are normal, have grown stealthily above their station and become demands. When ideals are not realized we do not generally regard ourselves as failures, but when these perfectionistic demands are not fully met, and they cannot ever be fully met, there is an inevitable and devastating sense of failure, known as 'neurotic guilt' because the person is not aware of the utter irrationality of the demands.

There is thus in the neurotic a constant and inconsolable fear of failure, which goads him on to more and more effort, to greater achievement or to defensiveness of some kind, even through aggression.

All through this grim evolution of neurotic attitude and behaviour there are inevitable consequences in the actual feelings of the person, which further increase anxiety, and still more in the reactions of other people, who find it impossible to understand his attitudes, even

[1] *Neurosis and Human Growth.*

though they are anxious to help him. Their criticism, in word and attitude, and their 'good advice' only make him feel still more 'isolated and helpless in a world conceived as potentially hostile'. In this way the neurotic process is spurred onward, all his efforts must go to maintaining and justifying this fictitious personality, to appearing rather than to being. He is constantly driven when he ought to be the 'driver' of his own self, he is like the confirmed spendthrift who 'has' to live more and more on borrowed money, knowing deep down that the day of reckoning must come but being 'unable' to do anything about it.

Ideals and ambitions then have become insatiable and perfectionistic demands on himself. He must never 'fail' or make any wrong decision. All decisions then are matters of tremendous importance, and can never be final. When made he can never let them rest, he must go back over the whole problem again and again in a worrying indecisiveness which 'strains at a gnat' (of the particular decision) and 'swallows a camel' (of his futile waste of time and energy).

Wishes and needs then have become demands on others, also insatiable and perfectionistic. Others, including the doctor and the pastor, must never say or do the 'wrong' thing, they must always 'understand', and must fulfil all his expectations. He feels entitled to happiness, rather than, as the American 'Declaration of Independence' wisely puts it, to 'the pursuit of happiness'.

Confidence (based on reality) has then become neurotic pride (based on phantasy), and he therefore needs repeated and endless confirmation of his own opinion of himself, and of other people's 'admiration' of him. He is excessively vulnerable to shame from within, and humiliation from without, and therefore he can never be at rest or feel at peace within.

Conscience and self-criticism then have become self-contempt, but he must hide this behind all kinds of evasions and defence-mechanisms without realizing what is going on, because these self-criticisms come into deep painful conflict with his neurotic pride. He has a vindictive feeling against other people, and a need to 'score' off them in some way, or to make them scapegoats for his 'failures'.

We have seen that many of these neurotic manifestations may have the superficial appearance of virtues, of good religious ideals and practices, but there is always something not quite 'right' about them when they come up against the challenges of reality, and there is always a sense of tension and vulnerability behind them rather than the 'fruits of the Spirit': love, joy, peace, and the rest.

The clinging compliant people may appear as deeply surrendered to the will of God, but it proves to be of very partial character, and motivated by great hopes of getting something out of it, as will be seen when they fail to do so.

The rebellious and aggressive people appear as deeply conscientious aspirants for moral righteousness, but again this is generally found to be superficial.

The withdrawn people may appear as dedicated to Christian acceptance and the cultivation of inner peace, but it is often a different kind of resignation: a refusal of the struggle of life instead of a dedicated search for higher goals and standards.

The pastor will recognize many of his people in the foregoing description, which is very largely based on the work of Karen Horney. But it must be realized that the neurotic cannot see the fallacies and inconsistencies behind his attitudes. Other people can see them all too clearly but cannot know the reason for their presence. Any direct attempt to bring them to the notice of the neurotic will do more harm than good. It will mobilize all his automatic unconscious defence mechanisms and compel him to make them stronger than ever, to justify himself at all costs. In fact the neurotic often uses the psychic mechanism of projection (described in Section I of this book), and to react to his own self-criticism by projecting it on others and imagining that they are criticizing him. He will very often imagine that the pastor and the doctor are despising him when in fact they had not thought of doing so. And no immediate assurances will convince him, so that mere acceptance of his idea is the best pastoral attitude.

The neurotic may be compared with a person struggling to keep afloat in deep water because he has never been taught to swim, and getting more and more frightened and hopeless as he does so. Those who can swim know that people do not need to struggle to keep afloat, because the buoyancy or the water will keep them afloat if they allow it to do so by lying flat or simply bending their heads backward. But however often and however forcibly the struggling person is told that he need not struggle he will not believe it sufficiently to put it to the test. Somebody must go out to him and support him until he can stop struggling, and then it may be possible to help him to utilize the buoyancy of the water and even to work his way slowly to the shore.

The neurotic may be thought of as struggling to keep 'afloat' in society because he has never been taught to depend on the 'buoyancy' of society, to 'swim' in life. It is obvious to everyone that he is selfish and self-centred, but he must be in the same way as the drowning man must be. Accusations of selfishness will increase his despair as they would that of the drowning man. Someone must go out to him and support him until he can relax his futile struggles, and then help him to 'learn to swim' in society.

The needs of the neurotic are those of the child: love, dependability, and reverence for his personality. These great qualities need to be applied with knowledge, patience, and wisdom, both for the prevention of neurotic illness and at all stages of its management. If ever the Christian injunction 'Judge not' needs to be kept, it is in dealing with the neurotic. We may well pray with Jesus: 'Father, forgive them, for they know not what they do!'

Here is where the Christian, be he minister or layman, has the essential resources for helping these unfortunate people. The ordinary citizen will accept people as long as he can 'understand' their attitudes and behaviour. But it is impossible for any man to understand any other sufficiently, and the Christian faith in its deep realism gives people the direction and power to accept other people's attitudes even when they cannot understand them. The trouble is that this great creative healing spirit is not always understood, or shown by Christian people in their dealings with those who may feel and think in ways that appear strange or inconsistent.

Prevention of Neurotic Illness. It seems obvious that we can do little at present to alter any possible constitutional factors in the causation of neurotic illness. But all that we have been considering about the mode of production of such illness should make it clear that one of the most important of all preventive measures open to the Church, to medicine, and to society itself, is the creation of first-class facilities for universal and comprehensive education for marriage and parenthood as outlined in Section II of this book. This should be the basic foundation on which is built all the help we can give people for growth to maturity and mental health.

The good home will then come more frequently to form the secure background for the more public training of children in baby health centres, kindergartens, schools and Sunday-schools, and in child guidance and other mental health clinics. Marriage counselling services will also have greater influence on the promotion of mental health when backed by a fuller pre-marital education service.

This universal education for marriage and parenthood is an immense 'combined operation' in which many existing organizations can have an important part. The medical profession will need to provide some of the special knowledge and training, and this will involve an extension of the ordinary medical training for those who may feel the call to service in this field of 'Social Medicine'. The Church would seem to have a very large part through fuller Christian pastoral educational work as indicated in Section II of this book, and in the promotion of better pastoral counselling. This will involve better pastoral training for ministers, and more pastoral training for laymen than has generally been available.

Social organization and services, such as housing, town planning and various welfare organizations will also have a part to play, and people themselves have the responsibility to seek better knowledge and to cultivate better personal and social responsibility, and more disciplined balanced living.

This is a staggering task, but we face a staggering challenge, the size of which will certainly become more obvious with the passage of time—when many golden opportunities will have been allowed to slip away. In a talk broadcast in 1950 by the British Broadcasting Corporation the Rev. J. Leycester King, S.J.,[1] made the situation very clear.

During the war, a committee, of which I was chairman, had the task of finding out whether, and to what extent, psychological factors were interfering with the war effort by causing absenteeism, loss of efficiency, lowered production, and so on. Our pilot survey disclosed so alarming a state of affairs that I was unwilling at first to accept the figures as accurate. But careful comparison of our results with those obtained by similar surveys conducted during the last few years both here and in America, have gone far to convince me that our conclusions were substantially correct; namely that from about ten to twenty-five per cent of the industrial population of this country are suffering from psychological troubles which disadvantage them to a more than trivial extent in their health, happiness and efficiency. The implications of this matter are simply vast, it is without doubt the most important human problem of our time.

Treatment of the Neurotic is a long, patient and comprehensive

[1] *The Listener*, 21st December 1950, p. 787.

matter, but it begins with the very first contact between the patient
and the doctor, even when that is an indirect one through being told
about him by someone else, or through making a telephone inquiry
with his nurse-attendant. It continues through all the diagnostic and
counselling and other therapeutic procedures, and through all the
other personal relationships, with pastors and with relatives and
friends. We have seen how sensitive, vulnerable, and 'defensive' the
neurotic is and how important it is that he should be offered an outgoing, accepting goodwill, not dependent on 'understanding'.

The physical surroundings come under some consideration by the
doctor, who must decide whether to have the patient in his own home
or lodging, or transfer him to hospital or rest home.

The personal relationships also need consideration, because every
person in contact with the patient has some part in the treatment. It
is often helpful for the doctor or pastor to have some discussion with
those nearest to the patient so that their attitudes to him will not be
so likely to hinder the treatment. Good team-work between all who
come into any relationship with the patient will increase the efficiency
of the treatment very greatly.

The physical health of the patient also comes under close consideration by the doctor, together with the relevant conditions of work and
finance, which often provide heavy burdens and worries.

The specific management of the neurotic is through what is called
'psychotherapy', which may be regarded as a deeper form of counselling, and is designed to provide an atmosphere of acceptance in which
the patient may unburden his feelings progressively and be encouraged and helped to gain better insight into all the self-deceptions
which have been built up in his efforts at self-realization through the
years. This may be very difficult indeed. The patient's defences will
often be so deeply laid and so powerful that he cannot realize their
existence except through some deep analytical therapy over a long
period.

The whole purpose of psychotherapy is progressively to help the
patient to become aware of and to disentangle his conflicting and
pressing emotions, and the manner in which they arose in him. He is
then in a better position to begin again, with the help and encouragement of his friends, to build up his personality on the basis of
reality rather than phantasy, of being rather than appearing. Here is
where the pastor, backed by the whole Church fellowship and possibly even more by a special pastoral or social group (see Chapter 11)

may have a priceless contribution to make to the progressive healing and the steady new growth of the person. It seems certain that there will be many further developments in this valuable healing work.

The goal of healing of the neurotic should be something more than his own peace of mind and general welfare. Actually he may be of very great help to other people by virtue of the insights and understandings which have come to him in his struggle for health. If he sets out, under proper supervision, to give what help he can it will do much for other people, but also for himself, as the world-wide 'Alcoholics Anonymous' fellowships have abundantly proved.

III. THE PSYCHOTIC REACTION TYPES

We have seen that the neurotic generally lacks insight into his own inner attitudes but that he possesses reasonable insight into reality. The psychotic may generally be distinguished from the neurotic, not so much by the apparent severity of the disorder (although it is often more severe and uncontrollable) but rather by the apparent lack of insight into reality as well as into his own inner attitudes. Because of this the psychotic is much less 'accessible' to psychotherapy than is the neurotic.

As usual with mental illness, however, there can be no sharp demarcation between these two reaction types. Neurotics often have psychotic 'episodes', and they may even become psychotic at times. Some authorities regard the distinction as only one of degree, but in many respects they seem to differ in kind sufficiently to warrant separate consideration and generally different treatment. The psychotics can also be divided for convenience into five main groups:

(*a*) *The Depressed*. Melancholia: Reactive, 'Endogenous', Involutional.
(*b*) *The Elated*. Hypo-mania and Mania. Manic-depressive Psychosis.
(*c*) *The Deteriorated*.
    i. *Schizophrenia:* Simple, Hebephrenic, Catatonic, Paranoid.
    ii. *Senile, Arteriosclerotic, and Chronic Alcoholic Dementia.*
    iii. *Other Organic Dementias:* 'G.P.I.', Encephalitis, Injury, Tumour, Degenerations.
(*d*) *The Acutely Confused*. Delirium, Alcoholic or Drug Intoxications.
(*e*) *The Defective*. Idiocy, Imbecility, Feeble-mindedness.

How does a Psychotic Illness come into being? Apart from actual damage to the brain by acute intoxications, poisonings, injuries, nutritional disorders, acute and chronic inflammations, and tumours and degenerations, we must again consider the two great groups of factors: constitutional inadequacy and the internal and external stresses of life.

It is generally believed in these days that constitutional factors exert a greater proportional influence in the production of psychotic illness than in neurotic illness, as compared with the various environmental stresses. An increasing amount of research work through careful observation of identical twins, some of whom have been brought up in different homes, and comparisons with non-identical twins, has made the influence of these constitutional factors almost beyond doubt.

But there is no doubt that the stresses of life also play an important part, at least in the precipitation of many psychotic illnesses, in much the same manner as they do in the production of neurotic illness.

General features of the different Psychotic reaction types. It is important for the pastor to have some knowledge of the main features of the different psychotic illnesses, so that he can encourage or even urge the obtaining of psychiatric help at the earliest possible opportunity. This knowledge will also help him to avoid the futility and harmfulness of attempts to deal with them at the pastoral level.

(a) *Melancholia*, the Depressive Psychosis. This disorder generally appears at some time in the second half of life, from the age of 45 onward. It often comes in a succession of attacks of varying severity, each lasting for some months, and separated by months or years.

Attacks of Melancholia may alternate with attacks of Mania or what is called Hypo-mania (a mild Mania). When the attacks of either Melancholia or Mania are mild it may be difficult to elicit the history from the relatives. This alternating sequence is called Manic-depressive Psychosis, or, as the French call it *'Folie Circulaire'*.

The onset of an attack of Melancholia is generally gradual, with the development in the patient of progressively deepening inconsolable sadness, with pessimism for himself and his relatives, apathy and listlessness. There is an increasing dullness and insensitiveness of his whole personality. He is well aware of this deadness of feeling, but quite unable to do anything about it. Attempts to interest him or to 'buck him up' only drive him into deeper despair. He is equally insensitive to joyful and to tragic news. In many cases the most obvious indication of the illness is a rapid loss of his previous initiative, and a growing neglect of all his interests and even his everyday personal activities such as dressing, shaving, eating, and washing. He is quite capable of logical reasoning except when delusions appear, and he generally knows what is going on around him quite well, although his thinking may be slowed down considerably.

There are often physical symptoms, such as indigestion, abdominal or thoracic discomfort, constipation, headaches, irritability and restlessness, and insomnia. There is a tendency to over-concern about these, amounting in some cases to definite hypochondriasis, and there is little or no response to well-based reassurance, often one of the first things to excite suspicion of the disorder.

The depression and other symptoms are generally most intense in the morning, and they tend to diminish during the day. He will be deeply puzzled at his 'laziness' and will generally develop greater and greater self-reproach and condemnation, in which every kind of activity of his past life may be magnified into justification for his remorse. It is probable that many of the delusions which further complicate the illness arise in this way, and they are usually delusions of heavy guilt, unworthiness, failure, corruption, or approaching disgrace and ruin for himself and his whole family. At this stage there is definite danger of suicide.

The medical treatment is generally complete rest with full acceptance of all the patient's ideas without any attempt at reassurance. Most of them do very well with a course of 'electro-convulsive therapy', generally in hospital. It is most important for pastors to understand that people with melancholia are made worse by attempts to reassure them or to argue them out of their delusions, and the same applies to all those who have any contact with the patient. It is very difficult to persuade people of this fact, and also of the fact that a person suffering from even mild melancholia is seriously ill, far more so than one who suffers from extreme grief from bereavement. The sooner they can be induced to have psychiatric help the less damage will be done, and the sooner will they recover. Many of them recover, but there is always a possibility of further attacks.

(b) *Mania and Hypo-mania.* This elated psychotic state also tends to appear in the second half of life, from about 45 onward, and to come in recurring attacks, generally of shorter duration than those of Melancholia, and sometimes alternating with it.

The onset is generally gradual, with progressive irritability and restlessness, leading to increasing elation and enthusiasm, in which everyone else is expected to share. The patient will seem to have tireless energy, impatience, and often reckless impulsiveness. With supreme self-confidence he will start all kinds of enterprises, and spend money freely and expansively, but few of his projects are ever completed.

He may tend to become aggressive in the face of any interference, and may become violent if he is forcibly resisted. In conversation he will show a 'flight of ideas', pouring out words in rapid succession, jumping from one subject to another, and talking, shouting or singing without regard to the time of day or night, or of the feelings of anyone else. There will often be increased sexual desire and exhausting demands on his wife.

There are often delusions of grandeur and power, which are quite beyond the reach of any reasoning. Eventually, if not brought under treatment he will generally become exhausted, but he will probably have brought everyone else to complete exhaustion before this happens.

The most important necessity in treatment is early recognition, and admission to hospital for sedation and generally for 'electro-convulsive therapy', which is generally most efficacious in this kind of illness. The pastor can often help greatly by early recognition and urging to obtain medical help, also by warning the family to take all possible steps to protect the finances against the craving of the patient for lavish spending. He may also help in some cases to persuade the patient to go to hospital, but this is more often done through certification.

At the beginning of an attack the wise pastor may be able to help the relatives to understand the nature of the illness and the initial handling and 'humouring' of the patient. Also to help the patient to live under less strain between attacks.

(c) *Schizophrenia*. This is the commonest psychotic illness of the earlier years of life, over seventy-five per cent of cases beginning before the age of 25, and some of them in the first decade of life. It is probably the most common of all serious illnesses in temperate climates, and about half the hospital beds of the world are occupied by sufferers from this mysterious and infinitely complex disorder.

The symptoms of Schizophrenia are many and varied, and often difficult to describe in words. Four types of the disorder have been described, which may overlap considerably, and the patient may change in the course of the illness from the simpler types to more complex ones. The four types described are Simple, Hebephrenic, Catatonic, and Paranoid. The recognition of the possibility of this disorder by the pastor may possibly be made reasonably simple by a brief description of the main features of each type. A good detailed description may be found in any recognized text-book on Psychiatry, one of the most recent being *Clinical Psychiatry*, by Mayer-Gross, Slater, and Roth (Cassell, 1954).

Simple Schizophrenia is the mildest form of the disorder, and includes many of the borderline cases. The most common picture is one of indifference and irresponsibility, with lack of initiative on the person's own, or anyone else's behalf. When a young person changes in character and ceases to show any consideration for his loved ones and his closest friends, or any regard for his social or vocational obligations for no apparent reason, the onset of this disorder must be suspected, and medical help obtained. When attempts are made to offer friendship and help to such people there is generally a complete lack of emotional response, or at best one that is shallow and fleeting. The person seems to have no perception of the puzzled bewilderment of his friends at his attitudes, and he may even perform acts of cruelty to children or old people without any twinge of conscience. He may accept complete financial dependence on struggling parents without any apparent sense of guilt or failure, and neither appeals nor threats have any influence on his attitudes.

Hebephrenic Schizophrenia generally presents all the manifestations of the simple variety together with definite indications of deterioration of the actual thought processes of the person. This form generally begins insidiously, often between the ages of 15 and 25. There is often some proneness to dreaminess, or vagueness of thinking, which may be noticed first in poor results at school or inefficiency and unreliability at work. At home it may be noticed that the patient has lost his ability to concentrate, and has become aloof, dreamy, and neglectful. In conversation he will switch off into bizarre side-issues because of some strange association of ideas, or even merely because of an alliteration or attempted 'pun'. When the listener is unable to understand these remarks the patient is often quite annoyed. There is often a 'thought blockage', a failure to answer questions directly, part of the strange unapproachability characteristic of the schizophrenic.

Later there are often delusions, it may be of his own ability to achieve great things, or of his own exalted status and position. The delusions are largely attempts at 'rationalization' or explanation of his thoughts and feelings, and are fleeting and inconstant. In later stages of the disorder there are often hallucinations, mostly of 'voices' which direct or interfere with his ideas, repeat what he says or mock him. He may be convinced that all his thoughts are 'broadcast' to other people, or that other people are exerting, or trying to exert, an influence on him.

Along with these signs of disordered thinking there are generally definite indications of disordered emotions, and their dissociation from his thinking. He will show what has been called 'emotional incongruity', giggling and laughing at nothing, at his own conversation and often in response to tragic or depressing situations. On the other hand there may be rage and hostility in response to attempted kindness. Grimacing is common, even when he is alone, and he will often show a fatuous, self-satisfied expression quite out of harmony with reality. He may spend hours simply looking into space, possibly with an open but unread book in front of him.

All these abnormalities of thought and feeling are also expressed in completely irresponsible conduct. He may go to bed late and lie in for hours in the mornings, indifferent to any obligations. He neglects his appearance and his cleanliness, and shows general deterioration.

Catatonic Schizophrenia. In this variety, or often it is this stage in the gradually progressive deterioration, the 'shutting off' from the real world is possibly shown most clearly in episodes of prolonged stupor, in which, when complete, the patient becomes completely immobilized or 'frozen', often in some strange posture. In early stages it may be partial and momentary, involving perhaps one limb, or the function of speech, and it may only occur when the patient is touched or spoken to.

There are many other characteristic signs of this condition, such as repeated 'stereotyped' movements, often of symbolic character, like a weird distorted miming or ballet dancing. The patient may also adopt symbolic postures. Another common feature is what is called 'automatic obedience', either to verbal direction or by mimicking the examiner's own actions or words, or allowing his limbs to be placed in some posture and leaving them so for some time.

At other times the patient may show the opposite characteristic: negativism, resisting all attempts to move his limbs, and all requests as a matter of principle. He may refuse to eat, to wash, or to go to the toilet, and often will soil himself soon afterwards.

These people will often write pages of material, repeating words, phrases and sentences over and over again. Their speech and their writing may be quite incoherent, or incoherent passages may alternate with more straightforward expression. 'Neologisms', or private additions to the language are fairly common, and some patients will express their disordered thinking and feeling in bizarre drawings or paintings, which may even be accepted as 'modern art'.

Paranoid Schizophrenia is generally more definite in form, and more constant in its manifestations than any of the other types. It is more common in middle and old age than in the young, and may gradually develop from the other types.

The main characteristic of this type is the presence of fixed and definite delusional beliefs, which are woven into the patient's total outlook on life, and are completely beyond the influence of any reasoning or assurances. The delusions are generally quite plausible at the beginning, and paranoid schizophrenics may cause very great inconvenience and distress to innocent people in their attempts to convey their ideas to others and to take action which they think appropriate.

When a paranoid woman tells everyone that she has proof that her husband is constantly unfaithful to her, or when another person is accused of some serious conduct and police are summoned to deal with the situation, or litigation attempted, it can be seen how much trouble and waste of social services can be brought about.

In many cases, however, the delusional nature of the beliefs is evident to everyone, for example the conviction that a body of super-scientists can see all that he sees, and that they speak through him, or that he is constantly persecuted because he knows so much that certain people cannot allow him to go on living. In a strange way these people seem to fit their delusions into their lives, and to go on reasonably quietly in spite of them. Many such people carry on for years without needing to be admitted to hospital. In others there is no such adaptation to their disordered thinking, and hospital care seems essential.

A schizophrenic illness of any of the four types described may apparently begin with a sudden or rapid 'breakdown' in mental health, or with some grossly abnormal or unexpected conduct. But careful inquiry will show that in most cases there have been earlier signs of abnormal attitude or behaviour at various times over the previous year or two, which were put down to some external strain, such as over-work, or the rapid growth of adolescence, or some shock or illness. These episodes, and the actual onset of the main illness, are generally regarded by the family as a 'nervous breakdown' which will pass off with rest and 'tonics'. This sometimes happens, but the dreaminess, aloofness, and shallowness tend to persist or to recur after a few weeks or months, and it is increasingly obvious that the person is ill.

There are few conditions in which early diagnosis and early treatment are of such far-reaching importance to patient and relatives alike, and unhappily there are few conditions in which it is so difficult to persuade the patient's relatives, let alone the patient himself, that he is suffering from a serious mental illness. The help of a fully competent understanding pastor who has already won the confidence of his people may be of the most vital importance in persuading them to seek competent medical advice and treatment without any delay.

Some of the milder schizophrenics, and those who have improved with treatment may live quietly in reasonable adaptation to a more or less protected environment for a long period. They are generally much better if encouraged to do what work they can without undue strain or fatigue. But there is always the possibility of relapse or breakdown in health. The more severely affected, and those who do not respond to adequate treatment may go on to profound deterioration, or may come to some kind of equilibrium with a completely protected hospital environment.

The essential treatment is entirely a matter for the highly qualified psychiatrist, assisted by hospital care when necessary, and by such accessory services as occupational therapy and social activities. The physical health of the patient is another important factor in the situation and is carefully supervised. It is generally agreed that psychoanalysis is likely to do more harm than good in this condition, so that any psychotherapy should generally be kept at a superficial level. For example the patient should be encouraged to adjust his life to his delusions and hallucinations, rather than to dig deeply into their possible meanings. The pastor may be of great personal help to many schizophrenics if he can offer them simple understanding accepting friendship, without attempting to criticize, advise, or preach. He can also help by initiating and supervising some good social fellowship on

S

the same permissive basis. In particular he may be able to offer very valuable help to the bewildered and grief-stricken relatives, who may be filled with a sense of remorse in the belief that some act or neglect of theirs may have brought on the trouble. Needless to say this is not the case.

(d) *The Dementias* are generally characterized by impairment of intelligence to some degree, the natural intellectual ability as well as the acquired knowledge and wisdom of those who suffer from them. These qualities are not generally impaired in early Schizophrenia, there is rather a deterioration of personality through which the patient is unable to use his knowledge and intelligence adequately because of a kind of splitting of the normal integration between the different faculties.

Senile Dementia is becoming an increasingly common problem with the greater proportion of older people in most communities. Another factor in the situation is the fact that there are often fewer facilities for their proper care, and consequently greater emotional and physical stresses. All too often they come to feel unwanted and unloved, and they tend to become bored and apprehensive.

The approach of senile dementia may be suspected when there seems to be an exaggeration of the normal psychological changes of old age, such as rapid deterioration of memory for recent events, and of the ability to grasp what is being said, or to reason things out. The imagination is also impaired and there is often an increasing self-centredness and rigidity of outlook.

The sufferer may develop increasing distrust and suspicion, which often extend to become delusions of persecution or injury. He may be quite convinced that everything is being stolen from him, or that people are trying to defraud him.

At the same time his emotions become shallow and unresponsive, and his general initiative and self-reliance become markedly reduced. He may be restless and wander about the house in an apparently vague purposeless manner during the night, and possibly be discovered cold and semi-comatose lying outside the back door when the family arises in the morning. Some of these nocturnal expeditions are probably for the purpose of emptying his bladder or bowel, or of obtaining food or a drink, but he may forget what he started out for and be uncertain as to where he is.

There are also many disorders of conduct in these people, firstly in the form of unjustified hostility or petulance, and then increasingly irresponsible and unpredictable behaviour. In some cases a sexual offence, such as exhibitionism, in a person of impeccable moral character may be the first indication of the onset of this disorder. With advancing deterioration there may be complete neglect of ordinary cleanliness, and loss of control of his bowel and bladder, which all contribute to a pathetic situation of incredible filthiness. Added to this he may degenerate to sexual perversions, which would have previously filled him with horror.

The course of this disorder is generally fairly rapid, and most of the sufferers are given a happy release by death, generally within two years of the onset. The main treatment is rest and care, proper feeding, and protection from injury or exposure. The patient may be happier in his own home at the beginning, especially if he can be relieved of loneliness, but with deterioration of his mental faculties it is generally necessary to have him nursed in hospital until the end comes.

The most important contribution of the pastor is a friendly understanding and acceptance, without any attempt to argue him out of his suspicions or delusions. He may also help greatly in reassuring the family, and sometimes the magistrate or the legal authority, that his deviations of conduct are not blameworthy, but simply a part of his serious illness. The doctors will generally have done this already, but some extra backing from the trusted representative of the Church will often bring increased comfort and reassurance.

The whole question of care of the aged and helpless is an inescapable social problem, in the solution of which the Church is taking a worthy part, but there is much still to be done.

The 'Pre-senile' Dementias. These form a varied group of conditions with dementia as a common factor, which occur generally during middle age and up to the age of 70. Like senile dementia they are characterized by some kind of damage to the brain. As a matter of general interest they can be listed as follows:

i. Associated with disorders of cerebral circulation:
    (*a*) Occurring in cases of high blood-pressure. Age 45–55.
    (*b*) Occurring in Arteriosclerosis without necessarily high blood-pressure. Age 55–70.
ii. Associated with previous injury to the brain.
iii. Associated with Cerebral Tumour.
iv. Associated with Disorders of Nutrition: Oxygen deficiency, Hypoglycaemia, Starvation, Vitamin B deficiency, etc.

v. Associated with Epilepsy.
vi. Associated with Chronic Infections: G.P.I., and other Syphilitic infections of the brain, Encephalitis of various forms.
vii. Associated with Cerebral Degenerations, from Chronic Alcoholism, Endocrine Disorders, some Hereditary Disorders, and a number of degenerations of unknown causation.

The pastoral attention to people suffering from these conditions is along the general lines already considered, and from the pastoral point of view no further description would seem to be necessary.

(e) *The Acute Confusional Insanities* form a group of conditions which are generally of rapid onset and short duration as long as the cause can be neutralized or removed. Here again we can list the most common varieties:

i. The acute intoxications, such as Acute Alcoholism, 'Delirium Tremens', certain Drug intoxications, such as Bromide, Barbiturate, Atropine and Hyoscine, Amphetamine, Morphine and derivatives, and Uraemia from renal failure.
ii. Acute Poisonings from Lead, Carbon Monoxide, Mercury, etc.
iii. Acute Fevers, such as Pneumonia, Typhoid Fever, Cerebral Malaria, and certain Virus infections such as Influenza. Generally Delirium.
iv. Metabolic Disorders, such as 'Insulin Coma' and Diabetic Coma.
v. Endocrine Disorders, such as 'Pre-menstrual Tension', and 'Puerperal Insanity'.

In many of these cases the acute confusional disorder is greater when there has been some previous mental instability. One of these acute stresses may even be the actual precipitating factor in a person who would otherwise have managed to keep his instability under reasonable control.

The treatment of these conditions is entirely medical, and the urgency and intensity of the illness generally brings the relatives or associates of the person to summon medical help without delay. The main interest for the pastor would seem to be in his realization that some apparently insane people may really be suffering from an acute 'medical' illness, the immediate proper care of which will bring a rapid recovery from the 'insanity'.

(f) *The Mentally Defective*. These form a class of their own, and it is generally obvious fairly early in life, if not actually at the child's birth, that there is some defect in the child's mentality. In doubtful cases there are many intelligence and aptitude tests which provide help.

These people are generally classified on a basis of the extent of the defect into three groups; the idiots, who are unable to guard themselves even against common physical dangers; the imbeciles, who are incapable of managing their affairs or of being taught to do so; and the feeble minded, who require care, supervision and control for the protection of themselves and others, and are incapable of being taught adequately in ordinary schools. These are the general terms in which mentally defective people are classified in the British Mental Deficiency Act, 1913.

Some mentally defective children are the products of genetic factors, but others are produced by stresses or deficiencies to which the child is exposed before birth, during birth, or soon after birth.

Before birth there may be the stress provided by certain infections in the mother, notably Syphilis and Rubella, or by Rh incompatibility between the parents (Father Rh positive and Mother negative), and possibly by defective intra-uterine nutrition or oxygenation, but these are not clearly recognized.

During birth the most common stress from this point of view is of course birth injury with some degree of intracranial haemorrhage. This is more common in premature births and in difficult and abnormal births, particularly breech presentations. Obstetricians are very careful to preserve all possible safeguards in these respects by the fullest ante-natal care and supervision, and by the most meticulous care in the whole conduct of labour.

After birth the child may be deprived of the chance to develop normally by being brought up in an inadequate social environment, by maternal deprivation in a physical or psychic sense, by gross lack of education, and sometimes by the non-recognition of deafness or blindness in the early months or years. Certain infections, notably Encephalitis and Meningitis, can also leave the brain damaged in such a way as to prevent the normal mental development.

The pastoral contribution to this complex problem is again divided between the patient and the relatives. Those patients who are not cared for in special institutions will need special pastoral understanding and care, and this provides an opportunity for many members of the Christian Congregation under the general leadership of the pastor.

The parents and other relatives, particularly brothers and sisters of the defective child, will also be suffering from considerable strain and bewilderment, which come very closely within the pastoral field of service. Above all the parents should be helped to a complete over-coming of any sense of guilt they may have had, and any resentment against God or against any human being. Such emotional tensions will tend to interfere greatly with their spiritual uplift and deprive the child (and often the other children of the family) of the most valuable inspiration for dealing with the whole situation.

The problem is complex, difficult, far-reaching and prolonged, and it provides a very vital opportunity for some first-class pastoral service to many people in urgent and intense need.

IV. PSYCHOPATHIC DISORDERS

These disorders form a rather vaguely defined group of persistent abnormalities of the human personality which do not fit easily into either of the groups already considered. The label 'psychopathic personality' is commonly applied to a rather mixed group of people 'whose disturbance is evident not so much in their own minds or feelings but in their conduct and in the adjustment they make between themselves and the rest of the world'.[1] Any consideration of these people must take into account the nature of the society in which they live, and its conventions and standards of conduct. What would be regarded as a psychopathic disorder in one society might be accepted as normal in another one, as the Cultural Anthropologists are clearly demonstrating.

Many deviations from conventional conduct are tolerated by society as long as it does not feel itself threatened. When society does feel threatened it reacts through legally enforceable measures, such as segregation or punishment, or in some cases both segregation and punishment. In less threatening cases the safeguard of some kind of bond is often imposed. With better understanding of the psychopathic personality there is less tendency to punitive reactions on the part of society and more to attempts at reform and reintegration into society. The growing science of criminology appears to be a healthy forward move.

[1] David Stafford-Clark, *Psychiatry Today* (Penguin Books, 1952), pp. 116-17. This book may be strongly recommended to all pastors, and to anyone who takes an intelligent interest in Psychiatry.

It is the province of the law, as represented by the judiciary and all the associated institutions and services, to make a full and impartial investigation into the actions of anyone who may be charged with offensive conduct, to allow him the opportunity to defend himself in fair trial, and then to pronounce whatever sentence is deemed appropriate. It is being increasingly realized that in many cases of apparent psychopathic disorder there is need for the professional assistance of a psychiatrist, a psychologist, and a social worker attached to the courts, with opportunities of investigating the mental processes of those who may seem to need it.

For the pastor who may come into contact with many people whose attitudes and conduct are suggestive of a psychopathic disorder, it is important that he should recognize that many serious abnormalities of conduct are of a more complex nature than they may appear, that the person may be the victim of urges which are stronger and more subtle than is usually assumed.

There is now some quite definite factual support for this view. The most definite is in the tracings elicited with a very sensitive apparatus called the electro-encephalograph, which records the electrical activity of the brain. It has been found quite consistently that a large proportion of those people who are regarded as suffering from some form of psychopathic disorder give tracings similar to those normally found in children, and show evidence of immature functioning of the brain. Those who recover from, or rather 'grow out of' the disorder show parallel improvement in their tracings.

Another interesting confirmation is found in the type of formation of the capillary loops in the nail bed of the fingers. This formation also changes with growth from childhood to maturity, and a large and significant proportion of psychopaths show the immature pattern of childhood in their capillary loops.

This immaturity is shown very vividly in the emotional reactions of psychopathic personalities. To quote Stafford-Clark again:

These people are impulsive, feckless, unwilling to accept the results of experience and unable to profit by them, sometimes prodigal of effort but utterly lacking in persistence, plausible but insincere, demanding but indifferent to appeals, dependable only in their constant unreliability, faithful only to infidelity, rootless, unstable, rebellious, and unhappy. A survey of their lives will reveal an endless succession of jobs, few of which have been held for more than six months, many of which have been abandoned after a few days; very little love but often a great number of adventures, very little happiness despite a ruthless and determined pursuit of immediate gratification. Such patients are all too often their own worst enemies and nobody's real friend. If, as sometimes happens, they are distinguished by some outstanding gift or talent they may achieve apparently spectacular success only to throw it away or spoil it at least for themselves by their turbulent and exacting emotional attitude. More frequently, despite a level of intelligence which is as often above average as below, they drift from failure and disappointment through one lost opportunity after another into drug addiction, alcoholism, suicide, or prostitution.[1]

It is difficult to classify these people in any satisfactory manner, and various attempts have been made. One reasonably simple classification is as follows:

(a) *The Active Aggressive Type:* Characterized by repeated irresponsible, impulsive or compulsive behaviour, often anti-social, violent, or even criminal. Many sex-offenders come into this group, and also many sadists and sexual perverts.

(b) *The Delinquent Type:* This group includes people who suffer from kleptomania and practise petty and unprofitable stealing. It also includes people suffering from drug addictions, including many alcoholics, and also many pathological liars and swindlers, who may be most convincing, plausible, and persuasive to their intended 'victims'.

(c) *The 'Accident-prone' and 'Illness-prone',* who are always in the hands of doctors and Insurance Companies. They are often 'masochistic' in character, and always being 'insulted' or 'injured'.

(d) *The Extreme Individualists:* Geniuses, and creative artists, lacking in emotional maturity and 'social ability', but often most valuable to society. Also the impracticable idealists, full of 'brilliant' but hare-brained schemes, which never come to any kind of fruition.

There is no sharp distinction between the psychopathic and the neurotic personality, and some authorities put these two kinds of disorder together. But in the more well-marked examples a distinction seems useful for purposes of discussion, and there is a clinical distinction in that the neurotic suffers from his abnormality, and

[1] *Psychiatry Today.*

generally seeks help for it, while the psychopathic causes society to suffer for his abnormality, and does not generally seek medical help for it. But many neurotics show psychopathic behaviour at times.

The many researches into possible causative factors in psychopathic disorders suggest that genetic and environmental influences each play a part, and that in some cases actual cerebral disease (encephalitis) or injury can be followed by a typical psychopathic disorder. The relative influence of these different factors is becoming clearer with further research, and will doubtless become still further clarified. A recent account of the various findings is given by Mayer-Gross, Slater and Roth.[1]

The works of John Bowlby already considered [2] suggest that maternal deprivation, actual or 'psychological', may produce a type of reaction in children very similar to certain types of psychopathic personality, and that when it is experienced for more than a given time by a child at the 'vulnerable' age (about 1–4) some of the changes in the child's personality become virtually irreversible.

It seems of great importance that the widest and fullest efforts should be made to prevent or to minimize the occurrence of these disorders by the promotion of the best possible care of children in their early years, and by looking out for the earliest indications of psychopathy in kindergartens, schools and Sunday-schools.

Treatment is generally difficult because the psychopathic person is not generally anxious to co-operate. It is probable that some kind of group therapy will prove most helpful, because one of the greatest needs of the psychopath is to learn to get on with other people. It may be that the Church will have an important part in any such group therapy through the quality of its fellowship, when that quality can be achieved.

When the psychopath falls foul of the law and is committed to some penal institution, it is necessary that the fullest consideration should be given to the nature of the disorder. In most cases there is an absolute necessity that the convicted person should be segregated in some way for the protection of society, and it is felt by many authorities that the sentence should be indeterminate, and reviewed regularly on a basis of his progress and behaviour. Punitive attitudes tend to deepen the alienation of such people from society, but if they

---

[1] *Clinical Psychiatry* (Cassell, 1954).
[2] *Maternal Care and Mental Health* and *Child Care and the Growth of Love*.

are segregated in a manner comparable with the segregation of a person suffering from an infectious disease, and given the best possible treatment, some of them may be helped to greater maturity. It has been noticed that with advancing years many psychopaths do tend to 'grow out of' some of their abnormalities, unless they are badly mishandled.

With the very frightening increase in the amount and seriousness of delinquency and crime in recent years, especially among young people, this whole problem has become of the greatest importance in the future welfare of the community. It is a problem in which the Church must be vitally interested, and to the solution of which it may well come to make a unique contribution. It is therefore worthy of constant and careful study and discussion.

CHAPTER SEVENTEEN

Marriage Counselling

WE HAVE seen in Chapter 6 that there is an increasingly urgent and widespread need for a first-class and comprehensive community service for the promotion of sound stable marriage and for the healing of the 'sick home'. The educational part of that great project was considered in that chapter, and we are now in a position to deal with the remedial part. The important and far-reaching work of Marriage Counselling is a special form of Pastoral Counselling, which can be and is being carried out with increasing effectiveness by selected and trained ministers and laymen in many parts of the world, mainly through organizations known as Marriage Guidance Councils, or Family Welfare Services. These have arisen in response to the increasingly felt need for education, counselling and research in connexion with the intimate, delicate, and complex relationships of marriage and family living.

The national importance of good marriage counselling has been recognized at the highest level in Great Britain since the presentation of what is now known as 'The Denning Report', the 'Final Report of the Committee on Procedure in Matrimonial Causes'—'Presented by the Lord High Chancellor to Parliament by Command of His Majesty, February 1947'—and printed by His Majesty's Stationery Office. Here are some relevant extracts from that report.

The reconciliation of estranged parties to marriages is of the utmost importance to the State as well as to the parties and their children. It is indeed so important that the State itself should do all it can to assist reconciliation.

There should be a Marriage Welfare Service to afford help and guidance both in preparation for marriage and also in difficulties after marriage. It should be sponsored by the State but should not be a State institution. It should evolve gradually from the existing services and societies, just as the probation system evolved from the Court Missionaries and the Child Guidance Services from the children's clinics. It should not be combined with the judicial procedure for divorce but should function quite separately from it.

The principal aims of a Marriage Welfare Service should be:

First, to make available a sufficient number of suitable persons to give advice and to see that their availability is generally known.

Second, to encourage young people to seek competent advice in preparation for marriage.

Third, to encourage married couples to seek competent advice as soon as serious conflicts arise.

Fourth, to attempt reconciliation whenever a break has occurred.

It should be recognized as a function of the State to give every encouragement and where appropriate financial assistance to marriage guidance as a form of Social Service.[1]

We have seen in Chapter 7 that there is an important distinction between pre-marital education, which is suitable for the reasonably mature candidates for marriage, and pre-marital counselling, which is necessary for those who are immature or who may be suffering from any 'bottled up' or repressed emotional tensions. This pre-marital counselling is generally carried out with each of the candidates separately, according to the principles and methods of pastoral interviewing and counselling already laid down in this book. This, when well carried out, will prevent many marital troubles and conflicts from happening, but not all. At the engagement stage it is impossible to prevent all marriages from becoming unhappy, because many factors in the choice of a mate are unconscious: they are hidden from the 'mate' as well as from the person who chooses. Any questioning at this stage of the wisdom of marrying may stir up very strong and deep defence mechanisms, and will tend to do more harm than good unless there is quite obvious and serious danger in allowing the marriage to go on.

Some inadequate motives for marriage may be known to either candidate, but felt to be too strong to be given up easily, such as loneliness, escape from possessive parents, desire to 'play the game' with regard to a girl whom the young man has made pregnant, or fear of being 'left on the shelf'. All such unworthy motives for marriage involve serious risks of failure, and even if they emerge in pre-marital counselling and the risks plainly stated by the counsellor, the two young people may still remain determined to accept them.

[1] The more recent Report of the Royal Commission on Marriage and Divorce 1951–3 (London: H.M.S.O., 1956), has even more strongly emphasized the need for Marriage Guidance and Conciliation (Part 4, pp. 93–102).

When such a situation arises, unless the risks appear to be such that the pastor cannot honestly undertake the responsibility of conducting the ceremony, it seems best that he should try to create the kind of counselling relationship through which the two people will feel able to come freely for help later if they need it.

The work of marriage counselling for the reconciliation of people in conflict demands a high degree of emotional maturity, personal integrity and stability, and considerable skill and patience. Those to whom the work is entrusted must therefore be very carefully selected and thoroughly trained, and then tried out for a period of probation under the supervision of experienced counsellors. Some people feel a strong desire to do counselling work as an unconscious compensation for deep personal frustrations or because of a deep emotional need of which they are not altogether aware. Such people generally show a degree of emotional instability, vulnerability, or inflexibility which make them quite unfitted for the work.

The necessary training involves a long course of instruction, together with some supervised practical work. Some people have a professional training which includes many of the basic principles of counselling, and some special knowledge of many aspects of marriage, and these assets are very helpful as a background.

What part can the Church play in marriage counselling? Many pastors will have a good background of emotional stability and maturity, and some training in interviewing techniques, possibly built up largely by their own experience. They may be able to undertake some counselling in their own pastoral work when the difficulties are not too complex or too deeply set. Some larger Churches may also be able to organize marriage counselling 'clinics', as long as those who do the work are very well selected and trained. Second-rate standards will not fulfil the Church's calling in the community, and may well bring more troubles than they help to solve.

It seems most appropriate that the marriage counselling work in any community should be a community project, non-sectarian and non-political, which offers help to all people who need it, Christians and non-christians alike, without regard to colour, creed, nationality, or political affiliation. It should be widely representative, and fully supported by Church, State, and all other community services. The best contribution of the Church would seem to be in the provision of a number of thoroughly suitable highly trained Christian Counsellors, ministers and laymen and women who are able and willing to carry out a full share of educational and counselling work, pre-marital and post-marital, and possibly some of the organizing work of Marriage Guidance Councils. In this way the Christian view of Marriage will be kept in the forefront of all marriage guidance work without any attempt to impose it on people. Any non-christian counsellors will also be brought more fully into contact with the Christian faith and the Christian view of God, man, and society. This is actually happening in many centres in many countries, and is proving its value for both Christian and non-christian counsellors.

A marriage guidance centre should be in a suitable place, central but not too public, and preferably on 'neutral' ground. Many needy people might feel diffident at venturing into church buildings. If possible there should be quiet pleasant counselling rooms, and a library and literature room, together with secretarial facilities. The work is generally financed partly by Government grants, and partly by donations from clients and from well-wishers. In some special cases it is carried on by 'private enterprise' of a professional kind for which fees are charged. This is generally the case when Specialist counselling, psychiatric, gynaecological, or legal, is carried out at the counsellor's private consulting rooms.

Clients may be led to come for help through a notice on the building where the centre is situated, through Press publicity, through the recommendation of friends, or they may be sent to the centre by ministers, doctors, solicitors or barristers, judges, or magistrates, or other organizations.

Marriage counselling does not set out to push two unwilling people together or to coerce them in any way. No person has the right or the power to interfere in other people's private affairs. The only exceptions to this are cases where a person's conduct is illegal or potentially dangerous, and then the help of the police force is sometimes neces-sary. In cases of insanity, not unknown in marriage guidance work, psychiatric help may be necessary and when the situation is potenti-ally dangerous the psychiatrist may find it necessary to have the insane person committed to a mental hospital for treatment.

The general aims of marriage counselling are as follows:

(a) To allow the release of emotional tensions in each partner, generally separately, by encouraging catharsis, and thus to pave the way for the necessary insight for a mature relationship to be re-established.

(b) To clarify and interpret the difficulties, tensions, and conflicts to each of the partners, and often to clarify their ideas about the nature of the marriage union itself.

(c) To help each to find a better understanding of the other one's feelings and attitudes as well as his own, and to mediate between them and encourage mutual acceptance. Not to give advice, but to draw out their creative resources for mental and spiritual growth, re-education, healing and reconciliation.

(d) Christian Counselling goes farther to offer the light, power, deliverance and fellowship of the Holy Spirit of Jesus Christ to each of them. The Christian Healing of the 'sick home' also goes beyond domestic reconciliation to include the wider integration with the community, including the Church, and with God. It stakes its claim on the conviction that service to the community and to God are necessary for abundant domestic life.

The application of the principles and techniques of counselling to marriage counselling is fairly straightforward. It is generally best to see each of the partners alone for the initial sessions, possibly after a brief introductory session with the two together. Most people will unburden themselves more deeply and effectively when they are seen in complete privacy. Quite often only one of the partners will come at the initial stage, and after the initial session the other one may be invited to come for a private session to find out how he or she feels about the situation.

Before the interview has gone very far the counsellor will have gained some idea of how far the trouble has gone. If it is at an early stage the two people may have become aware of some conflict or difficulty which is beyond their understanding or their ability to resolve satisfactorily. If there is no apparent emotional tension between them it may be possible to deal with the whole problem with the two of them together, but these cases are the exception, and will be until the idea of seeking help has become more fully accepted in the community.

In many cases the two people are willing to come, but the trouble has grown in spite of their attempts to find some mutually acceptable solution. They will probably be disillusioned and disheartened, each of them deeply wounded, even to breaking-point. They may only have come as a last resort, to please their relatives or friends. In spite of all their despair the results are generally good, but considerable patience and skill are needed before the deep wounds can be healed enough for full reconciliation to be possible. Such people should always be seen separately for as many sessions as required, until their emotional tensions are relieved, and insight achieved.

The ultimate and most difficult stage in the downward progress of a marriage conflict is the actual break in the relationship. In many such cases only one of the 'partners' will come, often unwillingly and without much hope or desire, and there is no direct contact possible with the other partner. It may be possible to obtain some contact through a simple kindly completely uncritical letter which offers the opportunity for him to say what he feels about the situation, and undertakes that everything will be treated in absolutely confidential fashion. The results in such cases are not as good as in the earlier stages of conflict, but are often better than first impressions would have suggested. Sometimes there is such a radical change in the attitudes of the one who comes for help that the other one is inspired with renewed hope and comes to the counsellor. In other cases the unwilling partner may be persuaded to come by a mutual friend. All these methods are worth trying.

If the person who comes is unwilling for the other partner to know of the visit at all the counsellor is placed in a dilemma. It is generally wise in such cases to try to find out why this unwillingness exists. Unless the other person is completely inaccessible or obviously incapable of any responsibility, the counsellor should put it to the client that further interviews behind the back of the partner might only add to the difficulties, and that he does not feel it right to continue unless the other partner knows about it. If this is not done there may be serious complaints from the other partner against the Marriage Guidance Centre and the counsellor.

We are now in a position to consider the actual counselling interviews with either partner. As with counselling in general the first impressions gained by the client are very important. He should feel welcomed with a simple natural friendliness, and there should be no impression of haste or impatience. After he has had time to settle and to collect his thoughts he should be asked the main details needed for the official record. The records are made under a number, and his name is kept on a separate card filed away privately. He should be assured that everything will be kept in absolute confidence. Any records of the actual details of the trouble are generally better made on a separate private card by the counsellor after the session.

The client should then be invited to tell his story in his own words.

In most cases this will prove at first to be an account of all the other person's faults and failures. Allow the story to flow and at the same time take in bit by bit the client's emotional state as shown by his movements and expressions as well as his narrative. The same kind of 'reflecting' comments may be made as described under 'Pastoral Counselling', and there may be room for an occasional question to find out what a particular thing means to the client.

At some point in the counselling, and no fixed rules can be laid down regarding the detailed conduct of counselling interviews, there may be a need for some definite questions about important aspects of the marriage relationships. This may particularly apply to the sexual relationship, which the client may find it difficult to describe without a little help and prompting by the counsellor. It is a good safeguard against overlooking some important questions if the counsellor has at the back of his mind a simple classification of the most common causative factors of marital discord. As the interviews with each partner proceed he will be trying to assess and evaluate these different factors, so that proper attention and help can be given.

The commonest causes of discord can be classified 'from without inwards' into three main groups, as follows:

Group 1. External or Environmental Factors: Bad housing, unsuitable neighbourhood, poverty and insecurity, over-heavy domestic burdens with insufficient help, interference by 'in-laws' or other people, over-strain at work, or a succession of accidents and illnesses. Many of these, and others like them, may be brought about through the people's own carelessness or stupidity, and most people are apt to blame external causes to the exclusion of deeper ones, but it is important to find out as much as possible about these causes as they appear to the client, because they cannot be ignored in any attempt at treatment.

Group 2. Disturbed relationships between the partners:

(i) Sexual Incompatibility is a very common complaint which is sometimes the first difficulty experienced in the marriage. In such cases medical help is often required. In other cases it is an expression of deeper emotional or personal conflict, or of actual neurotic, psychotic, or psychopathic disorder in one or both of the partners. This too needs medical help.

(ii) Personal Incompatibility: Rigidity and intolerance or possessiveness on either side with reaction from the other, or the absence of

T

sufficient common interests, or the lack of co-operation in the essential administration of the home, financial budgeting, domestic work, and the bringing-up of children.

(iii) Spiritual Incompatibility: Lack of the right kind of love, or divergent attitudes to life and to religion and morality.

Group 3. Internal Personal Factors: Ignorance, immaturity and inadequacy for marriage are still quite commonly found in people with marital problems, and of course trouble is almost inevitable when people marry who are unfit for the responsibilities of marriage. In some such cases the partners find their way to the required knowledge and maturity with the help of parents and understanding friends, but in others the strains are too great and the marriage reaches breaking-point. Other personal inadequacies come from, or show up in alcoholic excesses, over-addiction to gambling or other spending of money, immorality and infidelity, and other forms of psychopathy, and in some cases actual mental illness of neurotic or psychotic character. Much of the sadistic, mental and physical cruelty which brings strain and misery to many homes is attributable to such mental disorders, often in a form which only shows itself in the deep emotional conflict of a troubled marriage. An invariable symptom of emotional tensions is the inability to laugh at oneself, the lack of that priceless personal asset, a sense of humour. The most reliable indication of successful treatment is the recovery of a sense of humour.

It is clear that such a classification as this is very useful as long as it is remembered that all three groups are generally represented in any but the simplest marital discord. The third group represents problems of individual personality rather than primarily of marriage, and must obviously be dealt with on that basis as well as from the marital aspect.

It must also be remembered that many marital problems are greatly influenced by disturbed relationships in the household other than those between husband and wife. There may be conflicts between either or both parents and one or more of the children, or involving the relationships between the children themselves, or between parents or children and other occupants of the house or visitors to it or neighbours.

Each factor that is elicited provides a possible clue to some deeper underlying one, which must be given a chance to emerge through the catharsis or through asking the right questions. At the same time it will pave the way for the discovery of how the particular attitude came into being. This will involve questions about the client's childhood, his relationships with parents and siblings, his friendships or lack of them at school, his introduction to 'the facts of life', his parents' relationships to each other, his 'love life' before the present marriage, and all kinds of related questions.

When the catharsis appears to have come to an end, the various questions have been answered, and the client has shown some signs of positive insight, he is ready for some attempt at clarification of his situation, as long as the counsellor has had the opportunity of hearing the ideas and getting to know the feelings of the other partner. This clarification will generally begin with some kind of recapitulation of the client's story in summarized form to give him a picture of the working-out of the trouble. If the other partner is also at the point of some positive insight and emotional peace the clarification might be best carried out with the two of them together, as long as the counsellor remains sensitive to their reactions. This will naturally lead to some mediation between them when they are in any way out of harmony with each other.

At this point in the series of interviews, for all this cannot be carried out except in several interviews, there may be a wide-open opportunity for the Christian counsellor to offer the unique insights and attitudes of the Christian Faith in simple words which back up and extend his previous offering of the Christian Spirit throughout the whole counselling process. The wonder of Christian forgiveness and the Christian offer of a fresh start, and their complete rationality, will often come into the picture, and bring the whole counselling process into the essential realm of evangelism. Perhaps he can bring the clients to the greatest insight of all: their inescapable need of God, the priceless and yet free offering of God to all men through the actual historic Jesus Christ, and the invitation to accept His leadership in humility and faith.

It may be that these great insights, once awakened, will be strengthened to the point of committal through a period of silent meditation and prayer, possibly with a short prayer of thanksgiving and faith from the counsellor. This is a matter for good sensitive judgement, prayer should not be 'dragged in', but should express the spiritual atmosphere that has come into being, and the positive feelings which have been expressed by the clients. It is valid when they are ready to seek and to do God's will, and should lead to further positive questions about their willingness to serve God in the future in His Church.

The counsellor will generally need to stand by the clients until they are established in their new relationship, and have learnt to love many worth-while things together. Some old habitual attitudes may break through at times, but if the counselling has been successful they will generally be able to take such episodes in their stride.

At all points in the counselling it is valuable for the counsellor to have at the back of his mind the question of possible reference to someone with special knowledge and experience if that should seem advisable. This will also be affected by the availability of such help, and the willingness of the clients to seek it. In some difficult cases it may bring the one factor necessary for further progress, and the client may possibly return to the counsellor at a new level of insight and power.

Finally we must emphasize the constant need for the continuing education of counsellors. This can be helped by group case-conferences. It may sometimes be possible to obtain tape-recordings of counselling sessions for critical review and for teaching of counselling techniques. Typical case records can also be used for discussion.

There is also much help to be obtained by conferences with those who are doing educational work in marriage preparation, for the mutual benefit of counsellors and educators. And it goes without saying that the counsellor should continually study the available literature from other counselling centres, and take every possible opportunity for wider contact with other counsellors and specialists.

CHAPTER EIGHTEEN

Visiting the Sick

THIS IS a very wide subject. We have to think of all kinds of illnesses and accidents in all kinds of people, at all ages, and in all kinds of circumstances and places. There are the predominantly physical ailments, of short or long duration, and of mild or serious or fatal severity. At the other end of the scale there are the predominantly psychic ailments, ranging from sudden shock or tragedy with its burden of grief, through the various kinds of neurotic illness to the least accessible psychotic illnesses.

Beyond all our consideration of helping the sick or injured person we have also to consider the most helpful approach to his parents, children, relatives and friends, and also to doctors and nurses, and other people who may be looking after him.

And further still we can profitably think of the possible ways of dealing with the quite common situation in which it is impossible for various reasons to secure direct contact with the patient.

Visiting the sick, with all the other opportunities that go with it, is pastoral work of the most far-reaching importance, and an avenue of creative Christian service. It is a unique opportunity of reaching people when they are in great need and most open for help. Many of them will be otherwise out of touch with the Church, and largely unaware of what help it can offer, and they may be touched by the Spirit of God through well-conducted sick visiting in hospital or in their own homes in a manner not otherwise possible. In this Christian service there is therefore a great evangelistic opportunity which cannot be ignored.

In our Lord's vivid picture of the Judgement recorded by St Matthew, one of the great criteria of final commendation is given as 'I was sick, and ye visited me' and 'Inasmuch as ye have done it unto one of the least of these my brethren ye have done it unto me'. And this is underlined by the rejection of those who did not do the kindly acts (Matthew 25 [31-46]).

It is a tragedy that this great work is not generally being carried out as well as it should. All too often the sick patient's self-pity seems to be increased, and all too often he becomes the target of negative superficial advice, criticism, or gossip. This may be an indication of the general inadequacy of much of the present training of ministers and the almost complete absence of training of Christian laymen in this great work.

A vivid example of the ecclesiastical conservatism regarding the visitation of the sick is seen in the *Book of Common Prayer* in 'The Order for the Visitation of the Sick'. This expresses a Theology which is now quite inappropriate and obsolete, in a liturgy which might well hasten the end of anyone seriously ill if he were unfortunate enough to be subjected to it. It is only fair to say that the corresponding 'Order' in the 1928 Prayer Book is very much more appropriate in every way, but the Anglican Church is still unable officially to use it.

Many ministers teach themselves by reading and by 'trial and error', but this is not doing full justice to their calling, and many far-reaching opportunities are being lost every day.

SOME ESSENTIAL PRINCIPLES UNDERLYING VISITATION OF THE SICK

We may think of the underlying principles in terms of the three great entities—God, Man, and Society—and thus consider the Theology, the Psychology, and the Sociology of Sickness and Healing. Many of the principles have been touched on already in other parts of this book, but the more directly applicable of them will be recalled briefly.

(1) *The Theology of Sickness and Healing.*

This is a large subject with a vital influence on the Pastor's attitude to the sick and to those who attend them. It will also influence his clarifying of the ideas and feelings of the sick people with whom he talks. Some of the main points in the theology of sickness and healing may be summarized as follows:

(*a*) *A 'God's eye view' of Sickness.* We are fully assured by the attitude of Jesus to sick people and His recorded teaching about sickness that sickness is not 'the will of God', nor is it a 'visitation' of God. Sickness appears to be consequential rather than punitive, and often vicarious and unmerited. So of course are the good things of life, including the gift of healing. Some discussion about the deep mystery of unmerited suffering may be found in Chapter 14 of this book.

(*b*) *A 'God's eye view' of Healing.* We have seen that this goes beyond the 'human' view of healing to wholeness of the human personality and reconciliation with man and with God. It also sees it *'sub specie aeternitatis'* with death itself then to be thought of as promotion to a larger and fuller part of the unbroken life when men 'die in the Lord'. The God's eye view is also interested in what men do with their 'positive health' when they regain it, as it is with stewardship of all possessions

All healing is the gift of God, the *'Vis Medicatrix Dei'*, given with life and constantly being renewed with life, but it requires human co-operation from the sick person and those who seek to bring healing to him. The healing power appears to be governed by rational law-abiding processes in the overwhelming majority of cases, and we are justified in concluding that where we cannot fit any healing act into any known law it is an example of the working of a higher law so far beyond our knowledge or understanding. In other words we believe that miracles are super-natural, but not contra-natural.

The sick person is meant to co-operate with the known laws of health on the physical and chemical, mental, social and spiritual planes, and the 'healers' are agents of God and mediators of His power through the three great channels of environment, nourishment, and removal of hindrances to healing, as discussed in Chapter 11.

The pastor then is called of God to be one of His agents in His Healing, a vital channel between God and the sick person which must be kept open throughout its whole length (see Chapter 1). From his training and insights he has a unique opportunity to help counteract the evils of specialism in which the patient tends to be separated into parts for greater efficiency. The pastor can see him as a person among persons in God's world, and in this he can be a great potential ally of Medicine.

This pastoral ministry is intended to be backed and reinforced by the whole Christian Fellowship: the visible and tangible embodiment of Jesus Christ 'the Great Healer' in every age, God in human life.

The prayer of faith is a potent force for healing the sick, but it is not true that if only a person had enough faith every serious case of illness would recover. That erroneous doctrine must be fought at every point.

(2) *The Psychology of Sickness and Healing.*

This is also a large subject with a vital influence on the pastor's attitude to the sick and injured and to those who attend them. It will also influence his clarification of their ideas and attitudes. Some of the relevant principles will therefore be summarized.

(*a*) There is no clear distinction between physical and psychic illness. Illnesses and injuries can be classified on a sliding scale, at one end of which are the predominantly physical, with less marked but not negligible psychic components, e.g. the worry which may accompany a broken leg or an attack of influenza. At the other end are the predominantly psychic, with some physical components, such as weakness and rapid pulse. In between are many 'psychosomatic disorders' and others in which physical and psychic factors are more evenly blended.

(*b*) There is not generally one 'cause' for an illness, or even an accident, as most patients seem to expect. There are many causative and contributory factors in most troubles, and many hindrances to the natural tendency to heal. Some of these will be on the spiritual level and therefore within the scope of the pastor. The fullest and widest team work is needed for adequate healing, and this demands mutual confidence based on ability and efficiency.

(*c*) There are many psychic and spiritual factors in his illness which will not be recognized by a patient, or recognized and not faced by him. People have many powerful unconscious—and conscious— defence mechanisms, and may often expect to be made whole through some external means, such as a 'tonic', without having to face up to some inner fault or some wrong relationship. The pastor may need to give many a patient bread when he only wants a stone. The sick person is often deeply divided within himself, with ambivalencies, inconsistencies, conflicts, tensions, and anxieties, which have brought him to bewilderment and despair. He has often no fixed point on which to build his life.

(*d*) It is generally futile to try to present the Christian Religion in terms of belief to most non-churchgoers, and even to some church-goers. The 'Word' must be 'made flesh' to them, by the personal devotion and the personal relationship of empathy. These are the 'passports' of the Christian, the 'master keys' to the overcoming by the patient of his defence mechanisms and the gaining of the necessary insight. For, like the Prodigal, he must 'come to himself'. Empathy is a 'feeling into' the patient's feelings and attitudes, with a combination of sensitive understanding, tonic sympathy, and loving acceptance of all his feelings without criticism. This cannot be 'counterfeited', and the pastor needs to have some real awareness of his own emotional needs.

(e) Neurotic and Psychotic patients are best left to the doctor from the point of view of discussion of their condition. All pastoral visiting should be carried out as far as possible in co-operation with him. The 'pastoral' attitude, rather than a discussion of the problems, is generally more helpful in the 'acute' stage of a mental illness. This attitude should be mainly one of being a good listener. It is important to remember that the mentally ill are often very sensitive to 'atmosphere' and surroundings, even when they are apparently withdrawn or even stuporose. Many of them describe their experiences most accurately after they have recovered.

(3) *The Sociology of Sickness and Healing*.

This is also an important concern of the pastor, and needs some attention.

(a) Many sick people are out of harmony with society, they feel very sensitive to the attitudes and actions of other people. They are often egocentric, and battling to 'keep afloat' among their fellows. They are often deeply ashamed of their dependence, and of the extra burden which their illness lays on those around them, and feel guilty about it. They may be greatly hurt by thoughtless or selfish criticism, even if it is only implied, and they are helped very much by acceptance.

(b) The domestic relationships of the sick person are often the most sensitive. The patient may feel that he is bringing too heavy a burden on his loved ones, and may be very apprehensive about them. The other people in the home may feel worried and ashamed at their inability to give sufficient help or spiritual uplift. In their attempts to help they find all too often that they have said the wrong thing. It often helps them to be reminded that their best contribution is often in their devoted service, and that their own emotional involvement hinders their power for spiritual uplift. This is often best given by those who are not emotionally involved, which is one of the reasons why doctors do not undertake responsibility for treating members of their own families.

(c) The vocational relationships of the sick person may also be important in his recovery. He has been uprooted from his work, and may be worried about his prospects of being able to hold down his job, or about the financial consequences of his illness.

(d) Disturbed personal relationships of these and many other kinds

U

are a prominent factor in the causation and the persistence of a number of illnesses. For proper care and treatment these relationships need to be given full consideration. This is not always done by the medical men and women, in some cases they are investigated by psychiatrists, and in hospital cases they are sometimes dealt with by the almoners. A genuine interest by the pastor in these relationships, and a reasonable ability to help the patient to deal with them may well provide an important means to fuller and quicker recovery.

SOME PRACTICAL ASPECTS OF VISITING THE SICK

(1) *The Initial Approach.*

This will depend on various factors:

(a) The place—the patient's home, or hospital or institution. It is very important for the pastor to fit in smoothly with the administration of any hospital or institution, to ask the ward sister or nurse in charge whether it is convenient for him to see the patient or patients. In many cases he can find out what times are generally best and try to fit his visits in with them. The same applies to a smaller degree in the patient's home. The patient will be more relaxed and in a better state for pastoral ministrations when the room is tidy and all the routine nursing activities have been carried out. It is better also to try to time the visit so as to avoid clashing with a number of other visitors, which will hinder the more intimate discussion of the pastoral visit.

(b) The circumstances may also make a difference to the whole approach, for example whether the visit is by request of the patient or relatives, or on the pastor's own initiative.

(c) The personal relationship, whether the patient is well known to the pastor or not. If confidence has to be established it is most important that the pastor should allow it to take its time, possibly in more than one visit, and that he should leave the door open for the patient's refusal without embarrassment. When the sick person does not desire to talk with the pastor on a particular occasion he should accept this willingly and ask whether he may call again on some future occasion.

(d) The severity of the illness is a most important consideration. It is essential to try to find out first whether the patient is fit to talk or to listen, and to conduct the visit appropriately. If there is no information to be had before the visit the pastor will assess the situation by his own observations and be sensitive to the patient's energies and feelings. For very sick people it may be of great help if he simply stands for a few minutes with a sympathetic hand on the patient's forehead in silent prayer, followed by a short prayer or benediction spoken in a quiet voice before he leaves.

(2) *The General Attitude of the Pastor.*

This should be one of natural spontaneous friendliness and interest in the patient as a person. This will be shown further by intelligent listening and simple questioning without prying. The pastor should be careful to respect the patient's resistances on the one hand, and to be unshockable and 'uninsultable' on the other. He should radiate a quiet tranquillity, a steady strength and confidence, and a natural unforced cheerfulness. Through all his pastoral difficulties, trials and tribulations he should try to follow the excellent advice of Dr Oliver Wendell Holmes:

> And last, not least, in each perplexing case,
> Learn the sweet magic of a cheerful face.

The pastor should studiously avoid gossiping himself, however much of it he may have to listen to from the patient. He can safely leave that in the much more appropriate hands of other visitors. Above all he should not talk about depressing things. It is not unknown for a pastor to inform the patient that he knew of someone who had a quite similar illness to this one, 'and he had a terrible time and nearly died'. Of course a little introductory 'small talk' is generally very helpful, the recalling of mutual friends, mutual interests, and places known to the patient. If possible the pastor can reassure the hospital patient that things are going well at home. He should ask whether there is anything he can get or do for the patient, and use his imagination to anticipate some of his needs, and some of the things which might interest him, add to his comfort, and relieve the monotony of his illness.

Sick people are often acutely sensitive to smells, sounds, movements and vibrations, and also to having to strain muscles to look at a visitor. It is important therefore that the pastor should sit quietly, without fidgeting, in the patient's line of vision, and that he should not stay too long. Sick people are easily fatigued, and he should constantly watch for signs of it. Some sick people find it a strain to talk, and find great comfort from a sympathetic person who will simply sit quietly with them for a time, and allow them to absorb his personal fellowship.

In visiting any patient in home or hospital the pastor should take a friendly interest in all the other people in the vicinity, and be ready to use the opening to win their friendship and confidence, and possibly to feel into their needs.

(3) *Some Specific Opportunities in Visiting the Sick.*

The pastor should be constantly alert to the possibility of applying some of the general interviewing and counselling methods where they seem appropriate within the limits of a short visit. This may provide a good introduction to effective counselling later. If the patient's catharsis is concerned with the failings or imagined failings of doctors or nurses or relatives be content to reflect back their feelings without agreeing or disagreeing, and if they want something done about the situation it is generally best to refer them back to the proper person. If the question of possible death from the illness comes up the patient should be allowed to talk freely about it so that the pastor may be able to assess the patient's feelings about it.

The patient will probably have no other chance of talking freely about death to anyone, and such open discussion may enable him to lay hold on something not previously experienced or visualized, and to find a victory over fear and loneliness of spirit. Russell Dicks has some very worth-while things to say about the pastor's handling of this situation.[1] To a person who volunteered the statement, 'I think I am going to die', he said, 'You are not afraid, are you?', to which she replied, 'No, I am not afraid'. Another woman came face to face with death with the simple gesture of faith: 'It is all right; whether I get well or whether I die it is all right.'

Children should be treated as persons in the sense of the accepting relationship of empathy. In this feeling into their emotions a simple inquiry may be made into the 'health' of the favourite doll of a little girl, or about any other particular interests. Helping the parents may be of very great help to the children, because they are very sensitive to parental emotions.

Prayer is an important part of visiting the sick, and it is generally

---

[1] Richard C. Cabot, M.D., and Russell L. Dicks, B.D., *The Art of Ministering to the Sick* (Macmillan, New York, 1936), p. 298ff. This book is a mine of information regarding this important work.

expected and valued by them. If there is any doubt it is probably best to 'feel the spiritual pulse' first, and possibly to ask the patient if he would like it. Prayers offered in the sick-room should be prepared with the greatest care, as of course all prayers should be. They should fit the needs of the patient as he has expressed them, then offer positive affirmation and thanksgiving, and go on to petition and intercession. The main petition should not be that God will heal the person —that might be construed by the patient that prayer is the attempt to overcome God's unwillingness, which is bad theology.

The more fitting kind of petition is that the patient may be more and more conscious of and responsive to God's freely given healing power (which would probably have been stated in the earlier positive affirmation and thanksgiving). The petition could then go on to ask that the patient may be strengthened and enriched by the experience. Then there can be an intercession for every member of the healing team, for wisdom, skill, sympathy and courage, and finally for the pastor himself, that he may be able to understand the patient and to mediate the love, power, and fellowship of God to him.

Some sick people may be helped by what may be called a 'spiritual prescription', as carefully chosen to fit his need as the medical one would be. It can be written or printed on a small card, which is left with the patient so that he can look at it, and allow its message to sink down into his soul as the doctor's medicine is absorbed into his body.

The Bible is a fabulously rich storehouse of Spiritual treasure. It contains the best of the literature and poetry of a great nation of deep spiritual insight and cultural maturity: the product of a long and varied experience of triumph and failure, certainty and doubt, joy and despair. Above all it contains the one existing set of reliable records of the life and teaching of Jesus, in whom 'the Word was made flesh and dwelt among' men. The relevance of the Bible to present-day human problems, and its power to help anxious and troubled people, are still beyond measuring. But the same care is required in using the 'Spiritual Pharmacopoeia' as in using the medical one.

Here are a few suggestions for Spiritual Prescriptions:

(a) *For wakefulness and panics at night:* Psalm 4[8], 30[3, 5], 3[5], 46[10], 91[28], 121[5, 3, 4], 1 Peter 5[7], 1 John 4[18, 19]. The 23rd Psalm is very appropriate for this and many other troubles.

(b) *For Fear of Death:* Psalm 31[15], John 14[1], 10[28-9], Romans 8[38-9], Isaiah 43[1-3], 12[2], 1 Corinthians 2[9].

(c) *For Disappointing News:* Psalm 112[7], 37[8], 46[1].

(d) *Before an Operation:* Deuteronomy 33^{27}, Isaiah 42^{16}, 2 Timothy 1^{12}, Philippians 4^{13}.

(e) *For the Weary and Disillusioned:* Matthew 11^{28}, Psalm 19^{7}, Ephesians 6^{13}, 1 Corinthians 10^{13}, Hebrews 12$^{1-2}$, Isaiah 40^{31}, Matthew 6$^{28-9}$, Psalm 31^{7}, 2 Corinthians 12^{9}, Ephesians 3^{20}.

(f) *For the Sense of Guilt or Failure:* Isaiah 1^{18}, Ephesians 1^{7}, John 1$^{8-9}$, Psalm 103$^{2-4}$, Matthew 9^{2}, John 8^{11}, Luke 7^{47}, 15^{7}, Romans 12^{21}.

(g) *For Anxiety:* Isaiah 30^{15}, Philippians 4$^{6-7}$ (RV), Luke 12^{32}, Romans 8^{37}, Matthew 6^{34}, 1 Corinthians 3$^{21,\ 23}$, Job 42^{10}.

These are some examples, but every pastor will have his own favourite 'spiritual prescriptions' to add to them.

When the patient cannot be seen, the pastor can look for some other approach. He may be able to talk for a few minutes with relatives, or with nurses, or doctors. He can ask any of these about the patient's needs, and send some appropriate messages to help him feel that someone cares, that the pastor is in the fight with him. It may be possible for the pastor to leave a short note, a small booklet, a short prayer, or a 'Spiritual Prescription' on a small card with a short goodwill message. It is a good thing if the patient is fit for it, to try to arrange another visit as soon as possible in the hope that he can be seen on that occasion.

SECTION FOUR

The Evangelistic Ministry

CHAPTER NINETEEN

'Every Christian an Evangelist'

IT IS being recognized more and more urgently in these days that evangelism is much more than something that is carried out by certain specially gifted evangelists in special 'missions', it is the full-time, all-embracing calling of every Christian. It seems strange that this great truth should ever have been allowed to fade from the minds of Christian people when we consider the explicit directions of Jesus Himself to His disciples, the all-consuming evangelistic activity of the early Christians, and the great periods of expansion of the Christian Church in many countries throughout its history.

The certain foundation for the whole of our evangelistic vocation is of course in the actual bidding of Jesus to His disciples, who, with the company gathered together at Pentecost, were to be the nucleus of the Christian Church. 'Go ye into all the world', He said, 'and preach the gospel to every creature' (Mark 16[15]) and, as St Luke records it in the Acts of the Apostles, the last words of the Risen Christ to His disciples were, 'Ye shall receive power, after that the Holy Ghost is come upon you: and ye shall be witnesses unto me both in Jerusalem, and in all Judæa, and in Samaria, and unto the uttermost part of the earth' (1[8]).

In St Luke's account of the beginning of the Christian Church we find that the early Christians proclaimed the Kingdom of God in their vigorous preaching of Jesus, they showed it in their personal lives and in the quality of their fellowship, and in consequence 'the Lord added to the Church daily' (Acts 2[36-47]). We find after some 1900 years at a great Church Conference in Madras in 1938, the mission of the Christian Church is stated as 'to proclaim, exemplify, and build the Kingdom of God'.

When the Church has proclaimed and exemplified the Kingdom of God, the Lord has added to it, and we see the results of this steady missionary work over the years in the growth of what has become known as 'the World Church', so well described by the late Archbishop Temple at his enthronement as Archbishop of Canterbury:

As though in preparation for such a time as this, God has been

293

building up a Christian fellowship which now extends into almost every nation, and binds citizens of them all together in true unity and mutual love. No human agency has planned this. It is the result of the great missionary enterprise of the last hundred and fifty years. . . . Almost incidentally the great world fellowship has arisen from that enterprise. But it has arisen; it is the great new fact of our time.

The steady progress goes on, as the great world conference at Evanston in 1954 has clearly demonstrated. This is the great work which the Church of today is called to carry on. But any honest appraisal of the influence of the Church in most communities will leave no room whatever for complacency. Behind the advancing world movement are grave deficiencies in the home communities which might well spell ultimate failure.

This has been well recognized in many countries, and commissions have been set up to consider ways and means of dealing with the situation. One such commission in Great Britain published a full and well-considered report in 1945 under the title, *Towards the Conversion of England*, and the picture painted in that report could well be taken as representative of many other countries. It is probable that there has been no obvious improvement in the decade which has passed since it was first published.

An evangelist has been defined as 'one who announces good tidings, or good news', and this can be done in life and work as well as in words. Whether or not conversion will follow must depend on the free response of those to whom the tidings are given, but that does not absolve the evangelist from the duty of appealing for the necessary decision.

No would-be evangelist has any warrant for assuming that his witness and appeal, and all that are behind them, will provide all that the other person needs to reach the point of conversion. These things may constitute one factor in a long sequence of experiences, which may include trouble, hardship or tragedy, or personal contact with other people who have a special kind of witness appropriate to special aspects of his total need. The evangelist may 'plant', like Paul, or 'water', like Apollos, but it is God who gives the increase (1 Corinthians 3[6]).

Much of the current attitude towards evangelism seems to give the main emphasis to the propagation of the Christian Gospel by word of mouth, by preaching, and by personal witness in conversation or from public platform, backed of course by an appropriate quality of life. This of course is essential, but many difficult problems arise from the undoubted resistance or apathy of the great majority of people to the most eloquent and forceful presentation of the Christian gospel by word of mouth. Do we realize how the situation has been altered in modern times by the immense growth of propaganda of all kinds? In the early centuries the preacher had little competition, but now he has to reach a public immunized against much of the influence of the spoken and written message. But present-day men and women are not immune to Christian service. Is the better use of pastoral work the missing link in our whole evangelistic enterprise? Is our proclaiming possibly suffering a little because it has not been backed up by sufficient exemplifying of the Kingdom?

It has been suggested in some quarters that 'pastoral work' should follow evangelism, as of course it must, for 'the building up and strengthening of the convert within the worshipping community'.[1] But Canon Bryan Green does not appear to give much consideration to pastoral work as an actual channel of evangelism, or even as a resource for 'pre-evangelism'. It is implicit in this book that all pastoral work may be regarded as the work of the 'body' of Him who 'went about doing good' as well as proclaiming the Kingdom by word. And as such it is all evangelistic through and through. Much of the best fruit of such Christian service may well be lost if pastoral work is not so regarded by all who do it in the name of Christ. It has been suggested elsewhere in this book that the Word must be made flesh anew in every generation if men and women are to be inspired and attracted to the point of decision.

It has also been suggested in this book that pastoral work is something to which all Christian people are called. As with every kind of skilled operation we need the specialist for the more difficult and complex parts of the work, but there is a great deal of less highly skilled service for which the 'rank and file' can be trained. All Christian laymen can be trained to fulfil their total evangelistic calling, the proclamation of the Gospel by word of mouth, backed up fully by its exemplification in their lives, in the attractive quality of their fellowships, and in their pastoral service to their communities. How can this be done?

Some of the necessary training has already been dealt with in the earlier chapters of this book. Methods of making contact with

[1] Bryan Green, *The Practice of Evangelism* (Hodder & Stoughton, 1951), pp. 19–21.

people and winning confidence have been discussed in Chapter 1, some help toward deeper understanding of human motive is offered in Chapters 2 and 3, visiting and interviewing, the 'bread and butter technique' of human interaction, is discussed in Chapter 4, and all the other educational and therapeutic services described in the subsequent chapters have their particular parts to play in the total evangelistic project. Some of the most important and far-reaching of all 'lay evangelism' is discussed in Chapter 9, particularly the work of parents in the early religious education of their children in the home.

An attempt will now be made to link up all these aspects of pastoral evangelism with the evangelism through life and word in a form suitable for offering a reasonably comprehensive training to laymen, so that the slogan 'Every Christian an Evangelist' may become closer to being a living reality. It is helpful to remember that the layman often has contact with the non-churchgoer in ways denied to the minister and also that in these days of scepticism the witness of the layman generally has even more influence on the non-churchgoer that that of the minister who is 'paid to do that sort of thing'.

One more reminder is necessary to clear the ground. If, as we are convinced, evangelism is the full time job of every Christian, then the daily job, the domestic life, and all other activities among people are to be regarded as opportunities for extending the Kingdom. Also the main business of evangelism must be something very simple, because Christianity is open to the illiterate as well as the educated, the child as well as the adult. Many of the evangelists of the New Testament were people of little ability, notably the original disciples, but they were possessed by something which they felt impelled to pass on. The Samaritan woman was another example (John 4$^{28-30}$).

The fact that evangelism is essentially simple enough for all Christians to undertake does not mean that it is all simple. There is work for the adult as well as the child, for the scholar as well as the uneducated.

How can Every Christian Become an Evangelist? This important question may be answered to some extent in terms of two of Our Lord's own sayings:

(1) 'Follow me, and I will make you fishers of men' (Matthew 4^{19}).

(2) 'I, if I be lifted up, will draw all men unto me' (John 12^{32}).

Our part then is to follow Him and to lift Him up. He will make us 'fishers of men', and He will draw men to Himself. We may therefore look more carefully into each of these authoritative sayings.

(1) *'Follow me, and I will make you fishers of men.'* We can think of how we can follow Him in our lives and in our methods.

(i) *Following Christ in our lives.* The greatest evangelists have always been Christ-like men, possessed, like their Master, by an unswerving faith in God, and an unquenchable love of God and man. These qualities are open to all Christians, but there is an important condition attached, well expressed by St Paul, 'That Christ may dwell in your hearts by faith; that ye, being rooted and grounded in love, may be able to comprehend with all saints what is the breadth, and length, and depth, and height, and to know the love of Christ which passeth knowledge, that ye might be filled with the fullness of God' (Ephesians 3^{17-19}).

We all know how easy it is for our best efforts to become perverted. We try to be good Christians and, without always realizing it, we become pious, exclusive and pharisaical, concerned so deeply with details of authority and procedure, that we miss the all-embracing, all-inclusive love of God. We try to be kind, and somehow become patronizing, a fact to which the common expression, 'cold as charity', bears vivid witness.

The only safeguards are in the fullest worship and fellowship. We need the constant practice of the presence of Christ which is the perfection of prayer, the continual opening of our whole personalities to the inflowing tide of His Spirit, so that He can live in us and work through us. This will mean setting ourselves constantly to learn more and more about Him, and coming to know Him, His life, and His mind and heart and will as well as we know our own. Can our knowledge of 'the unsearchable riches of Christ' ever be complete?

This indwelling Spirit confers upon those who are possessed by it a vital infectious quality, compared by Jesus with 'treasure hidden in a field' and with a 'pearl of great price'. When people catch a glimpse of treasure hidden in a field they will sell all to get that field. When people see in us something of real value they will want it with all their hearts.

We, ministers and laymen, live and work alongside other people, and both we and they are at times beset by difficulty, trouble, suffering and calamity. If other people come to see that we have the inner resources to rise above these things, to turn our difficulties into opportunities, to become 'more than conquerors', to 'love our enemies and to do good to those that hate us', then some day one or more of our colleagues will see the thing they need, and open the door to our most effective witness to its source.

This is still more powerful when we can bring some of the dynamic healing power of Jesus Christ, the Great Healer, to people in personal trouble, or to the reconciliation of conflicting or broken human relationships.

An important part of following Christ in our lives is that we should follow Him in our fellowships. This will guard against our own self-deceptions, because a true fellowship of the Spirit will allow the kindly enlightenment referred to by St Paul as 'speaking the truth in love' (Ephesians 4¹⁶). The quality of our fellowship will attract those who are hungry for true fellowship if it is really a fellowship of the Spirit, and not a fellowship of formalism. There is little doubt that the quality of their fellowship was a great evangelistic force for the first-century Christians.

Our first duty as evangelists then is to be good advertisements for our own faith, to be a working model of the Kingdom into which we would welcome other people. We can only do this when we follow Christ in our lives, and accept His leadership in all that we do as individuals and in fellowship. In this way we cannot help becoming 'fishers of men'.

(ii) *Following Christ in our methods.* From the very beginning Jesus refused all superficial short cuts in the winning of men. Like every other leader He had to meet the subtle and beguiling temptations of bribery, force, and trickery, but He renounced them all, and set out to win men by love, never disguising the roughness of the path, or the sacrificial cost. How then can we follow Him in our methods?

(a) *We can look at people with the eyes of Christ.* Anyone who knows Christ and in whom Christ lives can learn to do this. The tragedy is that we look at other people with such human eyes, eyes which see their deficiencies so well that they often miss their less obvious good qualities. Jesus was not blind to the deficiencies of people. He knew men through and through, but He saw right through their superficial faults to the often hidden core of potential or actual goodness. He came primarily to bring abundant life, and He saw the goodness even in Zacchæus, which nobody else could see, and brought it into effective action.

We need to see right through the faults of other people to the hidden loyalties and decencies, the kindness and courage, which only need recognition and Christian love in many cases to be inspired into creative action. The faults, like the tares in the parable, are for God to deal with, and one of the greatest hindrances to the evangelistic efforts of many Christians has been their proneness to point fingers at other people, in attitude if not in word, instead of allowing the light of Christ to shine out of their own lives.

(b) *We can give lavishly of ourselves to other people*, in the Spirit, and following the method of Jesus Christ. He had an unquenchable passion for the welfare of all people, particularly the poor, the outcast, the blind, the suffering, and the helpless. He fraternized quite naturally with publicans and sinners, and told His critics that 'they that are whole have no need of the physician, but they that are sick' (Mark 2^{17}). His love was inclusive, not exclusive. He had a genius for friendship, which soared across all barriers of race, class, culture, colour, creed, and sex; and he has bidden His followers, 'Love one another as I have loved you', and made that the true sign of Christian discipleship (John 13$^{34-5}$).

We are called to show to one another in action the love of Christ and His friendship to all men. One of the greatest of all present-day world problems is that of race prejudice, and the peace and survival of the world may be dependent on its solution on a large enough scale. Can we hope to show the right example until we have overcome our lesser prejudices, particularly our denominational prejudices, throughout the nation? As the late Archbishop Temple once remarked; 'If the man who observes from outside sees no Christian graces in those who are inside, if congregations are quarrelsome or self-complacent, then no amount of preaching can counteract the harm that is done.'

Our example and our words will have much more influence on other people when we are able to create a positive relationship with them. People tend to imitate the lives and characters, and to take notice of the words of those in whom they have found confidence. Jesus built up such a relationship with the twelve, and even with publicans and sinners, and such 'quislings' as Zacchæus, and thus opened the way for His example and His ministry in word and action to go over to them.

This lavish giving of ourselves to others will involve taking initiatives, searching deliberately for points of contact with other people, visiting, writing letters, going out of our way to do them good turns, lending books, distributing pamphlets and other literature, using our homes as centres of friendly discussion and service, all offered with tact and consideration, patience and friendly tolerance. Nothing alienates people as much as the well-meaning Christian who overdoes it, and will not let them alone.

(c) *We can, like Jesus, respect other people's freedom.* We are bidden to let our light shine out of us, and that is a very different matter from trying to shine it or push it into anyone else. The other person may regard our 'light' as a lot of nonsense, and he is quite free to think that way. The familiar hymn of our childhood, 'Jesus bids us shine . . . You in your small corner, and I in mine', is full of good evangelistic treasure. As Dr Russell Maltby has pointed out, 'Christ in His saving work will do no violence to the natures He has given us, and His help, infinite as it is, must enter by the narrow door of our consent.'[1]

(d) *We can, like Jesus, seek not to destroy but to fulfil.* This will mean starting with people as they are, encouraging what seems good, and ignoring what seems negative or bad. Everyone who works in line with Christ's intention is to some extent on His side, even if their ideas seem unconventional to us. We do well to co-operate with all kinds of people who are working for social betterment of any kind, remembering that a Christian is known more by the calibre of his heart than by the colour of his shirt. We need to recover a great visible passion for social justice, not as a way of bribing people into the Christian Faith, but rather for Christian love of the outcast in the community and the world. When we do this people will be more convinced of the reality of our Faith.

(e) *Like Jesus we can co-operate fully with God.* Every man has in him some of the Spirit of God, however much of it may be covered up by resentment, greed, or fear. By the prayer of faith we can in some mysterious way link up with that fragment of God's Spirit in him which is capable of responding to God. But it must be the prayer of faith. All such efforts may be weakened and even ruined, by disparaging criticism of the other person, spoken or felt; or by impatience and doubt, or by wanting to play God; all of which block the flow of God's healing and reconciling Spirit.

In all these ways, which are open to all Christians for their perception and their patient cultivation, we can come to follow Jesus, in our lives and in our methods, so that He can make us 'fishers of men'. We can now think of His second great statement.

---

[1] *Christ and His Cross* (Epworth Press, 1935), p. 165.

(2) '*I, if I be lifted up, will draw all men unto me*' (John 12³²). We must do more than follow Jesus if we are to become evangelists. He will make us 'fishers of men', but we must do the fishing. This analogy seems appropriate except for one point: that it is to the advantage (in abundant life) for the human 'fish' to be 'caught'. As George Matheson put in his famous hymn: 'Make me a captive, Lord, And then I shall be free.' For successful fishing the bait must be put where the fish can see it, and presented to them in an attractive form for which they are hungry, so that it can 'draw' them.

For all effective evangelism Jesus must be 'lifted up', so that men can see Him. This is implicit in the generally accepted definition of evangelism: ''To evangelize is so to present Christ Jesus in the power of the Holy Spirit, so that men shall come to put their trust in God through Him, to accept Him as their Saviour, and serve Him as their King in the fellowship of His Church.'[1]

We need to lift Him up, to let men see Him, 'in the power of the Holy Spirit', or our witness will have little or no attraction for men. As we saw in Chapter 3, the events in Palestine in the first century are far away in time and space, and they have far less power as a historical narrative than they do when the 'word' is 'made flesh'. Men and women need something visible and tangible, as the early disciples had, to grip their imaginations, and inspire them 'to put their trust in God through Him, to accept Him as their Saviour, and serve Him as their King in the fellowship of His Church'. The great commission of the Church is to be His continuing 'body', to show Him afresh in visible and tangible form in every age, as a unique fellowship of the Holy Spirit. Is it true that the most frequently overlooked factor in all the evangelistic efforts of the Church is at this point?

It is essential that people should continually be told about the Historical Christ, the recorded facts concerning His life, death and resurrection, and about the utter genius of His teaching and His relevance to all aspects of our contemporary situation. They must also come to some knowledge of the unchallengeable evidence of His power in the lives of men and women across the world and throughout the Christian era. It is being slowly borne in on us how great is the general ignorance of these things even among those who confess to a vague admiration of His quality of life.

[1] *Towards the Conversion of England* (Press and Publications Board of the Church Assembly, Westminster, 1945).

x

Most of this, however, will take place after people have been sufficiently gripped by the visible and tangible quality of the Christian life, the attractiveness of the Christian fellowship, and the healing and reconciling and life-enriching power of Christian pastoral service of Christian laymen and Christian ministers alike. The first-class Christian preacher and the highly gifted Christian evangelist can draw large crowds, which include many who seldom go to Church except when they are thus drawn. The total long-term influence of these great experiences cannot be measured, but it is all too common to find that the number of such people who 'serve God as their King in the fellowship of His Church' is disappointing.

There are good reasons for believing that when the Church can express the highest quality of Christian fellowship, and be among people as 'one that serves' in devoted pastoral work on a much larger and wider scale and at a much higher standard than heretofore, the Lord will add to their numbers in a sustained and growing quality 'such as should be saved' (Acts 2[47]). These two great opportunities of Christian witness would appear to constitute the main evangelistic resources for today, and they will provide the setting in which the presentation of the Historical Christ will 'get through' to the mind and heart of modern man, indifferent to and largely suspicious of words which are not sufficiently 'made flesh'.

In that setting we can present Jesus as the supreme hero to the keen, hero-worshipping, formative, plastic mind of modern youth, as the one adequate foundation for the new world, which belongs to today's youth, and the one power which can bring man the victory over his most subtle enemy, himself.

Our verbal witness can be offered through private conversation, and many subjects of conversation can be gently guided to some of the fundamental things of life. The attitudes and methods of interviewing and counselling apply here, especially the art of creative questioning, questions being put where possible in such a form that the answer is very likely to be 'Yes'. For example, the question, 'Have you had much contact with the Church?' may quite possibly bring the answer, 'No', which will tend to block the steady crescendo of the conversation. If the same kind of question were put in slightly different form, such as, 'Your children are getting religious education at school, and you believe in the things Christianity stands for. Your identification with the Church would be a help to your children's Christian development, wouldn't it?[1] it would be much more likely to bring an affirmative answer, and lead to further development of the interview. We need to be 'wise as serpents, and harmless as doves' (Matthew 10[16]).

Our conversation should present Christ 'in the power of the Holy Spirit', so that we are offering a kind of 'Spirit Transfusion' to the other person as well as an account of the Historical Christ. This will generally require constant renewal in ourselves through our own devotional life in the quiet places of our own souls as well as in the living fellowship of the Church. Members of a dead or 'lukewarm' Church are not likely to have any great spiritual 'infectivity', and they will have no adequate fellowship into which to bring those to whom they offer their witness.

Members of some active Church congregations go visiting 'two and two', like the 'seventy' sent forth by Jesus (Luke 10[1-12]). This needs to be well thought out under the guidance of God, and the visitors well trained in their handling of the situations. They generally go as accredited representatives from the Church as a gesture of interest and fellowship, and offer an invitation to closer relationship with that, or any other Church which the people may prefer.

A recent example of this 'visiting evangelism' has been reported by Rev. Tom Allan from one of the suburban areas of Glasgow.[2] Many important lessons have already been learnt from this carefully designed project. One was the need 'for the development of a new pattern of life within the congregation' as a 'first priority'. A closely related lesson was that 'the only way to prepare a Church for evangelism is by the work of evangelism'. 'These two things are inextricably bound together.' Here is where any 'evangelistic group' which may come into being within a Church congregation will need to be closely related to and supported by such other living active groups as the 'social', 'prayer' and 'pastoral' groups already described in Chapter 11. Such groups, and any others which might be created or allowed to come into existence, might also help to solve one of the great problems of this kind of evangelistic work, what to give the new converts to do, and how best to assimilate them into the active fellowship of the Church so that they can progressively learn to 'be', which is the essential basis of all 'doing'.

Apart from the Christian witness of conversation there are often

---

[1] Dawson C. Bryan, *A Handbook of Evangelism for Laymen* (Abingdon-Cokesbury Press, 1948), adapted from p. 59.

[2] Edgar P. Blamires, *Changing Strategy in Evangelism* (Epworth Press, 1952).

opportunities for public witness from platform, pulpit, and in writing or broadcasting, for laymen as well as ministers. It will be remembered that St Paul made opportunities for Christian witness out of the most unlikely situations—imprisonment, shipwreck, and even his trial before King Agrippa (Acts 26$^{1-29}$).

But there is another important truth tucked away in the great words of Christ: 'I, if I be lifted up, will draw all men unto me.' While Jesus was on earth He did not draw all men. St John tells us that 'He came unto his own, and his own received him not' (John 1^{11}), and 'From that time many of his disciples went back, and walked no more with him' (John 6^{67}). When He said, 'I, if I be lifted up, will draw all men unto me', He said it 'signifying what death he should die'. Christ crucified, Christ the Saviour, has done and can do more to draw people to Himself than Christ the Teacher, or even Christ the Healer could do. The early evangelists all preached Christ crucified, and Christ resurrected, the Book of the Acts of the Apostles rings with it.

But they did more than preach Christ crucified, they were willing to share His sacrifice, and most of them did share it. The witness of sacrifice is generally the most convincing and powerful, and the words of Tertullian, 'The blood of the martyrs is the seed of the Church', have been proved over and over again to be true. In these days we do not find ourselves called to die for Him as often as we are called to live for Him, but it is when our witness costs us something that it becomes convincing to people as a witness of sincerity and truth.

In all our attempts to show Christ, in whatever manner we set out to do it, we need to be most careful not to show a distorted picture of Him. Often, with the best motives, people show the world, not Christ, but a Pharisee, deeply concerned with many superficial aspects of procedure, with narrow denominationalism, or even with a type of piety which blandly tolerates rank social injustice. Many people outside the Church accept Jesus as the embodiment of perfection, even if they tend to dismiss Him from the real affairs of life as an impracticable idealist. It is often a matter of admiration from afar, unaccompanied by any realization of His relevance to their own lives, but they see where the Church has distorted and misrepresented Him, where it has quarrelled and remained divided over matters which would appear trivial to His mind, and where it has bowed the knee to the secular gods of wealth, power, and prestige. They have missed the main point of course, their duty to help in the renewal of the Church, but often they have despaired of overcoming the complacent inertia of those within the Church.

These are hard words, but they do represent a very common idea in the mind of that symbolic human unit, the common man. And the common man, with all his peculiarities and self-deceptions, is endowed with a good stock of common sense, or democracy would for ever be a beautiful illusion.

Another common misrepresentation of Christianity is the suggestion that it is mainly a code of morality on the one hand, or a set of complicated philosophical beliefs on the other. Each of these constitutes a set of views, about which there is constant dissension and argument. But Christianity is first and foremost a Gospel, 'God's Narrative', Good News embodied in the person of Jesus Christ, and subsequently embodied from its beginning in the Christian Church, however much it has been obscured by the narrowness and blindness of fallible men. Christianity is primarily evangelistic and then ethical and philosophical; Morality and Theology arise out of the Good News, but do not and cannot take its place. A Christian is primarily, not a person who does something, or a person who believes a very great deal, but a person who has received and accepted something of which he could never be worthy, and who therefore constantly feels the tug of loving gratitude at his soul, urging him to self-giving service. 'We love', as St John wrote, 'because he first loved us', (1 John 4[19], RV), and He still gives to those who receive Him 'power to become the sons of God' (John 1[12]).

To set the ethical or theological before or apart from the evangelistic, to tell people that they must live up to a particular standard (presumably in their own strengths) or believe all the 'articles of the Christian Faith' (presumably through a simple credulity) before they come into relationship with Jesus Christ and the Good News which is embodied in Him, is very likely to do more harm than good to His great cause. The early disciples saw in Him something which gripped their souls and won their personal allegiance. Then bit by bit under His loving and inspiring leadership, they grew to Christian morality, courage and self-sacrifice, and they also came to know who He was, and is. The same unfolding sequence of experience has come to many people all over the world who have come under the spell of His personality and found 'the unsearchable riches of Christ' (Ephesians 3[8]).

This is the Christ whom we are privileged to show to men, to 'lift up' so that they can see Him. We are bidden to go forth, like the sower of old (Luke 8$^{5-15}$), to sow the 'seed' which is the 'word', the word made flesh and the word made vocal. And what we 'sow' will fall on different kinds of 'ground'. We have given some consideration to the word 'made flesh', but what of the word made vocal? What is the Christian Good News, and how relevant is it to the needs of modern man?

We have seen something of the relevance of Jesus to many aspects of modern life in earlier chapters, and we shall now give some consideration to the Good News itself.

The word news has come to mean something quite different in our day from what it meant in the first century A.D. Through the wonder of wireless it can be flashed across the world in a moment of time. The modern newspaper does its best, as Emerson once remarked, 'to make every square acre of land and sea give an account of itself at your breakfast table'.

These modern large-scale channels of news-dissemination have not done away with the ancient and more intimate methods. We still use the spoken word and the private letter, and there is always the 'grapevine', an incredibly rapid and efficient means of dissemination of certain kinds of news.

Day by day in fact people everywhere receive such a massive conglomeration of shouted, spoken and whispered news, headline and small print news, that they find it very hard to separate the important from the merely sensational, and to sift the news of permanent value from the evanescent and fleeting gossip.

In these days of sensationalism, in fact, we tend to overlook one particular kind of news altogether: news about life itself, possibly the most vital and important of all news, because in many cases it is literally life-saving.

Here is a familiar example of this life-saving kind of news. Before 1926 if a person became afflicted with the disease known as Pernicious Anaemia, he was doomed to die within two years in spite of the best medical treatment known at that time. But in 1926 in an American medical journal two doctors, Minot and Murphy by name, gave some vital news to the world: that they had proved in 45 cases that this hitherto fatal disease could be kept in check by a diet rich in liver. Many further developments have occurred since 1926 and many more will come, but as a result of this news about life the disease is no longer fatal, and sufferers can be kept in good health for the normal span of life.

The history of medicine is filled with news of this type. We may recall Lister with his news about asepsis, Banting and Best with their news about Insulin, and Fleming and Florey with Penicillin. But it is not limited to medicine: it may be found in all departments of life, and the Christian Gospel is a supremely important body of news of this life-saving kind. But before we look at the Christian Good News we may notice three important features of this life-saving kind of news.

First, it is news about how life has always worked. Minot and Murphy could well have echoed some famous words of St John, 'That which was from the beginning, that which we have seen and heard, declare we unto you' (1 John 1[3]). Unlike most of our modern news this kind of news can never become old or out of date, because it is quite independent of time. The news about liver is just as important to today's victim of Pernicious Anaemia as it was to his predecessor before 1926.

Secondly, this kind of news may be life-saving, but only if people know about it, accept it, and act upon it. It is not the news as such, but God, about whom it tells and man's personal response which save life. If the sufferer from Pernicious Anaemia has not heard the news, or if he 'knows better' and fails to co-operate with it, he will die within two years in the same manner as his predecessor.

The third feature of this life-saving news is that it is not just a lot of nice words, it is actually embodied and proved in human lives. The 'word' is 'made flesh', and dwells among people. The people who accept the news and live by it become themselves the news in each new generation. The sight of one patient rescued from serious illness by acting on the news will convince the doubter more than any fine words would ever do. This life-saving news will therefore spread most widely and effectively when it is shown in human lives for other men and women everywhere to see.

It is clear then that this kind of news has what we may call 'saving power', and that it can never become obsolete. Also that it needs continually to be propagated all over the world if all who need it are to receive 'salvation', and that this can be done when it is embodied in people as well as told in words. And finally, if people are 'to be saved' through it, they must believe and accept it in sufficient faith for them to order their lives by it. We make the best of life, as of such forces as electricity, not by trying to make it fit in with our devices and desires, but only by adjusting our lives to the way it works.

The Christian Gospel offers life-saving news about the whole range of personal and social life: about God, man and society, in the only way in which it could be really clear to men. It has been once and for all embodied in a Life, in and through which God has offered, and still offers the light, power, deliverance, and fellowship to meet men's deepest needs. For all who will accept it and order their lives by it, it is the one way to abundant victorious life.

This may be still clearer if we consider what we actually need for victorious living in the unceasing battle of life. We can see our needs in simpler terms if we think of the needs of the front-line soldier in another kind of battle. There are three vital items of news which mean everything to him.

The first is news about the cause for which he is fighting. He must be sure that what he is doing is worth doing, that the commander and all behind him know their jobs and will do their best.

The second is news about himself and his own status, that he counts for something, and will not be sacrificed unnecessarily, or used as mere 'cannon fodder'.

The third item of news is about his fellow-men, that they will stand by him and lend a hand if he is in trouble, as he would do for any of them. The sense of comradeship is vital to the morale of any soldier.

In the same way we need the right kind of news about the 'Cause' and the 'Commander', about ourselves, and about our society. We need to feel that life ultimately makes sense, that its ultimate purpose is worth living for, and even dying for. We need the faith that when we do our best our feeble efforts (like those of the soldier) will be reinforced by something greater than ourselves, and that even when we fail we can be rescued and given another chance to make good. In other words we need to know some vital things about God.

Then, like the soldier, we need to be assured that we count for something, that we are not made to be exploited, regimented, or 'pushed around', by the State, or by any other body of people. And thirdly we need assurance about our fellow-men, that we can count on them for help if we are in need, as we are ready to help them. Without the comradeship and co-operation of our human society none of us, particularly the helpless, could live for long, because we depend on our society for nearly all our material needs, and for everything which makes life worth living.

This greatly needed threefold news, about God, Man, and Society, is exactly what is offered in the Christian Gospel, and it is embodied, not in moral principles or in philosophical views, but in the Person of Jesus Christ: in Himself, His life, His work, His insights and His teaching, His attitudes to all kinds of people including His enemies, His sacrificial death, His resurrection, and His ever-active Holy Spirit.

Jesus gave to mankind the staggering news about God, that the majestic, all-powerful Creator and Ruler of the infinite universe is like a loving Father, with an unquenchable passion for the welfare of all His children. In the Person of Jesus we see the attitude of God to man, symbolized not in the awe-inspiring thunderbolts of Jove: powerful but aloof, but in a cross, the symbol of the most compelling devotion and the closest identification conceivable: Love which will go even to death. Even though life brings its share of tragedy and suffering is there not enough in the character of God as seen in Jesus to find a positive faith, an assurance that in spite of all its contradictions life ultimately makes sense, that a tremendous and worth-while purpose is slowly working out, and the battle is worth fighting when God is in it? In these days of struggle and despair on the world front, and conflict, anxiety and bewilderment in the human heart, the world needs more than ever the Good News about God which is offered for all time in Jesus Christ.

In His attitude to all kinds of people, and in all His dealings with men, women and children, Jesus also laid down for all time the most important and far-reaching news about Man: the essential dignity and sacredness of human personality. What a sensational and revolutionary bit of news that must have seemed to an age of slavery and oppression and low valuation of much human life! This news about man is that he counts for something, not because he is clever or good, not because he belongs to any particular race or class or creed, or period in history; but simply because he belongs to God and to nobody else. This explosive idea is the foundation of all our striving for human liberty, equality, and fraternity, and it has brought about the emancipation of women and children, the abolition of slavery, the progressive removal of sweating and exploitation from industry, and the development of great social services such as schools and hospitals. It has also generated a powerful crusade against all forms of totalitarianism and racial discrimination. There is still much to be done, and the world still needs the Christian news about the sacredness of human personality.

What of the news about Society? The Jews had expected a national deliverer, one who would free them from the Roman domination and lead them to what they regarded as their rightful prestige in the world. They found that Jesus looked far beyond any form of nationalism to what we now call 'one world', a world brotherhood of mutual encouragement, challenge, co-operation and help under the Fatherhood of God.

'The Fatherhood of God' is the key to all human brotherhood in the Christian Good News. All human efforts to build a workable ordered society of free men have failed, and will fail, unless they are under the direction and inspiration—and creative power—of something beyond human wisdom and skill. Jesus laid down the great fact of life, that when mankind will seek first the Rule of God, the needs of the human race will be supplied (Matthew 6³³). Only when most of mankind will accept the Rule of God will enough men and women care enough to co-operate willingly in production and world-wide distribution to use the God-owned and God-given resources of the earth to supply the needs of all. Can anyone point to any other way to such a goal without the sacrifice of human freedom?

This great News about the Rule of God in world society stands head and shoulders above all the "isms'. Without the direction and inspiration of Jesus Christ, even Democracy may well find that, as we saw in Chapter 5, 'the voice of the people' may be nearer to the voice of the devil than to that of God.

The Kingdom or Rule of God is not necessarily related to any particular pattern of society. With the inspiration and direction of the Spirit of Jesus Christ men will naturally work out the pattern of their society in terms which will best meet their needs at any given period, and in any particular circumstances, and the pattern may well be modified or changed from time to time in accordance with the constantly changing human situation.

This, expressed in all too sketchy terms, is the threefold Good News, which is offered for all time to mankind in the person of Jesus Christ, God in human life, and in His total ministry. This is the 'red-hot' news which we are called to offer to men and women everywhere in these days, as our Christian ancestors were called to offer it over the whole of Christian History. This is the 'seed' which we are to sow, the Word of God, continually being made flesh in the quality of our own lives, the gracious attractiveness of our fellowships, and the devotion and skill of our personal and pastoral service to men, women, and children. This is the Word continually to be made vocal in our personal witness and all the preaching and teaching of the Church and its people.

'The field is the world' (Matthew 13³⁸), the world of people, homes and families, of kindergartens, schools and universities, of churches and Sunday-schools, of hospitals and clinics, of factories, offices, institutions, shops and markets, of wharves and the ships that visit them, the fields of agriculture, and the Houses of Parliament and all the legislative organizations under its authority. The field is the world of Nations and the great assemblies where the international tensions are faced and considered. The Christian Good News is to go out into all the world, and to every creature at every age in the most simple and appropriate terms, from the emergence of man from the great unknown at birth to the time at which he stands at the gate of the other great unknown which we call death.

Our task, and that of all Christians, is therefore to find the light, power, deliverance and fellowship of Jesus Christ, and to let them shine in such a way before men that men may see our good works (and that is more important than our good words), and glorify God.

'We have this treasure in earthen vessels', wrote St Paul, 'that the excellency of the power may be of God, and not of us' (2 Corinthians 4⁷), and we may take comfort in spite of the burden of our unworthiness from some other words of that grand old evangelist, which sum up our whole justification for venturing on such sacred ground, in this and all our other pastoral ministry in His name,

For consider, what have the philosopher, the writer and the critic of this world to show for all their wisdom? Has not God made the wisdom of this world look foolish? For it was after the world in its wisdom had failed to know God that He in His Wisdom chose to save all who would believe by the 'simple mindedness' of the Gospel message. For the Jews ask for miraculous proofs and the Greeks an intellectual panacea, but all we preach is Christ Crucified—a stumbling-block to the Jews and sheer nonsense to the Gentiles, but for those who are called, whether Jews or Greeks, Christ the power of God and the wisdom of God. And this is really only natural, for God's 'foolishness' is wiser than men, and His 'weakness' is stronger than men.

For look at your own calling as Christians, my brothers. You don't see among you many of the wise (according to this world's judgement) nor many of the ruling class, nor many from the noblest families. But God has chosen what the world calls foolish to shame the wise;

He has chosen what the world calls weak to shame the strong. He has chosen things of little strength and small repute, yes and even things which have no real existence to explode the pretensions of the things that are—that no man may boast in the presence of God. Yet from this same God you have received your standing in Jesus Christ, and He has become for us the true Wisdom, a matter, in practice, of being made righteous and holy, in fact, of being redeemed. And this makes us see the truth of the Scripture: He that glorieth, let him glory in the Lord (1 Corinthians 1 $^{20-31}$).[1]

[1] J. B. Phillips, *Letters to Young Churches* (Bles, 1947).

Index